Diversity and Dominion

Diversity and Dominion
Dialogues in Ecology, Ethics, and Theology

Edited by
KYLE S. VAN HOUTAN
and
MICHAEL S. NORTHCOTT

Foreword by Stanley Hauerwas

CASCADE Books • Eugene, Oregon

DIVERSITY AND DOMINION
Dialogues in Ecology, Ethics, and Theology

Copyright © 2010 Wipf and Stock Publishers. All rights reserved. Except for brief quotations in critical publications or reviews, no part of this book may be reproduced in any manner without prior written permission from the publisher. Write: Permissions, Wipf and Stock Publishers, 199 W. 8th Ave., Suite 3, Eugene, OR 97401.

Cascade Books
An Imprint of Wipf and Stock Publishers
199 W. 8th Ave., Suite 3
Eugene, OR 97401

www.wipfandstock.com

ISBN 13: 978-1-60608-821-0

Cataloging-in-Publication data:

Diversity and dominion : dialogues in ecology, ethics, and theology / edited by Kyle S. Van Houtan and Michael S. Northcott ; foreword by Stanley Hauerwas.

xiii + 218 p. ; 23 cm. — Includes bibliographical references.

ISBN 13: 978-1-60608-821-0

1. Religion and science. 2. Human ecology — Religious aspects — Christianity. 3. Environmental degradation — Religious aspects — Christianity. I. Van Houtan, Kyle S. II. Northcott, Michael S. III. Hauerwas, Stanley, 1940–. IV. Title.

BT695.5 .D58 2010

Manufactured in the U.S.A.

To Hope, may you be wise in many ways

Contents

List of Illustrations / ix

Foreword—by Stanley Hauerwas / *xi*

Introduction—*Kyle S. Van Houtan*
 and *Michael S. Northcott* / 1

One Eyes Wide Shut—*William H. Schlesinger* / 13

∼ Response: Science Itself Is Only Half-Prophetic
 —*Jeffrey D. Vickery* / 21

Two Censuring Nature and Critiquing God—*Lisa Sideris* / 25

∼ Response: Wrestling with Evolutionary Biology
 and Theology—*Norman Christensen* / 42

Three A Walk on the Wild Side: The Idea of Nature Revisited
 —*Michael Jackson* / 46

∼ Response: Good Work—*Kyle S. Van Houtan* / 64

Four Thanks for the Dirt: Gratitude as a Basis for
 Environmental Action—*Norman Wirzba* / 69

∼ Response: Biogeochemistry on the Farm
 —*William H. Schlesinger* / 87

Five The Dominion Lie: How Millennial Theology Erodes
 Creation Care—*Michael S. Northcott* / 89

∼ Response: A False Dominion of Control
 —*Robert B. Jackson* / 109

Contents

Six   Anti-Imperial Themes and Care for Living Nature in Early Christian Art: The Good Shepherd as a Model for Christian Environmental Ethics—*Susan P. Bratton* / 113

∼   Response: Seeing through a Columbine Flower —*Makoto Fujimura* / 134

Seven   Nature and the Nation-State: Ambivalence, Evil, and American Environmentalism—*Kyle S. Van Houtan* and *Michael S. Northcott* / 138

∼   Response: Conservative Christians and Environmentalism, 1970–2005—*Seth Dowland* and *Brantley Gasaway* / 157

Eight   Biodiversity and the Kingdom of God —*Laura Yordy* / 166

∼   Response: Biodiversity and the Ministry of Reconciliation—*Fred Van Dyke* / 191

Bibliography / 199

List of Contributors / 211

Illustrations

1. Good Shepherds (I): Sculpture from Museo Pio Cristiano, Vatican. Detail of Jesus entering Jerusalem from the sarcophagus of Junius Bassus, Museum of the Treasury, St. Peter's Basilica, Vatican. / 129

2. Good Shepherds (II): Entry into Jerusalem. Jesus, in an inversion of the usual Roman triumphal entry on a warhorse, rides a humble donkey. Museum of the Treasury, St. Peter's Basilica, Vatican. / 130

3. Birds feasting on grapes. Fresco from the Christian catacombs, San Sebastiano, Rome, Italy. / 131

4. Imperial Roman violence towards animals. Detail of the Big Game Hunt, mosaic in the ambulatory of the Villa de Piazza Armerina, Villa del Casale, Piazza Armerina, Sicily, Italy. / 132

5. Armed gladiator slaying a leopard as part of a public display for entertainment. Museum, Sousse, Tunisia. / 133

6. *Columbine Dream.* 2004, 60.2cm x 72.6cm. Mineral Pigments, Gold, Oyster Shell White on Kumohada. Used with permission of the artist. / 135

7. *St. Jerome and the lion.* Roger van der Weyden. Oil on oak panel. Used with permission of The Detroit Institute of Arts. / 139

Foreword

Stanley Hauerwas

MANY CONCERNED ABOUT THE environmental crisis want religious communities to support measures biologists and ecologists think are desperately needed. Theologians and ethicists have responded by writing books, trying to convince Christians that the crisis is real and that there are good reasons to join a common effort in response to the crisis. While this book does not disdain such an approach, the questions Van Houtan and Northcott broach through the essays collected here go much deeper.

Wendell Berry pointed out some time ago that the very language of "environmental crisis" is deeply misleading. The language, according to Berry, suggests that the crisis is "out there" and humans must do something about it. The difficulty with putting the matter that way is it gives the impression that nature is one thing and the human relation to nature is another. By contrast, Berry argues that humans cannot be abstracted from nature.

This book drives home Berry's point by arguing even more radically that the very notion of nature is problematic. It is the peculiar character of modernity to presume a fundamental contrast between nature and history. Nature is assumed to be dumb and without purpose. History is thought to be the realm of human freedom and creativity that makes it possible for humans to act on nature in the hope of making it serve human purposes. The future, accordingly, is thought to be dependent upon human intervention. The result is that the solutions proposed for the environmental crises continue to reproduce the contrast between nature and the human—i.e., the very dualism that has brought us to the current crisis.

As a number of these essays argue, the fundamental challenge facing us is not simply convincing religious communities that there is an ecological crisis, but more important are the very descriptions used to help us understand why we are in such a mess. If we are to begin to understand how to rightly diagnose our plight, we must recover the understanding that creation is a more determinative description of the world than nature. For creation rightly reminds us that we are not in an environmental crisis, but rather we, meaning humans, bear with all that is a common story. Creation is the language necessary if we are to remember we are not our own creators. We are, therefore, challenged by the essays in this book to think through once again what it means to live in a world shaped by the virtues befitting those who have learned to be creatures—i.e., the virtues of humility and gratitude.

At the heart of the ecological crisis is the recognition of limit. How do we learn to live within limits? For those without the notion of creation, limits name challenges to be overcome. Ironically, however, the very attempt to overcome limits turns out to create limits from which we suffer. By contrast, the essays in this book help us see how limits, even limits from which we suffer, are resources that may help us better understand what it means to live in gratitude of the limits we've been given.

This is not a book of answers. Rather, it is a book of challenges to the answers we've been given. It is therefore a book of hope, which hopefully will be received in gratitude by those who are willing to explore these fundamental theological questions.

Introduction

KYLE S. VAN HOUTAN *and* MICHAEL S. NORTHCOTT

THIS BOOK EMERGED FROM a series of public lectures in the spring of 2005 at Duke University that were jointly sponsored by the Nicholas School of the Environment and Earth Sciences and the Duke Divinity School.[1] The concept for the lecture series was to address the ethical dilemmas in the human destruction of biodiversity through a set of exchanges between scholars from different academic disciplines—primarily addressing Christian perspectives in the Unites States. This project is also the first fruit of collaboration between the Environment and Divinity Schools at Duke, the aim of which is to grow the scholarly interface between ecological science and moral and religious perspectives on conservation. As editors we also reflect this interface personally, since one of us is a conservation biologist and the other a theologian. We believe that this interface is of the utmost significance in making headway in the global ecological struggle.

A chief motivation for this volume is our belief that purely scientific descriptions of widespread ecological destruction are inadequate. In our experience, this is primarily because natural scientists can neglect non-scientific epistemologies and the human dimensions of ecology. This seems symptomatic of a larger failure to acknowledge humans as a member species of their environs, or as a constituent species of biological diversity itself, and hence scientific descriptions often place humans outside the domain conservation scientists want to save from destruction. A further problem with the scientific narration of environmental catastrophe is that it has proven a poor motivator of cultural change and of public participation in nature conservation (Van Houtan 2006).

1. Ethics and the Environment Lectures. See http://www.duke.edu/web/ethics.

Our suspicion is that this is partly from the lack of attention to the human dimension, and in particular cultural, historical, and political perspectives, in scientific descriptions.

It is notable that nearly all of what conservation scientists call "biodiversity hotspots"—areas of combined biological uniqueness and endangerment (e.g., Myers et al. 2000)—have been colonized and administered by European powers over the last few centuries. A strictly scientific analysis of this difficult history neglects the cultural and political realities that are also implicated in the threats to biodiversity in these regions (Pimm et al. 2001). The genocide of indigenous tribes like the Huaorani in Ecuador accompanying oil exploration in the upper Amazon basin, the war and refugee crisis over mining and logging in west-African forests, the collapse of coastal communities from commercial overfishing in Polynesia, or totalitarian rule in the Indo-Burma peninsula are all symptomatic of ongoing postcolonial human injustice in areas which are also sites of high biodiversity. These crises indicate the problematic nature of the economic and political regimes imposed on many former colonial regions today by international financial institutions, and in particular structural adjustment programs which have seen large areas of forest and savannah converted to cash crops to meet punitive debt repayment regimes (Northcott 1999). Colonial and postcolonial governments have shown similar disrespect for the indigenous peoples who live in these regions, and have failed to recognize that indigenous guardianship of primal forests, ancient savannahs, and coastal estuaries has been more effective than colonial and postcolonial property regimes in preserving biodiversity. But the scientific construction of these areas as biodiversity hotspots or even "Ecoregions" (Olson et al. 2001) misses the vital role indigenous peoples have played as custodians in conserving the biological heritage of these regions. There is growing recognition among anthropologists and political scientists of the value of common property regimes and indigenous guardianship in conserving biodiversity while also providing a sustainable living for indigenous forest dweller and fisherfolk (Ostrom et al. 2002). But attempts to sequester nature from local guardians in the name of conservation still provide warrant for the continuing expropriation of "natural resources" by governments and corporations.

The concept of guardianship involves a very different understanding of the human relation to land and water sources, animals, fish and trees than the regnant accounts of private and state property rights in

Introduction

modern economic and political theory (Northcott 2006). Guardianship is a central and constitutive feature of common property regimes in indigenous cultures. In Western culture the most significant locus of accounts of guardianship are provided by religious traditions and sustained by participation in religious communities. But modern philosophers, like modern scientists, tend to believe that it is possible to narrate the human condition and nurture the young into full citizenship without reference to the ancient stories and traditions that have shaped earthly and human history. This neglect of predecessor cultures is ironically more pronounced in the United States, where, from the Puritans on, there has been an effort to reinvent the world without reference to the prior inhabitants of North America or even to the European past. This also helps to explain the profound role science has in framing the American story. Since Vannevar Bush penned his influential essay *Science, the Endless Frontier* (1945), governmental trust in science and technology has developed into a broad social optimism that science will take the lead in redeeming human structures.

The reality is that across the American continent there is a double ecological problematic developing. Within the continent, there has been a sustained assault against ecological diversity, and a looming and likely larger threat from global climate change. At the same time there is a sustained assault by conservative politicians, and by many of their conservative Christian backers, on such central pieces of environmental legislation as the Clean Air and Endangered Species Acts which are represented as unwarranted governmental interference in the rights of Americans to create wealth and enjoy their property unrestrained by public bodies or laws. In their view, such rights are inalienable, God-given, and grounded in the Genesis mandate of "human dominion." But this interpretation of the Old Testament entirely neglects the dimension of covenantal justice and its ecological implications as charted by the Hebrew prophets (Northcott 1996). Novels like Michael Crichton's *State of Fear* are powerful cultural exemplars of this problem, precisely because they refuse the link between individual or human welfare and the health of the biosphere. The central trope of Crichton's novel is that global warming (and the ecological crisis more generally) are drummed up as apocalyptic scenarios by progressive politicians and liberal intellectuals who want to justify the continuing power and invasiveness of government and regulatory bodies on peoples' lives and communities. For Crichton and his ilk the ecological crisis is a grand conspiracy whipped up by leftist politicians to justify their liking for governmental regulation of private property owners.

The Old Testament, unlike modern conservation biology, clearly narrates the connection between the tendency of wealthy private property holders to exclude the poor from their own environment and ecological destruction. In the postcolonial economic order an international corporate elite has increasingly taken hold of the political process to benefit their own interests in developed and developing countries. As in the empires of the old world, this new governing class of individuals is committed to the belief that the wealth of nations is advanced by the continuing amassing of power and wealth by the dominant institution of the market empire—the economic corporation. To its interest, everything else, including the poor and nonhuman species, must be subservient in the quest for the economic utopia to which borderless markets and global trade are said ultimately to deliver all human societies. The domination of government and the economy by a super-rich corporate elite fosters an attitude of dominion towards what are often called "natural resources," and to the earth itself, which has advanced even faster the rate of destruction of biodiversity as well as human cultural diversity in the last thirty years. This attitude and the geopolitical strategies it advances have also fostered continuing growth in violent conflicts over resources in this new century, conflicts which are in themselves major ecological as well as human catastrophes.

As Jacques Ellul argues in *The Technological Society*, science and technology play an important role in the rise and dominance of the corporate elite (1964). The sacrifices imposed on people and planet by this elite are legitimated by the unquestioned presumption that economic growth combined with technological progress will ultimately redeem the human condition from want. The continuing affirmation of this credo despite the evident social and ecological failures of the present era strangely mirrors the fundamentalism and irrationalism of some of the religious perspectives that are frequently derided by this elite. And this is indicative that both scientific description and modern religious discourses have been infected by a monocular mindset which obscures the true multi-layered and multi-sensory structures of human knowledge and the connections between the ways in which humans acquire knowledge and skill and the larger-than-human world. But the scientific narrative of technological progress, combined with the claim that scientific data and description of-

Introduction

fer a privileged and direct access to the true or fundamental nature of reality, obscures the tacit way in which earthly bodies and rhythms shape and mould human consciousness and cultures.

In an important sense the modern claim to certain knowledge of the laws which govern the biophysical world produces a fundamentalist quest for certainty both in religion and in economics. Religious and market fundamentalists adhere to their own paradigms and interpretations of favored texts regardless of empirical evidence which may disconfirm long-prized shibboleths. Both kinds of fundamentalism reflect a modern quest for certainty as a competitive response and an apologetic strategy for the analogous veracity of their convictions and claims about the laws which govern the moral and social world which was in part provoked by the claimed certainties of natural science. But although the planet increasingly suffers from the ecological limits of its technological transformation and subjugation to modern scientific knowledge, few are prepared to question the underlying epistemological assumptions which inform the quest for certainty in the human and natural sciences, or in religion (Toulmin 1990). It is on this terrain, rather than in debates about cosmology and evolution, that we believe engagement is needed between ecological science, religion, and ethics of the kind we seek to advance in this volume.

The particular way we challenge the quest for certainty in science and religion in this volume is to look at the metaphors of dominion, destruction, diversity, and humility. When we read the great books of biology—Aristotle's *History of Animals*, Linnaeus's *Systema Naturae*, von Humboldt's *Cosmos*, Darwin's *Origin of Species*—we find the observer has a primal respect towards the world that transcends their own being, and that this is analogous to the orientation to the earth that is manifest in biblical cosmologies such as those of Genesis, the Psalms, and Job. This respect, which we might call awe or wonder, calls forth in the one who experiences it humility, a sense of their smallness in the scheme of things, and prudence in considering the possible systemic consequences of their actions in this scheme. And this sense of humility is in tension with the claim of modern scientists that their methods represent a master discourse which trumps the knowledge frameworks of other disciplines and other eras.

Our project is particularly timely given the increasing recognition of the role of religion in the formation of political policies concerning respect for the environment and the need to conserve it for future generations, and not least in the United States where religious mobilization remains strong. The extent of religious mobilization in the political realm in the United States since 2000, and the rise of the Religious Right, though it may now be on the wane, has nonetheless at last caught the attention of conservation biologists and climate scientists as witnessed by a recent editorial by David Orr in the science journal *Conservation Biology* (2005), and the many responses this essay spurred.[2]

Another significant feature of recent public policy debates in the United States has been a growing sense among environmentalists of all stripes that the traditional liberal approach to ecological conservation is not working and is losing public support. It is as if environmentalists are pushing the wrong buttons of the American psyche. There is too much bad news, too much emphasis on state intervention, and not enough discourse concerning empowerment and the roles of citizens and local communities, and not enough hope that it is possible to turn the direction of industrial civilization around (Shellenberger and Nordhaus 2004). For us this recognition is highly significant, as it interacts with our shared belief that we have inherited from wise teachers that it is only possible to build a good society when the individuals of that society are themselves good. In the world of ecological thought, that recognition requires a much more profound engagement between the procedures of science and public policy making, the promotion of respect for the environment, and the beliefs, practices, and rituals of citizens, civil servants, and corporate actors in all regions of the globe.

At a crucial moment in human and planetary history, we offer in this book a series of prophetic encounters between ecologists, theologians, and ethicists. Against the imperatives of the market and wealth creation we present wisdom from the emergent tradition of conservation science, and from the ancient traditions of Judaism and Christianity which have evolved over thousands of years, and which in that time, as the growing body of scholarly work in religion and ecology has demonstrated, have manifested an ecological sensibility and human welfare which we could call human ecology. Far from being a distraction from earthly things as some secular scientists and philosophers have claimed, traditional reli-

---

2. *Conservation Biology* included a special section in the issue following Orr's essay, devoted to the many responses to his essay. See *Conservation Biology* 19 (2005) 1685–98.

Introduction

gions manifest an ultimate concern with the co-flourishing of creatures, human and nonhuman, that neither scientism nor capitalism are able to sustain. To put this differently, scientists and policy makers cannot conserve without attention to the kind of religious and cultural dialogue that we essay in this book.

What we are suggesting in this volume is that a multi-disciplinary conversation offers a better description of the multi-layered world that we inhabit and the multiple ways our knowledge of the world enables us to live and flourish in it. In our present ecological crisis both Scripture and empirical data require a larger multi-disciplinary vision which is open to mystery, metaphor, and analogy (Placher 1996) and which is also open to persons on the margins of human society, as well as nonhuman creatures. Such an approach should be prepared to see the fate of factory-farmed animals through the narratives of a persecuted church, to read a biodiversity hotspot from the perspective of a Huaorani indian, to see the soil through the husbandry of a rural farmer, to consider dominion through the humility of the Amish, or to imagine an Ostrich flapping its wings through the eyes of Job. Our approach challenges a narrow vision of life on earth seen reductively through disciplinary discourses and logics that are mutually incommensurable (Louth 1990). It is for these reasons this volume pairs experts with different training and sensibilities. Such scholars describe situations differently, and these descriptions together bring forth a fresh humility, willingness to learn from one another, and wisdom. This is our project.

The biogeochemist William Schlesinger opens the book with a personal narration of environmental awakening of the 1960s and a plea for political cooperation between scientists and persons of faith. Schlesinger's main context is the issue of climate change, or global warming, as he has studied the nitrogen and carbon cycles for decades, seen dramatic shifts in the data sets firsthand, and is somewhat beleaguered that this science has not produced appropriate public concern and policy. Schlesinger the scientist views the ethical landscape and wonders why Christians (in particular) aren't doing their part. They might. The philosopher Jeffrey Vickery responds to his essay and explains that science is only part of the story, and it fails as a worldview to inspire social change because it has no anthropological story. Science has no account of redemption.

In the second chapter, the religion scholar Lisa Sideris examines how Darwinian evolution raised theological concerns about theodicy, or the "problem of evil." For Darwin and many others, his findings raised the question of the beneficence of God as Creator, given the levels of cruelty and suffering involved in the origin and evolution of species. For Sideris the answer to this conundrum is that God does deliver us from evil, but that God does this through suffering. By contrast Sideris finds that many attempts to engage the ecological crisis theologically too often fail to take seriously the level of suffering that Darwin finds in the history of life, and that they rely instead on a romanticized biblical account of the world. Only by taking seriously the redemptive character of suffering in the Christian tradition, and in other theological traditions, is it possible according to Sideris to reconcile a Darwinian notion of evolution and traditional theism. The ecologist Norman Christensen responds through his experience of chairing a federal panel to manage Yellowstone's elk population after widespread fires in 1988. To Christensen, theologians are not alone in their struggle with suffering. Ecologists have long wrestled with animal suffering, and particularly how to manage carnivores. He reminds us that Darwin, unlike his competitor Lamarck, uses the word function over purpose. This, Christensen offers, should help us recognize that science will always be mute to certain questions, but that does not mean humanity does not ask them.

In the third chapter the cultural anthropologist Michael Jackson argues that human knowledge is far more limited than modern scientists imagine. Consequently it is still necessary for modern humans to attempt to conserve and guard their ecological heritage on the basis of imperfect knowledge. For Jackson nature is profoundly ambivalent towards humankind—it both gives and takes away life. And human actions have far less significance in the larger scheme of things than most moderns would attribute to them. In this sense they do not differ as much as moderns imagine from the "magical" thought of indigenous shamans in Australia or Borneo. The indigenous shaman and the Western celebrity scientist are both motivated by the same instinct: to do something. One of us, Kyle Van Houtan, agrees with Jackson's critique of the position that "Man is the measure of all things" and appreciates the humility in which Jackson approaches knowledge. Scientists could listen more to these lessons. But Van Houtan argues that Jackson's view leaves little room for what we the editors, and many others, call ethics.

The agrarian philosopher Norman Wirzba argues in the fourth chapter that it is impossible to understand how human beings cultivate such moral virtues as humility and gratitude apart from an agrarian appreciation of the cultivation of food and the tending of the soil. However much modern urban humans live apart from this seminal relationship to the soil they are still biologically sustained by what they eat. And unless they know what they eat, and where and how it is grown, they will be cut off from a significant source of their own identity, and their moral formation as embodied creatures. The ecological problem for Wirzba arises in particular from the disconnect between the modern epistemologies of food and place and the sustaining rituals of everyday life. For Wirzba, understanding these deep links evokes gratitude that can help to translate a conceptual knowledge of ecological problems into meaningful actions. As a biogeochemist, Schlesinger is sympathetic to Wirzba's argument of understanding our biochemical dependence on nature's cornucopia. But Schlesinger is no romantic and not preoccupied with nostalgia for times past. Surely, Schlesinger suggests, we cannot all return to the farm, or even maintain gardens to supply our own personal needs. The world has grown past this. We can however still inculcate humility towards nature through other practices, including the practice of science.

Michael Northcott in the fifth chapter notices a deep paradox in the lives of apocalyptic conservative Christians who develop industry and business to accumulate wealth for a future they consider will soon end in apocalypse. They both do and do not live like there is no tomorrow. He suggests that the cultural power of contemporary apocalyptic Christianity produces a public theology of dominionism which has in the recent past in the United States legitimated highly damaging attitudes to the non-human environment. Northcott argues that apocalyptic Christianity is a perverse variant of historic Christianity and that it is the consequence of a collusion between capitalist ideology and evangelical individualism. He then narrates the Christian practices of confession and repentance as an alternative response to the ecological crisis that this curious combination of ideas and practices has helped to sustain. The atmospheric scientist Rob Jackson responds by enumerating how biblical miracles have been replaced by science and technology. Manna no longer comes from Yahweh, but Montana. Water does not miraculously flow from a desert rock, but from hydraulic well pumps. By narrating our history of earthly dominion and control, Jackson believes that it is still possible to find humility from within modern science.

In chapter 6, the art historian Susan Bratton analyses the politics of the early Christian church through the paintings on the walls of the catacombs in Rome. The images she describes are Edenic and point to an afterlife through images of birth, fecundity, peace in human society, and fellowship with the rest of creation. Bratton suggests that this legacy demonstrates a resistance to the dominant values of Roman Empire as manifest in the glorification in Roman art of hunting, military prowess, and mighty beasts. And as Christianity becomes the cult of the Roman Empire after Constantine, Bratton finds that the empire infects Christianity, and Christ is increasingly portrayed as a worldly emperor whose followers enact the same rituals of killing and power as the emperors of Rome. The artist Makoto Fujimura responds to Bratton through his experience of being commissioned to compose funerary paintings for the Columbine High School shooting tragedy in Littleton, Colorado, in 1999. He describes one of his paintings, and particularly his inspiration to portray the confession of faith of one of the murdered girls. Like Bratton, he sees this as truth-telling that "maintains the bonds between the heavenly and earthly realms." And such truth-telling performs a true dominion by transforming a funerary work into a celebration of life—one that is and is yet becoming.

In chapter 7, Van Houtan and Northcott examine the ambivalent legacies of John Muir and Gifford Pinchot in order to provide an insight into American environmentalism. They find that Wendell Berry's agrarian ethics indicates the inadequacy of Pinchot's utilitarianism and Muir's wilderness fetishism. But they suggest that Berry's agrarianism is insufficient and requires some account of the way in which the communities of the kinds of people who do live sustainably on the land—such as the Amish—are formed, and how modern forms of statist and corporate farming are deformed. With the Mennonite theologian John Howard Yoder they argue for a robust account of sin that explains humanity's descent from responsive dominion to destructive domination. And they argue also for the significance of what Yoder calls "body politics" as the means by which humans can be formed in communities which are at peace in themselves and with the more-than-human world. The historians of American Christianity Seth Dowland and Brantley Gasaway write in response that both conservative and liberal American evangelical Christians have concepts of environmental stewardship. They describe the development of the Evangelical Environmental Network, which they characterize as "servant

Introduction

stewardship," and the Interfaith Council for Environmental Stewardship, which, in Orwellian fashion, characterizes itself as "caring dominion."

The theologian Laura Yordy argues in the eighth and final chapter that the theological themes of eschatology and redemption are central to the church's practice of biodiversity conservation. Yordy easily moves from the biblical stories to the present day arguing that all species take their ultimate meaning from a triune God who created them in mutuality, relationship, and peace. Creatures still show God's goodness, but this is dimmed and can only be fully restored by God's eventual work to redeem all of creation. Though this cannot happen by human efforts, it does not diminish human conservation efforts. Instead Yordy suggests that local parishes are capable of taking a lead in caring for creation and thereby working for the *Shalom* of creation in the here and now. The conservation biologist Fred Van Dyke responds that Yordy too easily accepts the ethics that scientists put forth. Van Dyke suggests the conservation community lacks a robust concept of species as creatures and merely considers them a part of the evolutionary process. For species, death is certain. Why bother with conserving them? All creatures, according to Van Dyke, have an ultimate significance. Acting in such a way as to conserve them is to act in accordance with the resurrection of Jesus Christ from the dead, which is the definitive event in which Christians discern from within human history that life and not death is the end of all things.

One

Eyes Wide Shut[1]

WILLIAM H. SCHLESINGER

AMERICANS BEGAN TO TAKE environmental issues seriously in 1969 when the Cuyahoga River in my hometown of Cleveland caught on fire. The water pollution of the Cuyahoga typified the problem of "point-source" pollution that was rampant throughout the nation. Corporations, municipalities, even individuals, regarded our air and water as a logical dumping ground for myriad wastes of a modern industrial society—"the solution to pollution was dilution."

With point-source pollution, blame was easily cast, appropriate remedial actions were obvious, and the regimen for cure, perhaps painful to initiate, was effective. Today, we have much reason to rejoice from the early success of the environmental movement. Few pollutants now spill unregulated into the natural environment, urban children have lower levels of lead in their blood, and whitefish have returned to Lake Erie.

Yet, even amidst this environmental awakening in the late 1960s, we had a foreshadowing of the larger, global environmental problems that now face us. Rachel Carson hinted at them in her seminal book, *Silent Spring*, predicting that the persistent nature of chlorinated hydrocarbons would lead to their global distribution and accumulation in animals living quite distant from the original application of DDT. Indeed, she foresaw the new era of global change—what some have called the *anthropocene* or the era of humans—in which a single species, *Homo sapiens*, would come to exert a dominant control on the characteristics of our planet—particularly its chemistry—and to usurp the natural habitat for other species that share

---

1. Some of the thoughts in this essay were presented earlier in a two-part series, "Earth Daze," (August 4, 2002) and "Eyes Wide Shut," (August 11, 2002) in *The Winston Salem Journal*, North Carolina, and in a public presentation at the Cleveland Museum of Natural History on September 25, 2005.

the Earth with us. We have conquered and subdued nature, and increasingly, we are leaving our mark upon the Earth. Climate change is but one manifestation of global problems wrought by humans, and we must not approach our global environmental impacts with "Eyes Wide Shut."

There is widespread denial about many environmental issues, which is easy to explain—the news is always bad, the cure is often unpleasant, and the consequences seemingly distant. The voting public is much happier putting jobs and personal well-being above the life-support system that sustains us on planet Earth. We pounce with fervor on Michael Crichton's *The State of Fear* or Bjorn Lomborg's *The Skeptical Environmentalist*. If they are right, let the good times roll.

Humans have a pretty good track record of subduing nature and living better for it. The first explorers of North America struggled with subsistence and survival. Just a few decades later, painters of the Hudson River School captured an idyllic pastoral landscape under human management and control. The Bible tells Jews and Christians that they have God's blessing and orders to dominate the planet, which is so wonderfully endowed to support our fruitful multiplication and well being. Why should we believe those who say that the old rules no longer apply?

Today's environmental problems stem from a rising global population of humans, now close to 6.8 billion, each with a desire for a higher standard of living. Our population continues to grow exponentially, whereas our planet, save for the receipt of a few meteors, doesn't grow at all. Our rising numbers leave less of nature in its natural state, fewer species to share the planet with us, and changes in the basic chemistry of Earth's atmosphere and oceans that form the evolutionary environment for all life now on Earth. Here I will focus on climate change, but I could just as easily address the current human impact on the ocean's fisheries, the global spread of mercury, the dispersal of exotic species, pests, and pathogens, or the loss of natural habitat from the overpopulation of the human species. The collective impact of 6.8 billion people on Earth certainly exceeds that of our forefathers—the old rules don't apply to a full planet.

The dominance of *Homo sapiens* on planet Earth leads to huge ethical questions that we must address seriously and very soon. We must ask fundamental questions about our role on Earth—in the past, now, and in the future. Beyond leaving a heritage for our children, do we have a basic responsibility to leave behind a functional environment for the future?

Are we to use the Earth's non-renewable resources at will, or is there an ethical responsibility to leave some for coming generations? If global climate change wrought by burning fossil fuels in the developed, industrial nations of the North impacts food production in the South, what is our moral obligation to feed those beyond our borders? Are we sure that our own agricultural production is secure? We need to consider our responsibility as stewards of the Earth. What is our responsibility to preserve other species? Do they even matter?

Certainly, we have faced some of these ethical questions before. If I go outside and shoot a wood thrush, I am in violation of the Migratory Bird Act and subject to severe prosecution. Someone, at some time in the past, thought that such behavior was unacceptable. But, if, as a developer, I cut down a tree containing a wood thrush nest filled with its begging young, I am regarded as important to "housing starts" and the growth of the economy. If, as a citizen of the United States, I am responsible for adding five or six tons of carbon dioxide to Earth's atmosphere (about the amount each of us now emits each year), contributing to global warming and the inability for wood thrushes to find proper habitat in all of eastern North America, is that acceptable or unacceptable behavior?

Climate change is a good example of a global environmental problem, for which more heat than light has emanated from the debate about what to do about it. Indeed, there are those who still argue that global warming is a myth, or merely a natural, short upward excursion of temperature in a long history of temperature variations on Earth. There are those who argue that somehow the human species will muddle through this type of global environmental problem, because we have such a good track record of muddling through lesser problems that have faced us in the past. Overlooking the plight of several billion of our number at the edge of poverty and starvation, we may focus complacently on the belief that more people are now living better than ever before. We may advocate the philosophy of Adam Smith—that the good of the whole will rise when each individual pursues life for his/her best personal advantage.

Americans may feel distant from other cultures—half a world removed from their problems—but we must realize that we occupy the same planetary ecosystem, which will respond to the global changes we make in it, especially its climate. I cherish an anecdote told to me by my good friend Ted Purcell of Duke University's Baptist campus ministry, which captures how I feel our government is behaving badly in the face of global climate change. Two men are rowing a boat. Suddenly one begins to bore a hole in the bottom of the boat. When the other man challenges him, he retorts: "This is none of your business. I'm drilling this hole under my own seat."

Our ability to dominate nature has led us to believe that we are not part of nature, but above it. How often do we see the human listed as a species in any local field guide to the mammals? But with the appearance of *Homo sapiens* a mere 150,000 years ago, we are relative newcomers to the Earth's biosphere. As Sallie McFague proposes, we are actually housemates with the rest of God's creations on Earth. And, as housemates, we "must abide by three main rules: take only your share, clean up after yourselves, and keep the house in good repair for future occupants. We do not own the house, we do not even rent it. It is loaned to us for our lifetime, with the proviso that we obey the above rules, so that the house can feed, shelter, nurture, and delight those who move in after us" (2001: 125–40).

Global climate change may appear slow and the threats may appear distant, but global warming is an example of how the human species is affecting the life-support system of planet Earth—the evolutionary environment for all of us. In Genesis (1:26–28) God said to humanity, "be fruitful and multiply, and fill the earth and subdue it, and have dominion over the fish of the sea and over the birds of the air and over every living thing that moves upon the Earth. Perhaps we have done too well in following God's word, when as Michael Northcott shows (1996), the correct Hebrew translation of "dominion" is steward, not ruler. We should see that dominion was an order for us to take care of Eden—for stewardship of our planet.

Let's focus on climate change. Carbon dioxide, CO_2—the main culprit in global warming and the main emission from fossil fuel combustion—has been rising in Earth's atmosphere since the dawn of the Industrial Revolution. For about 10,000 years, the concentration of CO_2 in the atmosphere remained between 270 and 290 parts per million (ppm), rising rapidly to today's value of about 382 ppm during the past 150 years (Fluckinger et al. 2002). It is easy to overlook CO_2; it is odorless, colorless, and non-toxic. No one gets out of bed in the morning and says: "Gee the CO_2 levels are awfully high today!" Its rise in the atmosphere is slow, about 1.5 ppm per year. In the atmosphere, CO_2 acts as a "greenhouse" gas—analogous to the glass that causes a greenhouse to get very hot inside during the summer. CO_2 is transparent to much of the incoming radiation from the Sun, but it absorbs heat radiation trying the leave the Earth, so that the temperature of Earth's atmosphere rises. Other gases, including water vapor (H_2O), methane (CH_4), and nitrous oxide (N_2O), have the same effect and are collectively said to add to the radiative forcing of Earth's atmosphere. It is fortunate that these gases are found in the atmosphere; without its natural greenhouse effect, the Earth's temperature would be below freezing, and the Earth would be a frozen ball of ice.

However, with the recent rise in CO_2, the Earth is getting warmer, as seen directly in the records of weather stations and ocean temperature, and indirectly in the earlier springtime appearance of birds, insects, and flowering plants (Parmesan and Yohe 2003). During the past century and a half, the overall history of rising temperatures largely parallels rising CO_2 in Earth's atmosphere, just as fluctuations in Earth's temperature have correlated well with fluctuations in atmospheric CO_2 during the past 500,000 years, spanning the last several glacial intervals.

Over the long run, major human impacts on climate may affect us indirectly, through shifts in forest cover, in the occurrence of drought and crop failure, and in the epidemiology of diseases, especially those which are spread by mosquitoes. The temperature in the U.S. is anticipated to rise about 5 to 9° F during the next hundred years, but the rise globally will not be uniform. A larger change is being seen at polar latitudes, where a lot of ice is now found. Satellite measurements of Earth's temperature—while not providing a long record—show a rise in temperature concentrated in the northern polar regions, where we also see a recent decline in Arctic sea ice. To the south, we see increasing fragmentation of Antarctic ice sheets. Penguins may feel it first, but humans will see the effects of warming, in rising sea level, very soon.

In 2004, the movie *The Day After Tomorrow* entertained us with a catastrophic scenario of future climate change. The scene was a Hollywood extravaganza, but the movie did capture some grains of truth. Studies of Earth's past show that global climate can change quite rapidly. Scientists have noted a recent freshening of the surface seawater in the North Atlantic, presumably derived from melting ice packs. This low-density water could slow or stop the global ocean circulation that carries tropical heat northward to warm Europe and North America. Global warming could paradoxically plunge these regions into deep regional cooling. Warmer or colder, it should give us great pause that humans have the potential to cause large, rapid changes in the Earth's climate, with inevitable effects on the world's agricultural production.

Rapid changes in climate are seen in the Earth's past, but not when we were trying to feed 6.8 billion people. We may think that we can adapt to or manage global climate change, embark on planetary engineering to do so, and even bring back DDT to combat a greater onslaught of mosquitoes and the diseases they carry, but will planetary management be as easy as prevention? Many argue that the economic costs of reducing carbon dioxide emissions are too high—too much of a cost to GNP. But, as captured in the title of his recent book, Eric Davidson reminds us, *You Can't Eat GNP.*

It is not at all surprising that we are so reluctant to give up the fossil fuels that have brought so much benefit to modern society and wealth that has been amassed by using them so effectively. The emission of CO_2 from fossil fuels is directly linked to economic activity: when times are good, we emit a lot of it. When times are slow, we emit less. A rise in per capita use of fossil fuels has paralleled the rise of human population during recent decades—a multiplicative cause of rising CO_2 in Earth's atmosphere. Some nations emit a lot less CO_2 than we do per unit of economic activity—that is, they use fossil fuels more efficiently—but overall, an increasing level of economic activity worldwide is leading to greater emissions of CO_2 each year.

Beyond recognizing the aesthetics of a pristine environment and the wondrous diversity of life that so fascinates us, ecologists are increasingly documenting the economic value of nature. Nature and natural lands provide "ecosystem services." The traditional cost-benefit analysis of economists often fails to include the benefits that the life support system of nature provides to the human species. The economic benefits of a forest extend far beyond the daily fee that an average citizen might pay to visit it on holiday. Forests store carbon that might otherwise accumulate in the atmosphere as carbon dioxide and cause global warming. Forests cleanse the air and water that sustain human society. Sure, we can do these things too, but only at a substantial, direct cost to our economy.

In many risk assessments of environmental pollution, the risk to humans is quantified but the risk to nature is not (Parker 2003). The costs of regulation need to be compared to the benefits of a healthy environment. Recently, Robert Costanza and his colleagues (1997) provided one of the few full-benefit accountings of the value of natural ecosystems—finding that each year the work that nature does for us far exceeds the GNP of the world's economy. The Bible tells us that on the evening of the sixth day of creation, "God saw everything that he had made, and behold it, it was very good" (Gen 1:31). Today, it seems crass for us to value nature at $33 trillion per year; rather, we should be stewards of nature so as to be stewards of the services that nature provides. We depend on nature to sustain the global lifeboat.

William Rees developed the concept of the "ecological footprint" to describe the amount of natural land that would be needed to supply resources and mitigate the effects of resource use by people on Earth. He originally calculated this for his hometown of Vancouver, showing that an area vastly larger than Vancouver's city limits would be needed to supply the needs of its citizens. Recently, a group of scientists led by Mathis Wackernagel (2002) calculated the global footprint of the human species. In 1980, it passed the size of planet Earth. More than 6.8 billion people now use more of the natural resources of our planet than the Earth can supply. This is clearly not sustainable, and we must stop drawing down nature's capital to support our lifestyle.

Why have we made so little progress on these and other global environmental issues? I believe that one impediment is our tendency, within the short lifespan of a human, to reset or shift the baseline of what is natural and acceptable. When I was growing up in Cleveland, my father used to take me to an area, fully suburb, where as a boy he caught toads. When I caught toads with him in the 1950s, we had to drive further to reach the countryside, to an area that has now sadly also succumbed to suburb. I suspect that if I lived in Cleveland today, I would have to drive even further afield to find toads. But, mentally, I set my baseline of a pristine environment not at the fields of my father's time, but to the fields that I remember. And today's generation would set it even further afield, creating, in the words of Daniel Pauly (1995), a "shifting baseline" against which to measure environmental degradation. We have lost track of what nature once was.

My suspicion is that continuous resetting of the baseline of environmental acceptability lessens our appreciation of the long-term degradation of Earth's ecosystems. This explains why those concerned with overpopulation tend to be among the older of us—those who can remember when the Earth's population was 2.5 billion folks, rather than the 6.8 billion of today. Our baseline is lower, our concern about the change greater, and our belief more passionate that time is short—before we too pass on and the acceptable baseline of population density and environmental degradation is once again reset to a higher level.

What can we do?

Scientists can show us how the world works and identify ways that humans are affecting nature. Concurrently, I believe that religious organizations have a major role to play from their teaching of the Bible, which casts humans as stewards of nature, to their ability to connect the current, conservative national agenda to a religious agenda that embraces the environment. Religious organizations can muster grass-roots support that will make a difference. If the communities of faith in America speak out, their voice will equal that of major corporations, and politicians will listen. Indeed, religious organizations are the only groups with the clout in numbers and finances that can equal the powerful corporate forces that foster environmental abuse.

How we tackle global issues may well determine whether our population will face the fate of a small population of reindeer, added to an island off the coast of Alaska in the 1940s. Their rising population, in a trajectory similar to our own, soon ate all their available food supply and destroyed the ability of their island ecosystem to sustain them. Collapse was inevitable and swift (Klein 1968).

For us, our island is planet Earth. It is not getting larger, nor do I expect an interplanetary delivery of life-sustaining resources from outside our sphere. We must manage our home well, and have our eyes open to degradation of the environment that will lead to the demise of the blue planet, which so marvelously sustains life against the dark backdrop of outer space.

Response

Science Itself Is Only Half-Prophetic

JEFFREY D. VICKERY

DR. SCHLESINGER PROPOSES A partnership between science and faith. And in doing so he is being half-prophetic. Why half-prophetic? The biblical prophets were both fore-tellers and truth-tellers. They spoke the truth about how God's people's actions affected the outcome of their situations. These prophets surveyed human activity and measured it in comparison to God's desire and design. If God's people continued in the same sinful direction, or participated in the ungodly activity they found themselves in at the present, very negative outcomes were the reality they faced. In this manner, Jonah was a prophet with a message to the people of Nineveh: "Forty days more, and Nineveh shall be overthrown!" (Jonah 3:4b). Prophetic truth-telling poses its warning.

The other half of prophecy, however, offered solutions that involved the people of God reconsidering their relationship to God and each other. These were theological and ethical re-evaluations of their personal and corporate responses to God. In the case of the Ninevites, avoiding the destruction of the city of Nineveh did not depend upon building their defenses, but changing their hearts. Unlike many prophetic audiences in the biblical record, the people of Nineveh, led by the wisdom of their king, responded appropriately to God and were spared destruction.

The intent of prophecy, therefore, is to speak the truth, and in speaking truthfully the people are warned about what is to come. Yet prophecy is also intended to change the coming calamity by altering people's understanding of their present situation—specifically in the religious community, their standing before God, and their relationship to one another. Rather than offering "ample precedent for pessimism about human activities leading to environmental degradation," as Schlesinger suggests, the prophetic strand seems to call us to look forward, anticipating the possibility for redemption, even the redemption of creation.

What has been offered in "Eyes Wide Shut" is, therefore, half-prophetic, but an essential half; it tells us what will be if we continue to sin against creation, but it fails to tell us how our relationship before God is affecting this crisis of possibility that awaits our planet. This oversight is intentional, it seems, and comes as an invitation for the religious community to join with the scientific community so that our collective response to global warming is more fully formed. Science, therefore, voices its warning prophetically and the religious community must respond to such prophetic words with the force of faithful action that reflects the reality of the scientific message and the character of God in our world.

The general Christian population, it seems, has shown little interest in global climate change or in a concerted Christian response to its slow but sure effects. This reality has little to do with denying the reality of global warming. Only the marginalized among Christians today agree that creation is given by God for humans to dominate. Fortunately most are convinced that the scientific evidence of global warming is a fact. Yet their inability to envision a response that can help reverse the damage inhibits their willingness to change.

Science needs to move from convincing people of faith that global warming is a reality to giving us practical ways to respond. Statistical data that show warming trends provide proof of the reality of global warming, but Christians and theologians are not often motivated to action or belief from data alone. Science has the ability to move from theories and experimentation into practical application, as has happened with everything from alternative light bulbs to hybrid-engine automobiles and less environmentally damaging refrigerants.

As I do not consider myself a conservative evangelical, I posed the following question to a fellow pastor who is both a knowledgeable and opinionated conservative evangelical: What is the typical evangelical response to global warming? "Well, it varies of course, but not many of us are still saying that global warming is not happening. And they're idiots if they deny it. We're just not convinced that we can do anything that's worthwhile to stop it. So why should we change what we're doing if it's not going to make a difference."

Herein we find the challenge for science. Christians care about creation, and the effect of humanity on global warming is now a given across broad Christian perspectives (Van Houtan and Pimm 2006). Yet we need help with practical ways to respond. Contemporary Christian theology has taken a practical and ethical diversion in the last fifty years. No more do theologians have the luxury of pontificating about theological truth without practical applicability. Nor can scientists expect to win converts about the effects of global warming without offering Christians a mechanism for response. President Bush's policy of refraining from nonessential travel may be in his mind an energy policy (Leonhardt et al. 2005), but it is not enough for most Christians just to suggest they drive less. Help us drive smarter and cleaner. It is great to think we could all follow the wisdom found in a Kate Campbell song, born from a phrase of William Faulkner's in *Knight's Gambit*, and "go out into the free world and farm" in order to depend again on the earth and its abundance and thus nurture creation as it gives us life. But this, too, is unrealistic.

Christian ethics and theology, therefore, have a role to play alongside science. Christians must learn to respond to something without it having to become a crisis first. Why is it that we care for the poor and homeless when their plight is the result of a hurricane, yet we have had thousands homeless in our cities for years and not responded with the same kind of care and generosity? Pastors and theologians and church-going Christians need to find the collective desire to respond to the realities of global warming without having it come to the point of crisis. Our theological foundations are in place already, yet our motivation for response is not equivalent to our stated belief.

Let me offer a few of these theological foundations that will help move the Christian community toward Dr. Schlesinger's hoped for redemption of creation. First, he is right with regard to stewardship. A proper theology of stewardship can focus the Christian on global climate change. At the same time, we recognize that the human ability to care for creation is much more delicate and demanding than simply to claim that we know the Creator. Caregiving is exhausting, often inefficient, sometimes inconvenient, but nevertheless necessary. Biblical dominion understood as partnership rather than domination is at the heart of stewardship (Hall 1986), and yet the perception of a partnership with creation is sorely lacking in our human community.

Second, neither science nor faith communities need to wait for politics to require us to respond. Our ability to care for and sustain creation does not come as the result of legal regulations. Our ethics call us to change our action before legislation requires it. We must do what we must do even if we are not required by law. In recent days Christians have too frequently shown an ability to look to politics to save us—this runs close to blasphemy. Politics will not save creation. Religion and science together will make a difference. But only God can save creation—though this holy work comes through the obedience of God's human creation.

Third, the biblical concept of Jubilee has been tied to issues surrounding poverty, the forgiving of Third World debts, and the meeting of the UN Millennium Development Goals (Collins 1999; Sachs 2005). It is equally applicable to a Christian response to global warming. The intent of Jubilee is not only to cancel debts and release prisoners, but to return land to its original owners, and to let fields lie fallow so as to rest the earth from its continued production (Lev 25:1–7). It is an Earth Sabbath, mirrored precisely on the human observance of Sabbath. In our current circumstances, however, humanity has not allowed the rest from pollution and production and misuse that God intends for creation.

Fourth, the Christian response to global climate change will likely come from the majority of Christians globally, who are not, by the way, Americans. Asian and African Christians are calling for more substantive responses to the stewardship of creation (Kyung 1994). Feminist Christian theologians worldwide, like Sallie McFague, have already taken up the call to a theological mandate to care for creation (McFague 1987). It is time white, middle class men like myself and Schlesinger realize that we do not have all the good ideas, and that times call for us to stand aside and be led rather than lead. We have much to learn from our sisters and brothers who are too often silenced by the church.

And finally, we humans have become perpetrators of neglect rather than partners in care. Our crimes are against God's creation, and hence against God. Perhaps, then, confession and seeking forgiveness is another place to start toward the redemption of creation. After all, what comes closer to the heart of Christian theology than the asking and seeking of redemption, and the restoration of life to that which we have harmed.

Two

Censuring Nature and Critiquing God
A Third Option for Ecotheology

LISA SIDERIS

"Improvement makes straight roads, but the crooked roads, without Improvement, are roads of Genius."

—William Blake

IN BARBARA KINGSOLVER'S NOVEL *The Poisonwood Bible*, a southern Baptist missionary brings his family to the politically volatile Belgian Congo of the 1960s, expecting to convert the Congolese to the unimpeachable logic of Christianity. Soon after their arrival, the minister and his young daughter Leah survey their new vegetable garden. Intended as a model for their neighbors to emulate, the garden is the product of good Kentucky seeds, honest Christian labor, and strange African soil. The vines stretch endlessly toward the hot sun, apparently thriving, but day after day they refuse to set fruit. As they ponder this horticultural mystery, their conversation turns to the size of heaven, and whether it is capacious enough to accommodate all who are saved. The minister confidently assures his daughter that there will always be room for the righteous, whom God delivers from every affliction. "But you know, Leah," he goes on to say, "sometimes He doesn't deliver us *out* of our hardships but *through* them." Leah has never considered the possibility that God's plan might *include* the suffering of the righteous, and she finds this idea as strange and unsettling as their funereal garden. It is her first inkling that

---

1. A similar version of this chapter appeared in Preston and Ouderkirk (2007). This version appears with the permission of Springer Science and Business Media.

hard work and sacrifice are not always compensated, that all things do not necessarily work together for the good of those who love God.

Christians have always struggled to find redemptive value in sacrifice and suffering, and ecological theologians are no exception. The need to affirm that deliverance from suffering, perhaps even a heavenly reward, awaits all righteous beings—human and nonhuman alike—is sometimes very strong in ecotheology. In much of this literature, as in Kingsolver's story, a desire to see all suffering compensated is intertwined with a longing to see nature recreated according to an imported and transplanted ideal. The ecological imperatives that issue from such expectations sometimes fail to find purchase in the natural world we actually inhabit.

Just as the minister's remarks seem to Leah an insufficient response to the problem of suffering and the meaning of sacrifice, a theology and theodicy more firmly rooted in evolutionary realities may be unsettling to many ecotheologians. Convinced that God is essentially good and praiseworthy, many ecotheologians find fault instead with natural processes. Restoring nature to its original, pre-Fall goodness brings it back in line with the intentions of the creator. Surely God would have us facilitate the flourishing of individuals as well as their communities. In nature, as in culture, we should dismantle destructive hierarchies, banish oppression and domination of the weak by the strong. Physical health must be recognized as a "basic right" for all individuals in the natural community, as in human communities (McFague 1997: 16). However in the view I am defending, God may not will the liberation of each organism from conditions of pain and deprivation, nor does God compensate individual loss. The (very real) existence of these "disvalues" ought not to be an argument against God. Nor is wholesale, eschatological redemption of nature necessary in order to realign nature with the "true" or "ultimate" plan of God. The natural world is godly precisely because of struggle and suffering, not in spite of it. In short, I wish to defend the possibility that the natural world, in its given ordering, rather than its past or future perfection, may reflect the ordering of God, even while elements of it remain troubling, or frustrating, or even improvident, from human perspectives.

Drawing on the work of Holmes Rolston, I explicitly reject this sort of redemptive environmentalism proposed by many ecotheologians, and I endorse Rolston's wariness of ecological ethics that are inordinately preoccupied with "saving" (theologically or biologically) individual organisms, over and above concern for natural systems and natural processes.

An emphasis on biological realities may not sit well with the soteriological and eschatological orientation of much of Christian environmental ethics. Nevertheless, I believe that the key to harmonizing natural selection and Christianity—while still offering a realistic environmental ethic—may lie in re-thinking a perennially thorny issue: the status of the individual organism, and its suffering, within the overarching processes of evolution. Many Christians encountering evolutionary theory—ranging from Darwin to modern day ecotheologians—have had difficulty facing this fact of nature squarely without either repudiating God or censuring nature. In order to appreciate what is so troubling to Christians about Darwinian nature, we begin by examining the theological anxieties of the best spokesperson for a Darwinian worldview, Charles Darwin himself.

DARWIN'S CRITIQUE OF GOD

Darwin, like ecotheologians and other evolutionary theists, was troubled by evolution's apparent indifference to the fate of individuals. This brutal fact of nature was a compelling reason for Darwin's creeping atheism, but it was also one of the best pieces of evidence for his theory of natural selection. But, in general, Darwin's response was not so much to critique nature but to critique *God*. In reasoning through the conflict between widespread natural suffering and belief in a benevolent deity, Darwin took some initial, tentative steps in the direction an evolutionary theology and theodicy, before retreating once and for all to atheism.[2] "Disbelief crept over me at a very slow rate but was at last complete," he reports in his autobiography. "I can indeed hardly see how anyone ought to wish Christianity to be true" (Darwin 1958: 87). He yearned for a "better God than God," but never found him in nature (Fleming 1961: 230). Portions of Darwin's critique of Christianity were for many years omitted from his autobiography at the request of his wife Emma, who deemed some passages too "raw" for public consumption (Darwin 1958: 87). Darwin somewhat wistfully recounts his naively "orthodox" and creationist views while a young naturalist on board the *Beagle*. But with time and careful observation, he came to believe that there is "no more design in the action

---

2. Darwin vacillated somewhat even after publishing the *Origin of Species*, though not so much between atheism and theism as between atheism and agnosticism. He attended church services all his life and some of his letters to friends and family show that he continued to think about the possibilities of reconciling belief with evolutionary theory. See Rachels (1990) for a discussion of Darwin's theistic, atheistic, and agnostic tendencies.

of natural selection, than in the course which the wind blows" (1958: 87). Nature's randomness in and of itself casts some doubt on divine providence, but the deal-breaker for Darwin was the presence of so much suffering in the animal world. Such suffering makes sense in light of natural selection, which as Darwin argues is "not perfect in its action, but tends only to render each species as successful as possible in the battle for life" (Fleming 1961: 90). But suffering was not compatible with belief in the Christian God because it "revolts our understanding to suppose that his benevolence is not unbounded, for what advantage can there be in the sufferings of millions of the lower animals throughout almost endless time?" (Fleming 1961: 90).

Though Darwin presents his findings as an open-and-shut case against God, some of his insights suggest that he probed the issue more deeply. In particular, he wrestled with the problem of "counterproductive pain"—pain that seems excessive, serves no obvious purpose. This category of counterproductive or dysfunctional pain suggests that there is also pain and suffering that *is* in some sense productive or functional. Indeed, despite Darwin's rejection of theism on the grounds of widespread natural suffering, he suggests that counterproductive pain is in fact anomalous. Here Darwin discerns an opening toward an evolutionary theodicy that I think he never completely steps into. His take on the role of pain (and pleasure) in natural selection is captured well in this account:

> If all the individuals of any species were habitually to suffer to an extreme degree they would neglect to propagate their kind; but we have no reason to believe that this has ever or at least often occurred.... Now an animal may be led to pursue that course of action which is most beneficial to the species by suffering, such as pain, hunger, thirst, and fear,—or by pleasure, as in eating and drinking and in the propagation of the species, or by both means combined, as in the search for food. But pain and suffering of any kind, if long continued, causes depression and lessens the power of action; yet is well adapted to make a creature guard itself against any great or sudden evil. (1958: 89)

As Darwin notes here, pain may be functional on different levels. If not so extreme or continuous as to cause "depression," it can serve as a warning system. And while individuals may not undergo *moral* improvement, they may very well learn how better to respond to pain, or avoid it in the future. Benefits may accrue to the *species* as a whole of which the suffering individual is a member. Those individuals who respond successfully to pain (whatever that entails) may survive and pass on their successful genes. Sometimes *only* the species benefits: it is improved by weeding out of less fit members, even while no benefits accrue to the individual (which dies and/or does not "propagate its kind"). Neither of these cases is *dysfunctional*, though the second case is clearly more tragic from the standpoint of the individual. Then again, predation, usually considered a primary *source* of suffering, may also mitigate it. For organisms weakened by injury, hunger, or disease, death from predation may be preferable to a lingering death, and we may thus "console ourselves," as Darwin notes in the *Origin of Species*, that "death is generally prompt" in the war of nature (Darwin 1987: 129). Note too Darwin's recognition that pain and pleasure are intertwined: the unpleasant sensation of hunger drives the organism to procure food which is pleasant to consume (and in turn, painful, even if only briefly, for sentient prey organisms). But rarely if at all, Darwin argues, do we find pain that stands alone, with no resultant or commingled pleasure or benefit; pain that is dysfunctional in the sense that no advantage is evident at *either* the individual *or* the species level is rare-to-nonexistent. Over time, it is not favored in the evolutionary process.

Darwin, it seems to me, has partly answered his own question—and the question he essentially puts to God—of what possible "advantage" there can be in the suffering of so many individuals. In fact, he argues that we find in nature a "generally beneficent arrangement" which "harmonises well with effects which we might expect from natural selection" (Darwin 1958: 89). But if nature is *generally beneficent*, as Darwin claims, then why is atheism alone compatible with natural selection? The sticking point for Darwin seems to be that this generally good system is nevertheless sustained at the expense of the suffering individual who may receive none of its benefits. Even in those cases (which, he concedes, are the majority) where suffering produces some positive benefit somewhere, the problem remains that a God whose goodness is "not unbounded" could surely have devised a better scheme. This is a concern that Darwin shares with eco-theologians, such as Jay McDaniel, who puts it this way: "God's love for nature cannot be limited to the whole of nature at the expense of nature's parts ... If the love of God is anything like that of an all-loving parent, God would want to redeem the parts as well as the whole" (McDaniel 1989: 41). Darwin does not deny that certain "improvements" emerge from suffering, but he remains uneasy with what seems their inequitable and impersonal distribution. Add to that the weight of those anomalous but deeply troubling cases of truly dysfunctional pain, and the scales tip toward atheism.

Still, Darwin would remind us, the natural world ought not to be faulted—it is after all merely the result of "fixed laws" that do manage to produce "endlessly beautiful adaptations" (Darwin 1958: 87–88). As Darwin concludes in the famous, final passage of the *Origin of Species*, there is undeniable "grandeur" in an evolutionary view of life. But the same cannot be said of evolution's author.

PEACEABLE KINGDOMS AND COMMUNITY ETHICS

Ironically, as I have suggested, this preoccupation with uncompensated individual suffering is one that Darwin shares with many ecotheologians who otherwise tend to ignore Darwinism. Rather than critique God, many take a dim view of natural processes and regard nature's apparent cruelty as a symptom of the Fall which corrupted its original goodness and perfection.[3] Consequently, their environmental ethics often seek to guide nature back to "pre-Fall" conditions that are biologically impossible (Sideris 2003).

Newcomers to the field might be surprised to discover just how rampant the belief in nature's inadequacy—its fallenness—is in ecotheology, particularly given recent efforts by many Christian environmentalists to attain greater scientific literacy.[4] The motif of the Peaceable Kingdom, in which predator and prey exist in harmony and nature is once more infused with a tranquil abundance, recurs throughout this literature. Above all, ecotheologians want to join the good of the individual and the good of the natural "community"—the parts and the wholes—in a way that dissolves all conflicts between them. The "problem" of predation is the most obvious, though not the only, form of conflict between the individual and the natural system in which it is embedded.

---

3. Darwin himself rejected any notion of nature's sinful fallenness, in part because the late appearance of humans on the evolutionary scene makes this explanation untenable, but also because he wanted to dissociate his own theory from theories of "devolution" that claimed certain lifeforms (including "savage" human tribes) had degenerated from a more perfect, former condition.

4. All of the ecotheologians cited here claim that their ecological views are scientifically informed. In fact some explicitly make claims to a Darwinian worldview.

For some of the most prominent ecotheologians, biblical stories of a lost paradise serve as a touchstone for environmental ethics. Rosemary Radford Ruether hopes for a final restoration of nature that will usher in "right relations" among all creatures, thus "healing nature's enmity." The book of Isaiah, she reminds us, promises that "even the carnivorous conflict between animals will be overcome in the Peaceable Kingdom" (Ruether 1994: 213). Sallie McFague offers a "subject-subjects model" drawing inspiration from biblical stories "in which the lion and the lamb, the child and the snake, lie down together; where there is food for all; where neither people nor animals are destroying one another" (1987: 158). Jürgen Moltmann awaits the time of *creatio nova* when the spirit of God "drives out the forces of the negative, and therefore also banishes fear and the struggle for existence from creation" (1993: 102). A "peaceable kingdom of shalom and ecological harmony" in which "predatorial behavior will no longer characterize human and non-human relations" comprises part of Michael Northcott's vision of God's will for creation (1998: 194). Charles Birch also anticipates a time when "paradise is regained, and everyone not only goes back to a nonmeat diet, but the friendliest relations subsist between all species" (1990: 67). Even secular ethicists such as Tom Regan have at times advocated animal rights as an important step in the "journey back (or forward) to Eden [and] God's original hopes for and plans in creation," though here the issue is more one of humans eating other animals than nonhuman animals eating each other (1990: 87). Ecotheologian Larry Rasmussen explicitly acknowledges that predation is "not a pattern of morality we praise and advocate" for our own communities—at least, he quips, "not on our better days" (1990: 347). Yet the sort of natural community envisioned by many ecotheologians could come into existence only if natural selection were somehow to cease. One way of at least mitigating natural suffering is discernible, some argue, in Jesus's radically inclusive community ethic. We ought to care for *nature's* marginalized, despised, and oppressed beings, "healing the wounds of nature and feeding its starving creatures," just as a Christian community would focus on "feeding and healing its needy human beings" (1990: 160). However, far less attention is given to the possibility that we might discern God's ordering in the patterns and processes—including natural selection—evident in the world we actually inhabit. This possibility receives sustained attention from Rolston. With ecotheologians' call for a restored, Edenic creation still echoing in our ears, we turn now to Rolston's response.

REDEMPTIVE ENVIRONMENTALISM

Rolston and Darwin agree that the Fall and the account of evil it implies makes little sense in light of natural history, given that struggle and suffering were extant in nature long before humans evolved. Biblical passages implying that nature is fallen and in need of restoration ought not to be read as a mandate for "redemptive wildlands management" (Rolston 1992: 131). A "peaceable natural kingdom, where the lion lies down with the lamb . . . is a cultural metaphor and cannot be interpreted in censure of natural history" (1992: 131). This reminder also casts doubt on the proposal that we minister to nature with the ethics of Jesus in mind. The feeding of hungry persons advocated in certain biblical passages does not require feeding wild animals. Pointless suffering in human culture ought to be addressed whenever possible, but a similar ethic of compassion toward the suffering individual may not be appropriate in nature. Humans are no longer buffeted by the forces of natural selection as our wild relatives are; for better or for worse, we have largely succeeded in removing ourselves—and our domesticated animals—from these refining fires. Suffering in nature, however, involves "pain instrumental to the survival of the species, even after it becomes no longer in the interest of the pained individual" (1994: 140). Redemption, then, cannot mean saving individual organisms from such conditions, which would only undermine evolution's way of adapting species to changing environments, and possibly create more suffering.

Still, environmental conservation might be seen as a kind of redemption, ensuring that natural goods are saved and passed on. Redemption in this sense enables nature's "biotic self-renewal," in Aldo Leopold's phrase. Redemption *qua* regeneration may even be linked to suffering, but not in the sense that redemption is a remedy for sin and suffering. Rather, it is more accurate to say that pain is sometimes a *prelude* to, an inauguration of, redemptive, regenerative processes, as with the birth process.[5] While environmental destruction resulting from human carelessness might be termed "sinful," nature itself is not sinful in the sense that its present predatory structure emerged as a postlapsarian phenomenon. On the contrary, those interactions are the very means by which nature con-

---

5. This is a suggestive parallel between the birth process and other processes in nature that cause pain, in light of the fact that the Genesis account explains pain in childbirth as a result of, and punishment for, sin.

tinually regenerates and transforms itself. In these processes, "corporate biological identity persists where individual and physical identity is transient" (Rolston 1987: 86). Along with this form of biological persistence there is also a persistence of value—a capturing and smearing out of the individual's value in the larger system. Beyond this, however, there is no further redemption or reward for the individual's sacrifice, no eschatological resurrection of its individual identity.

The question we ought to ask, then, is not: Why isn't nature a perfect Eden for all beings? Rather, Rolston would stress, we should ask whether nature exhibits "significant suffering through to something higher" (1987: 142). But what exactly is meant by "something higher"? Rolston does not mean that a more perfect, compensatory order awaits each sufferer, human and animal alike, but the phrase invites criticism from a Darwinian standpoint and I am in partial agreement with some such critics (though perhaps for different reasons). Darwin himself often avoided language of "higher" and "lower" forms in nature in light of the teleological and directional overtones of such terms.

SYSTEMIC VALUE, HOLISM, AND CRUCIFORM NATURE

The value of processes such as natural selection and ecological interactions can be understood as systemic and emergent—that is, values projected out from the whole system rather than residing individually in each part of it. This is not to say that subordinate parts, such as individuals, have no value or have only instrumental value. Rather, on this account, systems as well as their subordinate parts, have intrinsic value and these values are objectively real and not merely anthropogenic constructions. However, the value of the constitutive parts, including individual organisms, is less than the value of the whole, even when those individual parts are "tallied up." This is so because much of what is valuable about nature goes on in the processes that propel the system forward, not merely in the products. Some properties belonging to the whole are not manifest in the individual parts. A species, for example, has a collective "gene pool" which confers some flexibility in adapting to changing environments; yet any given representative of that species possesses only a subset of those genes. Thus an organism may or may not be a good evolutionary fit, but the species line has "options" and collective creativity. Species and ecosystems have emergent properties and therefore emergent values. Our duties are not just to species, but also to processes such as *speciation*.

Because evolutionary processes are themselves value-generating, interventions in such processes are warranted primarily when humans' past interventions have disrupted natural function: damage to nature (and attendant suffering) caused by humans should be addressed, but always with the somewhat paradoxical goal of managing nature so that it can manage itself. Genuine conflicts of intrinsic value occur infrequently in nature because natural values do not so much *clash* as blend or merge, becoming "transmuted" into something else. Thus, Rolston's view, many of the conflicts that generate "unjust" suffering in nature—suffering that ought to be redressed—are the result of past human actions that imperiled parts of nature. Seeking to resolve those conflicts engages us in a complex task of mimicking holistic, natural processes and this means, at times, treating the parts as relatively expendable, vis-à-vis the whole, just as nature appears to. (It may also lead to affirming very controversial actions in wildlife management.)

Emergent values of the system are bound up with and generated by the "disvalues" such as suffering. Yet if we take a long view, a systemic perspective, it is clear that local disvalues are often (not always, we must concede) transformed. Chief among nature's disvalues, of course, is predation. Another is the surplus reproduction of organisms that dooms so many to premature death. In predation, the value of a prey organism's life is not so much lost through predation as *captured*, to use Rolston's preferred term. Moreover, the individual prey that is consumed obviously "loses all; but [its] species may gain as the population is regulated, as selection for better skills at avoiding predation takes place" (Rolston 1992: 253–54). Darwin hints at much of this in his discussion of the pleasures and pains that drive evolution. But perhaps we can push the argument further, suggesting that predation drives evolutionary values onward *and* upward, toward greater complexity, intelligence, even beauty. In this light, not only are disvalues muted systemically, but evolution appears to be value-*enhancing*. Evolutionary "upstrokes," as Rolston calls them, are instances of value capture: lower intrinsic values are caught by the system and, in a sense, locked in, even though evolution does not *anticipate* these upstrokes. The predatory process allows species to "rise higher on the trophic pyramid, funded by capturing resources from below for greater achievements in sentience, cognition, and mobility" (Rolston 1992: 254).

Thus, the human species, while not the goal of evolution, could not have come to exist without predation in our evolutionary past.

Another disvalue is that of nature's apparent wastefulness and the suffering that results when far more organisms are produced than can possibly survive. Oak trees, for example, may generate 200 million acorns to replace themselves once or twice; a pair of birds may produce thirty eggs to replace themselves. Yet the largest surpluses of offspring occur among the least sentient species: acorns, for example, do not suffer when dined upon by squirrels. And in general, energy and biomass tend to be used by nature (not wasted). Often, in order to see these values transmuted, we must "transpose the question from one of human preferences into one about systemic processes" (Rolston 1992: 255).

I like to think that Darwin might find some comfort in arguments that highlight the capture and transformation, not mere loss or destruction, of values in evolution. But Darwin might well ask why God could not design a better system, such that these disvalues did not need to be transformed into something "better." Assuming that Darwin would still cast his vote for atheism, he might at least concede that certain affinities exist between natural selection and Christian theology—what Rolston identifies as the cruciform essence of nature. While we cannot be assured that *every* case of individual suffering is transvaluated, much less redeemed, in the next life, we can discern in evolution a type of redemptive transformation through suffering. Extrapolating over generations, or even millennia, pain and the drive to avoid it, can alter evolutionary history, as when prey species evolve structures or behaviors enhancing their ability to elude predators. Of course, predators too must hone their hunting skills to survive, and thus pain is never eliminated from the system. Like Darwin, Rolston maintains that counterproductive pain is relatively rare in evolutionary biology. He echoes Darwin in stressing that "any population whose members are constantly in counterproductive pain will be selected against and go extinct or develop some capacities to minimize pain" (Rolston 1999: 305). In *biological* terms, we can say that such pain tends to be maladaptive, while functional pain tends to be favored by selection. In more *theological* terms, we might say that life as a whole *suffers through to something higher*. Here biology and theology are not inconsistent.

This is so because the "Judeo-Christian faith never teaches that God eschews suffering in the achievement of the divine purposes," he reminds us (Rolston 1999: 145). Christians have misunderstood the tradition if they perceive religion as a shield against suffering; Christian teaching is "a call to suffer and to be delivered as one passes through it" (Rolston 1999: 221). In the concept of a Messiah we see life produced out of death, crucifixion and resurrection intertwined, new life rising out of old, "life suffering through toward something higher" (Rolston 1999: 135). To paraphrase Kingsolver's Baptist minister, God does not deliver life *out* of suffering but *through* it. Seen in this light, nature is cruciform because of struggle, not merely in its absence. However, seeing the transformed value demands expanding our usual, anthropocentric perspective to gain an appreciation of a broader, projective kind of value. Most of all, it demands that we consider that the way nature works is the way God works, even if it is not our way: In nature we see that "God writes straight with crooked lines" (Rolston 1999: 46, 129).

CRITIQUES FROM EVOLUTIONARY THEODICY

Of course, critics may object that Christianity loses its meaning if it fails to offer a promise of compensation for all cases of struggle and sacrifice. I want to briefly consider a few of these criticisms now. A reminder: It is important to keep in mind that I am seeking here a form of reconciliation of evolution and theism that *also* generates environmental imperatives that make sense in the world we actually live in.

We can put a very basic challenge to the systemic account: How do we *know* that the system is on the whole more valuable than disvaluable? How do we demonstrate this? One response might be to emphasize that evolution is not merely value-transforming but (as Rolston suggests) value-*enhancing*: in other words, we should not simply weigh the quantity of values versus disvalues but consider greater *quality* of certain values, the "higher values," generated in the transformative process. (However, insisting that some forms or modes of life represent higher values may land the systemic account in a different set of problems.)

Robin Attfield suggests a different way of showing the overall goodness or value of natural systems: Instead of pulling back to take in the broadest possible view of evolution's straight lines, Attfield wants to zoom in on the crooked lines with which God writes, and ask whether there isn't perhaps more happiness (and value) in those individual lives than is initially perceived.[6] He wants to give more weight to the lives of indi-

---

6. Attfield's argument seems to be the opposite of Ouderkirk's in this respect—i.e.,

viduals (prey included) without disputing the "impressive" case for systemic value. "What should be added to the balance of the argument here," Attfield notes, "is the *intrinsic value of the flourishing of each flourishing creature that ever lived*" (2000: 292–93). If I follow him, Attfield's locution here, "the flourishing of each flourishing creature," is not merely redundant. Attfield is *not* saying (as some ecotheologians do) that the system is a just one if, and *only* if, both the individual and the larger community can flourish simultaneously. If I have further understood Attfield correctly, he is distinguishing flourishing, on the one hand, from simple Darwinian fitness on the other. An organism can flourish—have a rich, pleasurable life—up to the moment when it is brought down by a predator, for example, or until the winter comes that finally proves too harsh. "The failure of most individuals to live long enough to reproduce," Attfield points out, "does not betoken that there are no elements of flourishing in their lives" (2000: 294).

I think Attfield is right. An individual's pre-mortem flourishing may not count for much in evolutionary *theory* where differential survival and reproductive rates and relative fitness are objectively calculated. But it ought to count for something in an evolutionary *theodicy*, where creation's (and the Creator's) goodness is at stake, regardless of the organism's inability, ultimately, to elude predators, survive a harsh winter, and pass on its genes. But would Darwin be convinced by this argument for the overall value of nature?

Assuming that Darwin has stubbornly remained in the atheist camp, Attfield's amendment here, combined with all foregoing arguments, might help tip the scales back toward some form of theism.[7] Darwin himself insists (or at least hopes) that while widespread suffering is a fact of life in the wild, there are "other considerations" that "lead to the belief that all sentient beings have been formed so as to enjoy, as a general rule, happiness" (1958: 88). Perhaps he just needed a little convincing.

Rolston has made too much rather than too little of these local disvalues. Both agree that given Rolston's own account of this system, the verdict on nature's goodness *in toto* could go either way, but Attfield's amendment tries to coax it in the direction of goodness.

7. This suggestion seems similar to McDaniel's (1989: 48) claim that even individual organisms that suffer and die prematurely nevertheless experience richness while they live, and their richness may contribute to the divine life—to God understood as an "ecological Whole." Though McDaniel *hopes* for an eschatological resurrection of the individual, he does not think it necessary in order to show the goodness of God. I suspect Rolston might be wary of McDaniel's process-influenced, close identification of God with the "ecological Whole," however.

However, Attfield raises a different concern here as well, and this brings us back to the issue of measuring quality and not mere quantity of values in nature. One could argue that since Rolston's theodicy maintains that human evolution required predation, then disvalues associated with predation are redeemed only in light of the emergence of higher lifeforms—especially humans—to redeem disvalues. Of course, saying that predation produced higher forms, including humans, is not the same as saying that these developments in evolution are valuable only because humans arose. But one must be clear about this, and on this point, Rolston himself is not always as clear as I would like. He claims, for example, that evolution is not orthogenetic but opportunistic: "chance favors the selective system that gropes for life . . . [and] locks in the upstrokes" (1987: 127). Yet, at times he maintains that through evolution God has "lured the ascent" of life, turning "protazoans into persons" (1987: 119; 1994: 228). I think a good Darwinian would do well to avoid this sort of directional and hierarchical language. Highlighting—as Attfield does—individual, subjective flourishing distinct from objective Darwinian (reproductive) fitness sheds light on the overall value of the system and its members, without resorting to teleological claims about the necessary appearance of higher lifeforms such as humans.

Before concluding, I want to look at one final criticism of systemic value and the alternative offered by that critic. Christopher Southgate proposes a system of biological and theological redemption in the here-and-now that harmonizes with some aspects of the account I am defending (2002: 803–24). However, he argues—correctly—that the systemic view "does not in itself 'redeem' the suffering experienced by individuals . . . does not comprehend all that is connoted by the word redemption . . . the suffering of individual organisms, even if it promotes the flourishing of others, must still remain a challenge for theodicy" (2002: 805). Southgate proposes to meet this challenge head-on, by constructing a genuinely Darwinian form of Christian theodicy that still ensures redemptive compensation for each individual victim of natural selection.

I have argued that Christians encountering Darwinism often critique either God or nature. Southgate engages in a bit of both. Like Darwin, he cannot reconcile the unredeemed suffering of millions of individual organisms with the existence of a God who remains worthy of our worship. He attempts to restore God's worthiness by means of two postulates: (a) God does not abandon victims of evolution, and (b) Humans are called to become healers and co-redeemers of the world. Specifically, our calling engages us in nothing less than "the redemption of evolution" in "real time" (2002: 815–19). This involves healing nature in keeping with humans' role as not merely *co-creators* with God but also "as co-redeemers ... of the whole evolutionary process" (2002: 818).

To his credit, Southgate concedes the problematic nature of his proposal to redeem evolution—after all, he notes, we would not expect to redeem "the law of gravity." But the idea "warrants further exploration," albeit with deep humility (2002: 818). We might, for example, adopt a vegetarian lifestyle as a form of real-time redemption; at the very least, he suggests, we should seek more humane methods of animal husbandry. Note that, while commendable, neither of these suggestions deals directly with *evolutionary* processes but rather with cultural practices regarding domesticated food animals. However, Southgate also calls for "wise conservation and repair of the environment" as marks of "redeemed human vision" (2002: 819). But it is difficult—at least for me—to imagine how we might "conserve" nature, or anything valuable therein, while at the same time shutting down *the whole evolutionary process*.

As if redemption of evolution in real-time were not a tall enough order, Southgate further endorses retroactive compensation, to "wipe the tears from the eyes of evolution's myriad past victims" (2002: 820). In other words, even if we could halt the violence of natural selection right now, we still must compensate all evolutionary casualties since the beginning of life on earth. Clearly this lies beyond human powers, so Southgate espouses as "necessary" the existence of an animal heaven in order to ensure that all of evolution's victims "are able to fulfill their being."[8] As co-redeemers of evolution, we do our part on earth and hope that God will follow suit and do his part in heaven.

Rather than humility, this proposal unfortunately resembles—if it's not too quaint a word—blasphemy. A theory of evolutionary, systemic value *already entails* a form of real-time, and this-worldly, transformation. The difference is that it lies within natural processes themselves, processes whose time scale may not be the same as ours and whose form

---

8. Ibid., 820. Southgate makes specific mention of "pelican heaven" following McDaniel (1989) who discusses the problem of the "back-up chick," the neglected second-born chick who usually fails to survive but serves as insurance for the parents when the first born dies. Rolston (1987) also discusses the back-up chick as a "discordant" case in evolution in *Science and Religion*.

of redemption may not satisfy us. Yet, of course, as humans we never do see the *whole* narrative of evolution but only pages of it. But in seeking to "redeem" evolutionary processes and render God more worthy of worship, Southgate, and many like-minded theologians, would put an end to this story, to the very system that generates and maintains value, beauty, and sentience in our world. Such proposals for reconciling evolution with religion, while holding tenaciously to human perspectives on suffering and individual justice, require so many additional theological postulates and such tweaking of biological data that they become unwieldy and unconvincing. Like the Ptolemaic model of astronomy requiring numerous epicycles, gears upon gears, in order to maintain the conviction that everything revolves around Earth, these solutions become cumbersome in their attempts to save the phenomena.[9] The simpler, and more elegant, solution would be to admit that humans, and their particular concerns and judgments and experiences, are not and ought not to be central in environmental ethics.

~

In the scene from *The Poisonwood Bible* with which I began, the minister and his daughter eventually solve the mystery of their garden's fruitlessness: though their African mission is overrun with a fearsome array of insect species, not one of them is the sort that pollinates their Kentucky Wonder beans. Their hard work and sacrifice has been for naught. In a sudden rage over his recent string of failures, the minister turns on the pet parrot Methuselah, a native of the Congo passed on to them from a previous missionary. He pulls the terrified bird from its cage and hurls it skyward. With some instinctive memory of flight still lingering in clipped wings, Methuselah manages a soft landing atop their fruitless vines. For months afterward, he hovers pathetically near their home, no longer able to survive in the wild. One day, a pile of bloodied feathers confirms that Methuselah's life has been cut short by an anonymous predator. In Kingsolver's narrative, Methuselah's ill-fated "freedom" is symbolic of the newly gained, dubious independence of the Republic of Congo. But at another level, the story contains an important message about wildness

---

9. Intellectual honesty compels me to note that historians of science routinely point out that the Copernican model eventually became quite cumbersome as well, perhaps as cumbersome as the Ptolemaic model it replaced—at least until Kepler clarified things.

and cultivation, nature and culture, and the way in which these overlapping categories complicate our human sense of fairness. Kingsolver's story is one of humans raging against, and sometimes blaming, God for the wrong things. If anyone is wronged in this scenario it is surely Methuselah—not so much because he was devoured by a predator, which is a common enough fate of jungle birds—but because humans stripped him of his natural powers and cast him off. The minister's misdirected anger is really a rebuke of God—a rebuke not unlike Darwin's—for failing to provide a natural world that conforms to human expectations of justice and fairness.

Environmental ethicists ought to be more circumspect about censuring nature—or God—for processes that fail to match human preferences. Perhaps God is also interested in the larger currents of life, the overall sorting rather than the local shuffling, the *supervival* of the system as a whole, as Rolston calls it, rather than the survival of each and every individual part. Perhaps the conflict we perceive between individual flourishing and systemic flourishing is a problem only for human culture—not for nature or for God either.[10] To be sure, it is not easy to construe the world from non-anthropocentric perspectives or to accept nature as it is. We may struggle to see God in nature's struggle, to see how God writes straight with crooked lines. But it is not the place of humans to erase or re-write those lines, even if we could. By holding fast to this conviction, Christians may have more success in bringing evolution and theism closer together while moving environmental ethics away from inappropriately human-centered concerns and values.

---

10. It may not even be accurate to say that this "conflict" has posed a problem for *all* human cultures. I am grateful to Greg Mikkelson for pointing this out.

Response

Wrestling with Evolutionary Biology and Theology

NORMAN CHRISTENSEN

IT IS FASCINATING THAT we are at once awed by the "balance of nature," but often repulsed by the processes—predation, pestilence, and decay—that maintain that balance. In the final sentence of his *Origin of Species*, Charles Darwin exalts in the "grandeur in this view of life, with its several powers, having been originally breathed by the Creator into a few forms or into one; and that, whilst this planet has gone cycling on according to the fixed law of gravity, from so simple a beginning endless forms most beautiful and most wonderful have been, and are being, evolved." But Darwin abandoned whatever belief he may have held in that Creator because that grandeur is achieved through the "sufferings of millions of ... animals throughout almost endless time." Given the high rates of predation on young birds, that His eye is on the sparrow can hardly be reassuring.

Aside from their theological implications, ecologists have had a long and difficult history of understanding and coping with predators and predation. None other than Aldo Leopold spent the first half of his professional career trying to rid ecosystems of predators. This he did as part of a seemingly unholy alliance between the animal protection community which was concerned about the suffering of prey and the hunting community which disliked competition from other predators, or—to use their word—varmints.

In a poignant essay on this topic, Leopold describes the moment at which his understanding of predators was transformed. He was charged with the management of a National Forest that he referred to as "the mountain." On sighting a wolf with her cubs, Leopold and a companion empty their rifles. In his words:

> We reached the old wolf in time to watch a fierce green fire dying in her eyes. I realized then, and have known ever since, that there was something new to me in those eyes—something known to her and the mountain ... I thought that because fewer wolves meant more deer, that no wolves would mean a hunter's paradise. But after seeing the green fire die, I sensed that neither wolf nor mountain agreed with such a view. Since then I have lived to see state after state extirpate its wolves ... I have seen every edible bush and seedling browsed ... and, the starved bones of the hoped for deer herd. I now suspect that just as a deer lives in mortal fear of its wolves, so does the mountain live in mortal fear of its deer. (1966: 129)

Some years ago, I chaired a federal panel charged with determining whether the National Park Service should establish feeding programs for the Elk herd in Yellowstone National Park following the 1988 fires (Christensen et al. 1989). Many people and organizations expressed concern that the loss of winter range coupled with a hard winter would result in widespread starvation in the herd. For a variety of reasons, our panel's strong recommendation was that such a feeding program was contrary to the mission of a Park dedicated to the conservation of wild nature. We further pointed out that the elk population was, by many estimates, well above the carrying capacity and that the increased mortality, by removing sick or aged animals, would improve the overall health of the herd.

Shortly after our recommendations were published, I was called by a Washington Post reporter who seriously questioned the panel's logic. Central to his concerns was the morality of our position that it was appropriate to "cull the herd" in the interests of the population or the ecosystem. He wondered how this was different than arguing for eugenics, forced euthanasia, or ethnic cleansing in human populations. Although I remain convinced that our panel's recommendation was appropriate for the future of both the elk and the Park, I understand the logic of his argument and the dilemma that it presents us.

My fundamentalist Christian parents reject evolution quite simply because it proposes a process and timeline that is inconsistent with a literal interpretation of the Genesis creation story. This clearly was not Darwin's problem with God. I think many of us would agree that creation stories serve primarily to tell us why we are where we are and to justify in some sense the way we are. The author or authors of Genesis seem to me more interested describing and justifying changing gender roles and our relationship to nature than they are in a dispassionate presentation of the history of our origins. In comparison, evolution fails as a creation story. It is intended first and foremost as an objective history of life on earth, and, quite secondarily, we are forced to ask what it means for the "why we are the way we are" question. Our answers are necessarily paradoxical and certainly less than satisfying.

Darwin's ultimate rejection of God was as much about his personal suffering over the loss of his young daughter to disease as it was over his concern for suffering in nature. Lisa Sideris posed the question of what Darwin might have decided about God had he thought about evolution or competition differently. What Darwin believed or might have believed about the Creator is of course interesting to us because it is a metaphor for the possible reconciliation of evolutionary biology and theology.

Like many others in this room, I have and continue to wrestle with that reconciliation, and my final comment on this matter is quite personal. As we consider this mystery, we are tempted to focus on the most repugnant features of nature—disease, predation, and the like—and neglect other mysteries of nature, and our own nature, that we might indeed celebrate. We are prone, perhaps with some justification, to see ourselves as unique among the products of creation or evolution, calling particular attention to such features as intelligence and self-awareness. As an evolutionary biologist and a theist, it is our capacity for empathy that I find most intriguing and, shall I say, promising. It is, after all, that capacity to project our own feelings on to others, beyond our kinship and even beyond our own species, that forms the subtext for the dilemma that Lisa Sideris has presented.

There are, of course, elements of altruistic behavior in organisms besides ourselves, and heated arguments continue regarding the genetic basis and evolutionary origins of such behavior. However, demonstrating that our capacity for caring for one another or the suffering of other species is attributable to the actions of some specific set of gene alleles that owe their existence to either natural selection or genetic drift should not diminish our commitment to the Great Commandment.

Evolutionary biologists are careful to avoid the word "purpose" in favor of "function," the former implying Lamarckian intent. Unlike

Larmarck, we are adamant that giraffes with long necks were better able to eke out a living in their struggle to survive and reproduce (function), rather than that giraffes grew long necks so that it could reach the high leaves (purpose). By extension, we may conclude that life in general, and our lives in particular, have no purpose. On this point the science of evolution is and always will be mute. While I struggle to understand suffering in the world, I struggle equally to imagine purposeless life, especially my own.

Three

A Walk on the Wild Side[1]
The Idea of Nature Revisited

MICHAEL JACKSON

"... in a sense nature is independent of thought."
—Alfred North Whitehead

IT WAS IN SWITZERLAND—or, more precisely, on an excursion to the summit of Rigi Kulm, 5,906 feet above Lake Lucerne—that I found myself thinking about the place of nature in European romanticism and the idea of human nature that is so intimately related to it. It was here that countless nineteenth-century visitors making the "grand tour" spent a night in order to watch the sunrise over the alps. An ecstatic Victor Hugo compared the scene to a monstrous ocean of gigantic waves, and likened them to the petrified breath of Jehovah that had stirred on the original face of the waters of the world, while William Wordsworth's heart "leap'd up" at "the terrible majesty" that met his eyes on his tour of the French Alps in 1791, and in *The Prelude* confessed that the mountains revealed to him "the universal reason of mankind" (Book VI, line 476). By contrast, an irreverent Mark Twain describes how he and his travelling companion were so exhausted by the climb to Rigi Kulm from the lakeside town of Wäggis that for two mornings in a row they slept in and missed the fabled sunrise altogether. On the third day, they woke in darkness and hastened

---

1. This essay appears in Jackson (2007). Used with permission of Duke University Press.

to the summit only to discover that the sun, which they thought was just rising, was in fact about to set (2003: 143–62).[2]

Twain's tomfoolery apart, it is tempting to see the European "thirst for the Alps" as a response to the political and social turmoil that had accompanied urbanization and industrialization from the late-eighteenth century. Recoiling from the horrors of the French Revolution, whose ideals he had initially embraced, Wordsworth's Jacobinism and utopian communism quickly passed, via an infatuation with the rural working class, into a faith in nature. Thus, with "melancholy waste of hopes o'erthrown" and good men on every side falling off to selfishness, he wrote: "I yet/ Despair not of our nature; but retain … a faith/ That fails not,/ in all sorrow my support,/ The blessing of my life, the gift is yours,/ Ye mountains! Thine, O nature!" (*The Prelude* Book II, lines 449–62). That the turn to nature implies a return to God is suggested, not only in Wordsworth's images of "God and Nature communing" (Ibid: line 446), but in the poetry of Gerard Manley Hopkins. In *God's Grandeur*, written over seventy years after Wordsworth's *Prelude*, Hopkins also invokes a world despoiled:

> Generations have trod, have trod, have trod;
> And all is seared with trade; bleared, smeared with toil;
> And wears man's smudge and shares man's smell: the soil
> Is bare now, nor can foot feel, being shod.

Yet for all this, Hopkins writes, "nature is never spent", and "there lives the dearest freshness deep down in things"—the inscape and instress of God—through which we may recover our original humanity.

In his 1849 essay on nature, Ralph Waldo Emerson defined nature as "essences unchanged by man" (2003: 182), and he argued that every generation longs to "enjoy an original relation to the universe" (181), which is to say, a direct and sensible relationship with the natural world that allows "the knapsack of custom" to fall from one's back (1995: 260) so that one becomes "part or particle of God" (2003: 184). Similar ideas inform the work of Mary Shelley who, in the "wet" and "ungenial" spring of 1816 when "incessant rain often confined" her, Percy Bysshe Shelley, and their infant son William to their villa on Switzerland's Lac Léman, wrote her

---

2. Fourteen years after Twain's misadventure, Georg Simmel (1991: 96) would publish his own devastating critique of the alpine experience, which Simmel saw as an expression of capitalism's infatuation with private property—an egotistical and hedonistic pursuit of subjective experience, disguising itself as a desire to build character or acquire moral virtue.

terrifying indictment of the presumptions of science and its mainly male advocates, observing that "the effect of any human endeavour to mock the stupendous mechanism of the Creator of the world" would be "supremely frightful" (Hindle 1992: xvii). And like Wordsworth, Hopkins, and Emerson, she conflated nature not only with the divine, but with the feminine. Nature was always a mother, or at least a "she."

Nowadays we are perhaps less inclined to polarize nature and culture, seeing the first as some pristine essence that becomes overlain or corrupted by an artificial or secondary reality that we call culture or civilization. New reproductive and genetic technologies, and medical advances in organ transplantation, seem to have dissolved time-honored distinctions between nature and culture and demand a new synthetic vocabulary of biosociality, hybridity, and biopower.[3] Even the line between biological kinship, based on natural or consanguineal bonds, and adoptive, assisted, fictive, and artificial kinship seems impossible to draw (Strathern 1992). Yet despite those who argue that contemporary social and technological innovations render the nature-culture dichotomy outmoded, voices continue to be raised in protest against the destruction of "natural" habitats and biodiversity, and against the "unnatural," abominable, and uncontrollable repercussions of genetic modification.

Historians of ideas have often seen these very different conceptions of nature not just as signifying postmodern and premodern worldviews, but as defining different stages in human history. Thus, R. G. Collingwood outlines three quite different ideas of nature, each based on a different root metaphor. The ancient Greeks compared nature to mind. Nature was "saturated and permeated by mind" (1944: 3) and possessed a soul or life of its own. By contrast, the thinkers of the European Enlightenment compared nature to a machine created by God, but requiring rational human management. From the late-eighteenth century, the modern scientific view emerges of nature as a counterpart to history—evolving and developing over time. The trouble with Collingwood's model is that it is

---

3. In a compelling paper that documents a Suyá man's experiences of receiving a kidney transplant in Brazil, Scheper-Hughes and Ferreira (2003) show that Suyá notions of the shamanic transmigration of souls enabled Dombá to come to terms with the biomedical transmigration of organs (132), suggesting a surprisingly "fluid and open-ended" conception of "reality, nature, human/animal, and self/other relations" (131). Even kinship identity, for the Suyá, is remarkably fluid, since it is based less on descent than on the sharing of intimate bodily substances, including milk, semen, blood, urine, sweat, spit, pus, vaginal secretions, and feces (146).

so deeply grounded in the modernist notion of teleology that it fails to recognize that though different epistemes may dominate public or scientific discourse in different epochs and in different societies, each exists everywhere and at all times as a potentiality that may be realized under certain conditions. Thus the Hellenistic worldview finds expression in contemporary Western notions of the earth as a living organism (the Gaia hypothesis), or the idea that the same reciprocal and ethical relationship that informs human intersubjectivity should govern our relations with the natural world (Abraham 1987), while the Enlightenment view of nature as something to be domesticated and dominated for the benefit of humanity underwrites the exploitative ethos of modern capitalism (Horkheimer and Adorno 1972).

My interest is not in the debate over whether nature is something to be manipulated and managed, or something to be protected and preserved; rather, I want to explore how both these modes of relating to the natural world are ways of addressing phenomena that lie at the limits of human comprehension and control. The word "nature" is, of course, not the only word that may be used to mark the extrahuman domain.[4] In medieval thought, it was the macrocosm—the great world within which the small world of human existence was embedded. For Karl Jaspers, this is "the Encompassing" (*das Umgriefende*)—a "subversive" term for demarcating the limits of knowledge and reawakening us to that which makes Being possible but which Being can never grasp through "the perspective of the conceptual" (1955: 73, 60). In Aboriginal Australia it is the Dreaming, the largely invisible and ambient field of ancestral essences and presences into which life passes at death and from life is drawn out in rituals of increase and rebirth. In West Africa, it is the bush, a domain of wild energies and nature spirits that anthropologists would, a generation ago, have called the supernatural. The words are less important than the phenomenological force-field they cover—appearing to be *at the same time* a domain of dangerous alterity *and* a source of the vital energies without which human life and human sociality cannot be sustained.

4. This way of construing nature echoes the sixteenth-century sense of nature as "all matter that exists in the world without the intervention of human agency or activity" by contrast with culture "which commonly refers to human activity, products, and accomplishments" (Bennet et al. 2005: 236), but rather than define nature and culture as designating extra-human and human realms my focus is the space between that which can and cannot be controlled, and I treat the ways in which this relationship is named as a secondary matter.

Diversity and Dominion

My argument is that our lived relationship with nature—whether we construe this psychologically as within us or physically as without—is, like any intersubjective relationship, profoundly ambivalent. On the one hand, genes, emotions, landscapes, and climates give us life; on the other hand, genetic mutations, ungoverned emotions, and wild nature in the form of hurricanes, tornados, tsunamis, volcanic eruptions, earthquakes, bush fires, and floods may destroy both lives and livelihoods.

Let me begin with two quite different ways of relating to nature (understood as that which is felt to lie at the inner or outer limits of one's physical and conceptual grasp). The first is predicated on the notion of affinity, the second on the notion of antipathy. I can best sketch what I mean by back-tracking to Switzerland and the Rigi Kulm.

My excursion to Mount Rigi returned me to my native New Zealand. This wasn't just because the alpine scenes were so similar, the same soundless collisions of cumulus cloud over the distant peaks and cloud shadows flowing down the grassy slopes of the high valleys. It was because, as a child, I developed a deep identification with the land, so that when I thought of the world to which I was naturally heir I did not think primarily of family or lineage, but of a quiet bend in a local river, a pine plantation, a remnant stand of native bush, a hill from which, on a clear day, I could see mountain Taranaki. These *physical* elements defined a *social* microcosm of which I felt intimately a part. Winter and summer, I explored, charted, named, and absorbed this world of mine until there wasn't an acre I did not know by heart. This was at once my lifeworld and myself. Animate, attuned, and entangled. So when I threw myself down in the long grass above Rigi Kaltbad, inhaling the odors of fescue, red clover, buttercup, and lucerne, catching a whiff of cow dung from the half-timbered buildings at the foot of the slope, hearing the drone of a light plane rising and falling on the breeze, I was a child again, yielding to the Taranaki landscape and finding in its sights and sounds and smells the elements of a stable world to which I felt I completely belonged. It was undoubtedly this yielding or submission to the contemplation of nature that attracted many of the nineteenth-century pilgrims to Rigi Kulm. There was a strange comfort to be had from experiencing oneself in relation to the immensity of what lay before one's eyes—the accidented roof of the Alps, scalloped, serrated, snow-flecked, with its scree slopes and cirques, and the forests and pastures far below where a window glinted in the sun and you heard the syncopated clonking of cowbells. But smelling the wildflowers, basking in the sun, or taking in the view—all images of participatory acquiescence—define only one side of the modern attitude to nature. For nature is also something to pit oneself or test oneself against, a kind of proving ground for a masculinist ethos that sees nature as something to be conquered and converted, tamed and transformed—an ethos captured in Edmund Hillary's remark to George Lowe after his ascent of Everest in 1953 with Tensing Norgay, "Well, we knocked the bastard off" (Hillary 1975: 162).

From where I was lying I could make out on the horizon the peaks of the Eiger and Jungfrau. While many visitors had come to the Rigi to see the sunrise over these Alps, others had sought to be the first to knock them off, often at considerable risk to their lives. The Matterhorn, for example, was conquered by the English climber Edward Whymper in 1865 after six failed attempts and at the cost of the lives of seven of his climbing companions.

Two contrasted modes of relating to nature are suggested here, the first characterized by union and yielding, the second by duality and dominance. While the first suggests a willing submission to a nature that is allowed to enter and even take over one's body and soul, the second implies standing out from or standing over a nature that has been subdued or backgrounded. This is the classical panoramic or perspectival standpoint, involving a separation between subject and object, observer and observed, actor and acted upon.

These contrasts apply equally to our relations with others, which is why I prefer to think of them all as intersubjective. Indeed, the co-presence of *three* dimensions of relationship—the individual body, the body politic, and the body of the land—is typical of cosmologies in all human societies. Thus the classical Chinese notion of "inner and outer worlds of experience as having identical systems of physiology" (Rawson 1968: 231), Hindu and Hippocratic images of the world as a human body, the Dogon view of the earth as made up of minerals that correspond to different bodily organs, rocks being bones, small white river pebbles being toes, and a family of red clays being the blood (Calame-Griaule 1965: 27–57), and Indo-European metaphors of the foot or brow of a hill, the mouth or arm of a river, a brooding or angry sky, and family trees with branches and roots. Rather than treat these synecdochic sets as poetic forms of expression or as markers of a palaeological mode of thought, I want to show how they provide a rationale for action in contexts where human beings come up against the limits of their capacity to comprehend and control their lifeworlds.

My first example is from the year my wife and I spent living with an Aboriginal family in the rainforests of southeast Cape York peninsula in Australia. Although Kuku Yalanji people do not think of nature and culture in the abstract, my suggestion that we might usefully construe nature as that which lies at the limits of our understanding and our power to act is consonant with the way Kuku-Yalanji see their lifeworld. Culture (a term many Aboriginal people have now adopted) covers everything *within* one's lifeworld, including land, language, kinsmen, and affines, and the ocean or rainforest ecosystems in which one lives. Although this lifeworld is divided into moieties based on an ecological distinction between rainforest-dwellers (*ngalkalji*) and coastal dwellers, everything and everyone in this lifeworld is thought to be intimately or affinally interconnected. That which lies outside this lifeworld, however, obeys "different laws" and constitutes a threat, although outsiders may be gradually accepted into one's family as affines or as friends (*jawun*). Kuku-Yalanji express these social distinctions in olfactory terms. Sea people smell of salt water and sea fish; land people smell of marsupial meat; strangers have a strong odor that is quite different. "How different," I once asked my informant Harry Shipton. "Old people said waybala smell like the slim of an eel," he said, "but they smell like bama after they bin live with us for a while."

"What about me?" I asked.

"You smell like bama," Harry said

From the beginning of our fieldwork my wife and I were struck by the linkages and lines of communication that existed within the Kuku-Yalanji lifeworld. Moreover, it became clear to us that knowing how to decipher these correspondences was vital to one's everyday life and livelihood.

Most afternoons and evenings we went fishing on a nearby beach or on a jetty on the Bloomfield River. Lacking the patience and ability to fish, I would sometimes drift into reverie, listening to the wind in the casuarinas, gazing at the long sweep of Weary bay or the dark mangrove reaches of the Bloomfield. But such an aesthetic engagement with our surroundings was foreign to our hosts, who were on constant alert for the vital signs that pointed to a hidden danger, revealed a food source, or presaged some social event. People would silently scrutinize the sea or river for signs of mullet jumping, stingray basking, or schools of herring, and if we were in the rainforest, they would be on the lookout for the spoor of deadly snakes or signs of bush tucker. Before long, I lost my habit of daydreaming and became absorbed by the pregnant meanings of the environment. A frilled lizard on a palm leaf was an augury of a coming storm. A hammer bird heard in the cold months meant that mullet would be plentiful. Bean trees flowering or the wild tamarind ripening meant that scrub hen eggs could be found. The flesh of the parcel apple turning pink meant that that liver of the stingrays would also be pink, and therefore good to eat, though eating stingrays in the preceding months (October–November) would bring storms.

With the approach of the wet season, I became increasingly fascinated by the family's preoccupation with thunder and lightning. Whereas I saw storms as natural phenomena, our hosts interpreted them in social terms; they were expressions of human malevolence and of tempestuous states of mind. Thus, the phrase *jarramali bajaku* (literally, "exceedingly stormy") is used of persons who lose self-control when drunk or drugged, while the term *jarramali* denotes any cyclonic or monsoonal storm, all of which may embody the illwill of outsiders. Questions of control thus entail allusions to individual psychology, relations with others, and relations with the elements of nature.

In Aboriginal communities one is often struck by people's extraordinary tolerance of aberrant or unruly behavior, and I was sometimes reminded of my experience among the Kuranko in Sierra Leone where incorrigible individuals would draw such comments as, "He came out of the *fafei* like that" (i.e., even initiation failed to make him mend his ways), or "That is how he was made (*a danye le wo la*) or "He is blameless; he was born with it" (*a ka tala; a soron ta la bole*). But while both Kuranko and Kulu Yalanji explain dispositions that resist socialization by invoking notions of innateness, there are practical limits to people's tolerance of antisocial behavior which, in both societies, is seen as a form of deafness to social values.

It was Christmas 1993. The heat and humidity were oppressive. Sweat dripped from my forehead onto the pages of my journal as I wrote about the tension that had built up in our camp, breaking on Boxing day like a storm, with Sonny in a fist fight with his brother-in-law, his elder sister heaping abuse on his head, another sister throwing a couple of punches for good measure, and then the youngest sister Gladys and her husband driving off to Ayton to get away from it all. As the first thunderstorm of the wet season approached, the sky turned indigo and the wind veered and picked up. There was a rattle of dry leaves and dry leaves falling, for which Kuku-Yalanji use the word *yanja*, followed by the crumpling sound of distant thunder, like heavy furniture being moved around in an upstairs room—a sound that also has its own specific ideophone, *kubun-kubun*. Painstakingly, people tracked the course of the storm, discussing where it was coming from and where heading, identifying its sounds, observing its effect on the foliage, comparing it with storms in the past. Indeed, the character of the impending storm was analyzed in the same way that people analyzed strangers—trying to read their intentions, second-guess their motives, identify their mood. As this discussion went on, various members of the family made forays into the bush in search of wild grape (*kangka*) vines, ironwood bark (*jujabala*), and grass tree (*nganjirr*). Sonny, now sober, applied himself to the business at hand, burning knotted hanks of grass, ironwood bark, and grass tree outside our camp. As the sweet smell of the grass tree pitch (*kanunjul*) spread across the clearing, I assumed that it was meant to repel mosquitoes. But Sonny told me that the storm would smell the smoke and go away. I later asked McGinty, who was not Kuku Yalanji, if he could explain to me how burning grass tree could ward off storms. The idea seemed to both amuse and embarrass him, partly because his own people on Princess Charlotte Bay used a different method of warding off storms (a certain kind of shell), partly because he did not want to give me the impression that he was a superstitious *myal*. That evening, as I was helping him put up his tarpaulin and tent at the beach, he joked about the ominous rainclouds hovering over the range. "Might rain soon," he said laconically. "Better tell that storm to wait until I get my tent up."

At Gladys's house in Ayton, however, the mood was somber. Most of the family had gathered behind closed doors, huddled and anxious as the storm approached. One of the children gave my wife a clue as to why they were so fearful: "If you eat things you are not supposed to eat, a storm will come and punish you." Was lightning an agent of retributive justice, seeking out those who might have broken a food or sex taboo, or transgressed a story place? Such matters are difficult for any anthropologist to divine, for who knows what guilty secrets a person may harbor, and whether these get projected as fears of external retribution. One thing was clear, however, and that was the association of thunderstorms and vengeful outsiders.

One morning, McGinty told me that a stranger from Kowanyama came to Wujal a few years ago. He was rumored to be a burri-burri man (a sorcerer), able to manipulate storms for his own nefarious purposes. That afternoon, Sonny opened up to me and explained the link between storms and affinity—a link that would make immediate sense to anthropologists long familiar with the ambivalence and uncertainty that marks relations between in-laws. As the Mae-Enga of the western Highlands of Papua New Guinea famously made this point, "We marry the people we fight" (Meggitt 1964: 218). Like affines, then, thunderstorms originate *elsewhere*.

Among Kuku-Yalanji, two analogous domains of relationship are posited: relations between social categories and relations between environmental elements.

The key terms, and the relationships between them, may be posited thus:

Mother-in-law : son-law :: thunderstorm : grass tree.

When thunderstorms approach, it is feared that social categories that should be kept apart are coming dangerously close together: oneself and one's enemies, insiders and outsiders. This situation is compared to the infringement of the avoidance relation between mother-in-law and son-in-law, and by association any transgression of things that should be kept apart, such as people and forbidden fruits.

The problem: how to drive the thunderstorm away?

The solution: activate the analogies alluded to above.

The practical action: grass tree logs are burned. Grass tree (as well as iron tree bark and wild grape vine) is son-in-law to the thunderstorm. The thunderstorm will smell the grass tree smoke. And just as mother-in-law will avoid her son-in-law if she smells him, so the storm will move away when it get winds of its son-in-law, the grass tree.

This brief excursion into Kuku-Yalanji ethnography enables us to see that the wild powers of what we call nature are (1) both intrapsychic and intersubjective, (2) social and physical in character, and (3) potentially destructive and creative. At the same time we have seen the ingenuity with which people seek to control wild nature, whether the momentary madness of a drunken and berserk individual or the passing danger of a cyclonic storm. However, control may take two quite different forms. It may entail repression and sublimation—which are strategies of avoidance—or it may entail management and mastery—which are strategies of engagement. In psychoanalytic theory these two themes are paradoxically entangled. As Róheim observed, it is "in the nature of our species to master reality on a libidinal basis" (1971: 105)—deferring immediate gratifications and discharging instinctual energies in non-instinctual activities and objects. For Freud, civilization is "built up upon the renunciation of instinct," which "presupposes precisely the non-satisfaction (by suppression, repression or some other means?) of powerful instincts." This "cultural frustration," Freud observes, "dominates the large field of social relationships between human beings . . . [and] is the cause of hostility against which all civilizations have to struggle" (1961: 44). But Freud's dictum, "where id is, let ego be," fails to acknowledge the extent to which our inner nature is not only a set of instincts to be repressed but a source of vitality to be channeled and liberated (Marcuse 1966). In existential terms, this implies that human beings can never find complete fulfillment in slavish conformity to socially-constructed, external patterns of behavior, for there must be, for every individual, some sense that he or she is not merely thrown into a world that has been made by others at other times but enters into it actively and vitally as someone for whom the given world is also a means whereby his or her own particular destiny is realized.

But let me return momentarily to thunder and lightning.

My theme is the paradox of power—that the same forces that threaten one's being—whether from within as libidinal energies or from without as natural elements—can, if harnessed and channeled, not only provide protection but generate and regenerate life. In the 1890s, the ethnographer W. E. Roth reported (1903: 8) that in many parts of northern Queensland, thunder and lightning were means of sorcery, but that people sometimes summoned these same forces to drive white settlers from their land (1897: 168). I heard identical stories from Harry Shipton in 1993. Many years ago, Harry told me, a white rancher, exasperated by *bama* spearing his cattle, rode up to a river encampment and shot a young girl dead. Bent on revenge, the girl's father went to the rancher's place as thunder. The rancher fired shots at the thunder but his bullets passed harmlessly through the thunder's body. Then, with a single lightning bolt, the thunder speared and killed the rancher. In another of Harry's stories, a certain white man who "messed with many *bama* girls," getting them pregnant and causing trouble, was sought out by lightning as he was driving his tractor in a Mossman cane field. "Bang! he dead, just like that."

Among the Kuranko of northeast Sierra Leone, thunder and lightning are also means of sorcery,[5] and among the most formidable masters of this power were the warrior chiefs, Bol' Tamba Marah and his younger brother Firawaka Mamburu Marah (known as Belikoro ["Mighty Elder"]), both of whom smote their enemies with lightning bolts and intimidated their own subjects in the same way.

What is fascinating here is the ambivalent and vexed relationship between secular and occult power. Ordinarily, these powers are separate and complementary, somewhat like church and state in modern Europe. Indeed, a strict distinction in Kuranko is drawn between the domain of wild powers (*suwage*[6]) associated with magical medicines (*bese*), bush spirits (*nyenne*), and secret societies (*sumafan*) and identified with the bush (*fira*), and the domain of custom (*namui* or *bimba kan*) and law (*seriye* or *ton*) associated with secular power (*noé*) and chieftaincy (*mansaye*) and identified with human settlements (*sué*). But though these domains are said to be essentially different, they are, in practice, interdependent, and each is equally vital to the Kuranko lifeworld.[7]

The Kuranko "bush" corresponds to nature seen as a force-field that lies on the margins of human comprehension and control—a source both of the energy that sustains life—in the form of game animals, medicinal plants, and rice (the staple food crop)—and of the powers that can destroy life—in the form of witchcraft, wild animals, and intractable bush spirits. For Kuranko, then, the paradox of power is that the locus of greatest insecurity and danger is also the place most vital to one's life and livelihood. To phrase this cybernetically, the social system—defined as a domain of non-negotiable roles, fixed rules, ancestral values, and received wisdom—drifts toward entropy unless it perennially taps into and draws upon the vital energies of the bush—the fertility of its soil, its natural resources, and even the *genii loci* who claim it as their own. But while Kuranko generally conceptualize the bush as an *external* domain, the term also covers *internal* powers such as the "natural gift" of intelligence, the reproductive capacity of women, the potency of men, and the disposition of magnanimity that defines personhood itself (*morgoye*).

---

5. Sangbalmatigi (lit. "thunder master").

6. Suwage connotes both witchcraft and anti-witchcraft powers—an indication of the ambiguity surrounding the domain of extra-social forces.

7. A direct analogy is with the public spheres of men and women (*ke dugu* and *musu dugu*), for while these are strictly separated, they too are functionally complementary.

Indeed, in Kuranko myth, personhood is exemplified not by ancestors but by totemic *animals* that saved the lives of clan ancestors in times of danger long ago. And it is the bush that is the source of life in rituals of initiation. For while initiation is the apotheosis of sublimation, in which instinctual tendencies are brought under strict control—sexuality finding expression in marriage and child-bearing, the body disciplined, the emotions cooled, speech measured and selfishness transcended—it is also the moment when one encounters, in cult associations, the wild powers of the djinn who, like totemic animals, are also means of imparting to ordinary human beings extraordinary powers.

The quasi-human figure of the djinn (*nyenne*) embodies what one might call natural, wild, or libidinal power. All such power is ambiguous: it may work for or against one. In Kuranko terms it is hard to know whether such power will be a good cause (*sabu nyuma*) or a bad cause (*sabu yuge*). One hears plenty of anecdotes about djinn giving a wrestler strength, a dancer grace, a diviner insight, and a musician inspiration, and there are sites in every Kuranko chiefdom, associated with djinn, where the unfortunate may offer sacrifices of food in the hope that they will be helped, or where the fortunate repay the djinn for help received. Several of the diviners with whom I worked had received their gifts from djinn that appeared to them in dreams during a bout of sickness, and both music and musical instruments are often said to have originally come from the bush. The great Malian musician Ali Farka Touré attributes his genius to the djinn. In his thirteenth year a series of visions and strange experiences transformed his playing, and he entered a new world that he compares with a prolonged sickness or epileptic seizure. "It's different from when you're in a normal state; you're not the person you know anymore" (Touré 1996). Despite such testimonies, the djinn are capricious, and their help often comes at a price. Sometimes, they simply withdraw their favors and disappear. Sometimes, as in European stories of selling one's soul to the devil, or Columbian stories of "baptized banknotes," such Faustian pacts bring a sordid boon (Taussig 1980). Among the Kuranko, a djinn that has done you a favor may demand the life of one of your children or kinsmen in return. As the original inhabitants of the land, the djinn may allow human beings to make their farms on condition they make sacrificial offerings at the beginning of each farm season, but even then a djinn may cause a farmer to cut himself with a machete or injure himself with a hoe. A djinn may possess a person, driving him mad or causing fits of delirium. A djinn may appear in a dream in the form of a beautiful woman (succubus) or handsome man (incubus), but the sexual encounter may lead to impotence or barrenness.

What is at play here is a struggle for being that involves a struggle between what is simply given to a person—his or her role, temperament (*yugi*), or birthright—and what a person desires, over and above what he or she has or who he or she is. The contrast between town and bush implies a contrast between centripetal and centrifugal forces—the first finding expression in custom and convention, the second in antinomian possibilities. Nature, in the sense in which I have been using the term, signifies a no-man's land between the known and the unknown, necessity and desire.[8] While any social system requires dutiful conformity to ancestral protocols, social life would become empty of meaning unless each person realized in himself or herself the capacity to bring the social world into being. But this capacity draws not only on what is tried and true, but on hazardous encounters with extra-social sources of power—bush spirits, wild places, limit experiences.

That one's being has its origin not only in one's position but in one's disposition, in one's standing within the established order of things as well in one's relationship with forces that have not been tamed, domesticated or socialized, is nowhere better illustrated than in the case of spirit possession, for as innumerable ethnographic studies have shown it is by allowing oneself to be overcome, taken, infiltrated, or ridden by wild powers that one discovers the resources to go on with life in the face of quotidian hardship and oppression. Thus, in Janice Boddy's compelling account of the Zar cult in northern Arabic-speaking Muslim Sudan, we learn that humans and *zar* spirits exist in parallel but contiguous worlds, the latter "within the realm of nature" and normally invisible to humans, much like the Kuranko djinn (1989: 3).Through possession, Sudanese women are taken out of their everyday lifeworlds, transcending their everyday sense of who they are, and seeing the world through new eyes.

---

8. Among the Bambara the term *sako*, which connotes social necessity, translates as "death matter," while the complementary term *dunko*, connoting inward personal desire, translates as "depth matter" (Cissé 1973: 148–49, Kassim Kone personal communication), while among the Dogon the domain of imperfection and disorder, associated with Yourougou, the pale fox, lies outside the domain of reason and social order associated with Nommo (Calame-Griaule 1965).

When the drums are beating, beating, you hear nothing, you hear from far away, you feel far away. You have left the *midan*, the place of the *zar*. And you see, you have a vision. You see through the eyes of a European. Or you see through the eyes of the West African, whichever spirit it is. You see then as a European sees—you see other Europeans, radios, Pepsis, televisions, refrigerators, automobiles, a table set with food. You forget who you are, your village, your family, you know nothing from your life. You see with the eyes of the spirit until the drumming stops (Boddy 1989: 350).

As Janice Boddy's work suggests, the world of spirits has become increasingly globalized, so that nature marks not merely the boundary between town and bush, but between local and global worlds. One also sees the widening of horizons in the changing form of witchcraft fantasies in Sierra Leone. Instead of the self-styled witch imagining that she journeys by night in some ethereal or animal shape and with her coven drains the life from some sleeping victim in another part of the country, contemporary witches imagine traveling by witch airplane across what Rosalind Shaw calls "unbounded and alluring global space" (Shaw 2002: 202).

> They often [describe] a prosperous city where skyscrapers adjoin houses of gold and diamonds; Mercedes-Benzes are driven down fine roads; street vendors roast "beefsticks" (kebabs) of human meat; boutiques sell stylish "witch-gowns" that transform their wearers into animal predators in the human world (no-ru); electronics stores sell tape recorders and televisions (and, more recently, VCRs and computers); and witch airports despatch witch planes—planes so fast, I was once told, that "they can fly to London and back within an hour"—to destinations all around the globe. (Shaw 2002: 202)

Such flights of fancy may well appear bizarre to us—on par with Kuku-Yalanji attempts to drive away thunderstorms by burning logs of grass tree. But human beings tend to think and act in remarkably similar ways when they come up against the limits of what they can understand or what they can control. Whenever our actions are ineffective or thwarted, and our understanding fails, we typically fall back on our own emotions, bodies, and thoughts as means of changing our *experience* of the world we cannot change. We thus move constantly between actual and imaginary modes of engagement with the world, depending on what circumstance and our own capacities allow. This kind of opportunistic switching between direct action and strategic inaction brings to mind Aristotle's distinction between "active" and "passive" agency[9] (*Metaphysics* (Book V, ch.12), the first referring to a subject's action on the world that changes it in some way, the second referring to a subject's being subject to the actions of others—suffering, receiving, being moved or transformed by external forces. Hannah Arendt speaks of this contrast between being an actor and being acted upon as a difference between being a "who" and a "what" (Arendt 1958: 181–86).

THE COMING ENVIRONMENTAL CRISIS

Widespread Western anxieties about global warming, environmental degradation, and polluting technologies have given rise to numerous forms of eco-activism and eco-philosophy, not to mention a proliferating literature that celebrates the virtues of the natural world while decrying its desecration. Within the academy, environmental studies has become a growth industry in science and arts faculties alike.

In March 2006, one of the doyens of this field—the Japanese-Canadian scientist and environmentalist, David Suzuki—was awarded the Roger Tory Peterson medal from the Harvard Museum of Natural History. In an impassioned acceptance speech, Suzuki observed that we had reached "a remarkable moment in the history of life on earth" and called upon his audience, as well as the developed world at large, to embrace an environmental agenda based on notions of sustainability and stewardship. In Suzuki's global conception of humanity, his invocation of our power to determine our collective fate, and an idealism that presumes some future vantage point from which it is possible to pass judgment on our times, one sees something of the intellectual hubris that writers as different as Sartre and Bourdieu have called into question. For Sartre, the bombast of intellectuals is a sign of overcompensation for their *lack* of political or social power (1983: 229), an argument that echoes the idea that the romantic infatuation with nature was a way of escaping the unmanageable mire of urban-industrial life. As for Bourdieu, his question is: "How can one avoid succumbing to this dream of omnipotence, which tends to arouse fits of bedazzled identification with great heroic roles?" How can one avoid what Schopenhauer called "pedantic comedy"—the

---

9. "Potency" is the usual translation of Aristotle's term for "a source of movement or change" (Aristotle 1941: 765).

absurd pretension of believing that there is no limit to thought, of seeing "an academic commentary as a political act or the critique of texts as a feat of resistance, and experience revolutions in the order of words as radical revolutions in the order of things" (Bourdieu 2002: 2).

My own argument is somewhat more sympathetic to public intellectuals like David Suzuki, though it is no less critical, since I repudiate the notion that enlightened thought operates solely from the standpoint of reason.

To those committed to saving the planet from ecological catastrophe, it might seem outrageous for an anthropologist like myself to question the rationality of their actions or of the scientific knowledge on which their actions are predicated. Still more outrageous would be the suggestion that their actions might be compared with the magical actions of, say, Kuku Yalanji attempting to ward off an impending thunderstorm by burning logs of grass tree. But the comparison *must* be made, if only on the grounds that there is, in both cases, little likelihood that the actions envisaged will necessarily avert the forces that are threatening the local or global lifeworlds in question. In other words, though human action is always subject to rationalization—in the Kuku Yalanji case, an argument that people can act on the forces of nature because those forces are essentially social and hence susceptible to human counteraction; in the Western case, an argument that people can avoid environmental disaster by using scientific evidence and democratic processes to pressure governments into making policy changes—*human action is motivated primarily by an existential imperative to do something rather than nothing*, and it is only secondarily a matter of which intellectual, cultural, or ritual *techne* makes the most sense, or is the most reasonable. Because our actions follow from a *need* to act before they follow from any conception of *how* to act, all action is to some extent "magical," which is to say that any action cannot be entirely explained by reference to the models adduced in justification of it. Accordingly, action implies an element of faith (one acts without being absolutely certain of the outcome), while working on the world *obliquely*, via the actor's own subjectivity. The ritualistic or magical aspect of action involves two moves. First, the scale of the macrocosm—the locus, in my examples, of both thunderstorms and global warming—is reduced to the scale of the microcosm, which is our most immediate environment, the world within our reach, the world at hand. Second, by changing our experience within this immediate world we conjure a sense of having made a difference to *the* world. It is by working on our own nature, as it were—showing concern, anguishing publicly, speaking out, affirming solidarity with like-minded souls—that we transform one's experience of an external nature that is, in fact, much more resistant to comprehension and control than we are ever likely to admit.

This is precisely how Bronislaw Malinowski explains the efficacy of Trobriand spells. Although the spells are addressed to a newly planted garden, an ocean-going canoe, or an agricultural implement, it is the *immediate subjective* effects of the spells that really matter—the ways in which they supplement action by boosting confidence, raising spirits, increasing hope, or inducing discipline. As Malinowski observes, "it is human nature on to which the force is directed" (1922: 401).

Like Trobriand Islanders, we undoubtedly need to believe that our actions can have real effects on the wider world, but global transformations are the product of such a multitude of causes and unforeseen effects that the power of conscious redressive human action is far more limited than we allow. But such skepticism as to the scope of our responsibility and agency should not be read as an argument against human action and human speech, the necessity of which both precedes and transcends our knowledge of their consequences. We must act, even if our actions only create the illusion that something has been done, some change has occurred, whether within or without.

It is for this reason that I have identified nature with the borderline between the worlds we know best and the worlds we know least, between the local spheres where our speech and actions make a difference and the spheres that lie largely beyond our grasp, much as we wish it were otherwise Nature is not, therefore, as Aristotle defined it, an essence[10] (*Metaphysics* Book V, ch. V), either deep within or distantly without, but a threshold where thought and language falter and mystery begins. If anything is in our nature it is that we are fated to live betwixt and between, as undone by what we do, what we think, and what we say as we are compelled to act, driven to understand, and bound to speak.

---

10. Compare this to the Arabic word for nature, *Tabi'ah* (literally "that which is stamped or impressed [with a quality]," and, like the Greek physis and Latin natura, referring to innate tendencies in beings.

Response

Good Work

KYLE S. VAN HOUTAN

During the construction of Emerson Hall at Harvard University in the late 1800s, the philosopher G. H. Palmer suggested Protagoras's claim, "Man is the measure of all things," serve as the inscription above the new building's entrance. Emerson Hall is the philosophy department at Harvard and is named after one of Harvard's most acclaimed sons, the great American philosopher Ralph Waldo Emerson. But the line of Protagoras never rested on Emerson's brick columns. As the story goes, Charles Eliot, then-president of the college, chose instead a verse from the eighth Psalm: "What is man that thou are mindful of him?" Though Emerson the transcendentalist may have endorsed the verse, it is likely that Palmer did not (Land 1936).

In the previous chapter, Michael Jackson chiefly argues against the idea that "Man is the measure of all things" and makes repeated claims for humility in our understanding of the world. As a scientist in my own training, I appreciate the careful way that Jackson sees nature and culture, implicitly critiquing a strong sense of scientific objectivity. Science often views itself as unique in the business of observing our lives and fashioning tools for improving it. But Jackson's stories are interesting as their vivid descriptions do not exclude the possibility that the observer influences the stories being told.[1] Whether it is consciously restrained or not, one's own life seems to surface in the telling. Observations always seem tempted by autobiography.

Hence when Jackson shares from the journals of Hugo, Wordsworth, and Twain, we see that climbing the alpine wild was not an objective

---

1. Among other fields, this insight is discussed at length by the discipline of science studies philosophy, a great example of which is Ziman (1984).

retelling of the landscape, it told us something about the writers themselves. It is as we might expect. The same Hugo who wrote *The Hunchback of Notre Dame* is somewhat dark and cosmic, almost undone by the jagged peaks. The same Wordsworth who wrote countless lines of romantic poetry is overflowing with piety. And the same Samuel Clemens who wrote *The Adventures of Tom Sawyer* is satirical and irreverent. In these stories and in the others Jackson portrays, the narrators' own character affects the characterizations they make. As an anthropologist, Jackson is well-prepared to teach this lesson, and it is one that experimental scientists could appreciate more.

This brings me to the several elements of ambivalence in Jackson's essay. In his travels and research among indigenous cultures Jackson sees nature as both the source of life and of death, capable of rousing both deep ecstasies as well as soulful turmoil. The Kuku-Yalanji people, as Jackson observes, constantly search their surroundings for "pregnant meanings" that judge human behavior or foretell future events. Approaching thunderclouds warn of human misdeeds and distant birds herald plentiful fishing. Sights and smells and noises all have vital importance in this world; interpreting them is essential to survival and peace. By comparison, Jackson's own habits were not as serious. Lying in fields of alpine wildflowers Jackson smells his childhood explorations of New Zealand mountain meadows. Bored with a day's work of fishing with the Kuku-Yalanji, Jackson happily escapes to dream of the bays and trees around him. All in all, Jackson's take on his surroundings is far less consequential than of the peoples he studies. As a result, Jackson is deeply conflicted towards work.

Jackson's conclusion of his cultural wanderings is that humans are forced to interpret their surroundings, and however accurate the interpretation, are compelled to act. Certain aspects of the human condition are inescapable—making judgments and acting—but any greater meaning here is up for grabs. This pessimism might become something like Reinhold Niebuhr's: "Man's capacity for justice makes democracy possible; but man's inclination to injustice makes democracy necessary" (1944). But Niebuhr's account of sin and his response to it do not influence Jackson. No, Jackson's conclusion is not that sin requires the wisdom of many, like Niebuhr. Rather, Jackson implies that wisdom or justice or sin do not exist. Jackson's take is that any human action is merely of our own making and for our own expressed benefit. In Jackson's view, human actions are all equally "magical" serving only to calm our anxieties that we must make some difference in the places we are. Jackson sees much work, but he sees no *good* work.

What then of the so-called ecological crisis? More than 16,000 kinds of plants and animals in this world are threatened with extinction and require human conservation efforts for their survival (IUCN 2007). Are human efforts here just some psychological salve to make us feel better about ourselves? Are ethics merely some sort of fiction? Focusing on many of the same themes as Jackson—culture, local life, work—Wendell Berry has argued for some time that conservation rests on the practice of good work.[2] For Berry, conservation "keeps work within the reach of love" (1992: 24). He continues:

> The name for our *proper* connection to the Earth is "good work," for good work involves much giving of honor. It honors the source of its materials; it honors the place where it is done; it honors the art by which it is done; it honors the thing that it makes and the user of the made thing. Good work is always modestly scaled, for it cannot ignore either the nature of the individual places or the differences between places, and it always involves a sort of religious humility, for not everything is known. (1992: 35)

Because of his observations of work, Jackson's drawing inspiration from a Gerard Manley Hopkins poem is ironic. Hopkins was a figure of astounding literary gift but was tormented by inner conflict. He lived in the second half of the nineteenth century and died early from typhoid before his poetry was either published or appreciated. Hopkins's turmoil was his perceived conflict between his literary talent and his vocation to become a Jesuit priest. Hopkins viewed the enterprise of writing as self-absorbed vainglory, something to reject in the Society of Jesus. This denial was a

---

2. Berry is not alone in arguing that modernity has stripped rural communities of the goodness of work. Schumacher (1979) previously articulated this idea in several influential articles appearing in *The Atlantic Monthly*. Schlosser (2001) and Scully (2002) more recently wrote that the entire process of animal agriculture has become intentionally industrialized and impersonal to keep costs low and labor uneducated and unorganized. What was once an artisan's vocation is now filled by disconnected foreign laborers. This change has chiefly abetted the demise of rural farming communities across the American prairies. The new labor force, however, has blossomed. This group, largely from Mexico and Central America, itself becomes an industrial cog, where workers are separated from their families and stripped of their emotional and physical health. Like Schumacher and Berry, Scully and Schlosser emphasize that good work is linked to health of people and their communities and environs.

discipline in which Hopkins painfully toiled, climaxing with his renunciation of poetry altogether and the ceremonial burning of his poems. But when Hopkins learns of a shipwreck of nuns exiled by the German Chancellor Bismarck, he is deeply moved and writes poetry anew. It is in writing *The Wreck of the Deutschland* that Hopkins seems to glimpse that his avowed life of prayer and his poetry are not at loggerheads, but that the working out of his poetry is itself a form of prayer (Hansen 2008).[3] In essence, it is the very good work he seeks. From the *Deutschland* forward Hopkins continues to write, pouring into it all his honesty, capturing the grandeur of nature even when it is hard pressed by the industrialization of the British Empire. It is his work where Hopkins situates his turmoil and is healed from it.[4]

What I take from this story of Hopkins's life is that we seem unable to shed our own skin, to be free of being the creatures that we are. By contrast this seems not a choice, as Jackson offers, between a human union with and complete submission to nature or a duality and mastery over nature—two classically flawed environmental positions. Nor does it seem a meaningless journey undone by our misdeeds or by life's uncertainty—Jackson's strongest suggestion. When confronted with the world's despair Hopkins did something interesting. Hopkins did not avoid the world's wounds and he did not ignore his own. He worked through uncertainty, anxiety, tragedy, and death and found meaning and beauty and joy. Hopkins encountered, captured so clearly by Buechner, that good work is where "our deep gladness meets the world's deep needs" (2006). In this way Hopkins became a psalmist.

This is what makes the story of Emerson Hall intriguing. We can only speculate as to why Charles Eliot chose from the eighth Psalm for his new philosophy building. Adding to the legend is that Eliot was not a philosopher himself, nor even a theologian, but a former professor of chemistry and mathematics. Eliot seemed humbled that the work of the

---

3. Hauerwas's *Prayers Plainly Spoken* (1999) further develops the idea that prayers can indeed confront the realities of this world with honesty, conviction, and peaceableness.

4. Since, Hopkins's work serves as a guide to others in their work to heal the world's wounds. Conservationists in particular draw inspiration from Hopkins's poetry. One example is Peter Harris, founder of the Christian conservation non-profit A Rocha. Harris details the influence of Hopkins on his own work in two books titled from Hopkins's verse; *Under the Bright Wings* (2000) and *Kingfisher's fire* (2008). Hansen (2008) also discusses Hopkins's poetry becoming prayerful inspiration for others.

university—whether it be in humanities or in the sciences, in research or education—was good work to serve society. This is wisdom for us today.

Four

Thanks for the Dirt

Gratitude as a Basis for Environmental Action

Norman Wirzba

WHILE IT IS FAIRLY common for people to voice general concerns about environmental degradation and destruction, their concerns do not often enough translate directly into effective personal and social reform. Though people will say that issues like global warming, species extinction, depleted fisheries, habitat loss, soil erosion, deforestation, aquifer depletion, and biological pollutants are causes for worry, it is just as likely that when they vote or shop they will choose in ways that directly undermine or compromise their concerns. How are we to account for this disconnect, and what can environmentalists do to help people bring their practical living into closer alignment with their stated concerns? Clearly, given the scope of ecological damage and the great risks we run leaving it unaddressed, environmentalists need a fresh approach if we are to move from general, abstract concerns to concrete, political and economic action.

The reality of popular ignorance, apathy, and inactivity with respect to ecological issues should be of concern to environmentalists, since it suggests that think-tanks, publicity campaigns, education efforts—all costing millions of dollars and volunteer hours—have not gotten us very far. Not surprisingly, Michael Shellenberger's and Ted Nordhaus's manifesto, "The Death of Environmentalism," touched a raw nerve when they argued that even after several decades of very hard work, especially in the last fifteen years, environmentalists had "strikingly little to show for it" (2004). National legislation, for the most part, has not moved in a direction that would substantially reduce greenhouse gases, improve the conditions of our soil, water, and air, or enhance the health and resiliency of organisms and habitats. Environmentalists are at a critical crossroads, Shellenberger and Nordhaus contend. What we need to do is rethink in a most fundamental and expansive way how a compelling vision can be drawn and presented to the broader public that will draw them and their wallets in and effect significant change.

Even if we do not accept all the analyses of their report, Shellenberger and Nordhaus are clearly correct in warning that environmentalists must not be perceived as yet another special interest group pleading for their due at the trough of political consideration and clout. The environment is not a separable "thing" out there that we can or cannot choose to defend. A meaningful environment always begins with the sense that every given place is first a home, and thus a source of nurture for ourselves and the many organisms we share our places with. The environment is not some abstract or general space that surrounds us (and thus can easily be taken for granted). It is, rather, a specific, life-giving place that through particular fields, forests, waterways, vegetation, and animal life feeds and sustains us with gifts of food, nurture, and productive and aesthetic enjoyment. I don't drink water "in general," but the water that (in my case) comes from the Elkhorn Creek watershed. This watershed connects me to specific farmers of the region, as well as to the Toyota manufacturing plant in town and to the thousands of homeowners who douse their lawns with fertilizers and weed-control products. All of our actions together, plus the gifts of natural habitats and weather, contribute to every drink I take.

When we talk about something like an environmental "crisis," therefore, we need to understand that what we are really dealing with is a crisis of culture, a failure to be properly "at home," and a distortion of what it means to be embodied beings living (necessarily and beneficially) in a geo-chemical and biologically driven world. For us to exist at all as bodies that breathe, drink, and eat we need to be sure that the sources of air, water, and vegetation are properly cared for and maintained. To think otherwise is to invite not only ecological but also human collapse. Saying this does not narrowly reduce ecological concerns to the human realm. Environmental activism is not simply about or for us. What I am suggesting is that we—the "public"—need to learn to see our living as more deeply implicated in the living of other organisms and their habitats, and vice-versa, so that when the one is under threat so too is the other.

In other words, we need to overcome the ecological amnesia that supposes our bodies can thrive while all other natural bodies languish or die. We are not self-standing, autarchic beings, but creatures profoundly in need of the nutrients and help that others give to us. We must recover the ancient ecological insight, an insight previously taken for granted due to the practical contexts of hunter-gatherer and agricultural life, that humans and habitats share a common, perpetually co-mingling past and future fate. We live *in terms of* our bodies, which also depend on other, innumerable bodies. The health and vitality of humanity depends on the health and vitality of the ecological systems upon which we depend.[1] This is the truth we must all internalize and be inspired by.

There are a great number of dimensions to what the intermingling of humanity with geo-biological systems and organisms means. I would argue that figuring them out, and being able to present them in a coherent and compelling way to a broad public that naively, and sometimes arrogantly, dismisses or underestimates ecological limits, will be key for a future environmental agenda. This essay will explore one aspect of this problematic. What interests me here is the question alluded to at the start of this essay: why is it that individuals, even when they profess some understanding of and commitment to addressing ecological problems, fail to act on those beliefs? Why this discrepancy between belief and action, and what can be done to address it? As I will later argue, our lack of gratitude, or more fundamentally, our inability even to see the need for gratitude, has a lot to contribute to our understanding of these questions. Gratitude is the clearest sign that we have come to appreciate, however incompletely, the range and vitality of the memberships that join people to their natural life-giving homes.

Having taught environmental ethics and philosophy for a number of years, it is a source of frustration to see students nod their heads in agreement as the litanies of ecological destruction or exhaustion are trotted out in depressing detail, and then leave the class with personal or economic habits unchanged. Though some of them "get it"—they recognize that the problems "out there" intersect deeply with choices we are making as individuals and as groups—many simply are unable to understand that ecological issues go to the heart of who or what we understand ourselves

---

1. Sir Albert Howard, grandfather or the organic gardening/farming movement, gave a classic statement to this position when he argued that that we must treat "the whole problem of health in soil, plant, animal, and man as one great subject" (1947: 11).

to be and how and where we are to move in the future. I can't really fault them, however, because it has been ingrained in us (partly owing to the academic specialization and compartmentalization that characterizes university/college life: how often do humanities disciplines seriously engage the natural and agricultural sciences?) that humanity in its essential nature exists apart from or in conflict with our natural homes. Whether we believe ourselves to be immortal souls, disembodied intellects, or highly sophisticated (mechanical/ computational) processors, the assumption in many instances is that humans are not really natural or biological beings at all. In fact, if futurists like Ray Kurzweil are to be believed, eventually we will shed ourselves of bodies altogether so that we can live in a techno-virtual paradise. Our perennial temptation is to think we exist at a higher or deeper or spiritual level, a level that renders us exempt from the limits, possibilities, and challenges of ecological life.[2]

The *idea* that we can live in relative disregard of our biological homes has (especially in the last two centuries) taken on dramatic *practical* forms as societies have become urbanized and people reduced to the status of consumers. While urbanization is not in and of itself evil, what is clear is that several forms of urban life facilitate the illusion that we don't really depend on soils, watersheds, forests, glaciers, earthworms, bees, and butterflies. What we need is available on demand or on tap. The view from our comfortable, climate-controlled cars, offices, and homes has the effect of shielding or insulating us from ecological realities, or distorting their ecological meaning (as when rain is primarily understood in terms of its potential to disrupt a golf outing). We expect that whatever we need will be cheaply and conveniently available at the store, and have no thought or concern for the health of ecological systems that make our living possible. We all want to believe that simply by shopping at Sears (or some other superstore) we can enjoy "The Good Life, at a Great Price, Guaranteed!"

To live in a postmodern world is to live the life of a spectator who is constantly on the move scanning for possibilities among realities that are "virtual" or not (the line between them is sometimes hard to know). Numerous sociologists and cultural critics have observed that it is the precarious, transient, frenetic character of so much contemporary practical life that makes deep knowledge and understanding so difficult. Lacking the deep bonds that are built and sustained through time and communal

2. I have developed this theme in my 2003 essay "Placing the Soul: An Agrarian Philosophical Principle."

effort, many of us are simply not in a position to appreciate the effects of what we do (Best and Kellner 1997; Bauman 1998, 2000; Harvey 1990; Giddens 1990). We live, for the most part, in the bubbles of our own or someone else's (usually a successful marketer's) making.

Can we be responsible agents who will care for each other and our biological homes when we live with such ignorance? Among ancient Greek philosophers there was a widely shared assumption that to know the good is also to do it. What this means is that abstract knowledge, the sort that comes strictly from books or screens or that is acquired as a spectator, is a deficient form of knowledge, particularly when it comes to matters of moral significance. In an important sense, for us to really know a moral truth or claim we must come to it through daily practices that involve us intimately in the realization of a good. We don't know why an action is good until we see, from the inside, the effects of our acting or not acting in a particular way. Upon seeing first hand how what we do has the potential to contribute to the good or flourishing of others, we will, almost automatically, be inclined to do that good action again. After all, who does not enjoy seeing the good in another develop and thrive?

This point can be made clear by considering the requirements of good farming. Farming that is good, and not merely profitable, will have the health of fields and animals firmly in view. What health means, however, cannot be known in the abstract because every farm and herd is different, having particular needs and limits. A good farmer is therefore one who carefully attends to the farm's potential and does not try to impose on it an abstract or foreign motive (such as quotas or stock share). By working carefully the farmer learns what makes and keeps soils and animals productive without their exhaustion or degradation. This is knowledge that cannot come from books. It is acquired through daily contact and committed, patient work. Through this sort of work the meaning and requirements of a *good* farm come into view and are deeply known.

If the people of this nation are to develop the kinds of understanding and knowledge that will overcome the belief/action divide (and thus lead them to care for natural habitats), there will need to be a period of appropriate training in which certain kinds of sympathies, acuities, affections, and character traits can develop. We need to learn to see how our living connects in multiple ways with ecological realities, and we need to appreciate how our economic choices have ecological effects. For this to happen we will need to get out of our cars and homes more often and follow the trails of our consumer choices. Where did the stuff we buy come from and how was it made? Was it made in ways that honor the integrity of natural places and human communities? We will need to develop the sorts of imagination that appreciate the agricultural worlds of soil fertility, water availability, and rural development presupposed by something so basic as a loaf of bread, just as we will need to develop the complex knowledge of coal fields, blown-up mountains, shattered communities, and corporate profits that lies behind the flip of an electrical switch.[3]

To summarize so far: while people openly profess care for the environment, their actions as voters and consumers suggest a different, often destructive, set of priorities. One reason for this discrepancy has to do with the superficiality of our knowing and outright lack in understanding of the deep connections between human health and the health of natural habitats. Practical conditions of contemporary life entrench and make highly likely the continuation of our ignorance. If we are to move forward in a way that will bring healing and vitality to our habitats we will need to develop practices that encourage deep and rich forms of sensitivity and sympathy for the natural and social places we call home.

Let's now make this all more concrete. When I consider the life of my grandfather, and the many agrarians like him, I see a much more seamless connection between what he thought and what he did. He understood, appreciated, and valued his land and his animals because he worked daily, intimately, and practically with them. This last point is especially important. He knew in a way that few of us today do that human life is possible because of the many connections that bind us to microorganisms, earthworms, humus, plants, chickens, pigs, cows, water, and sunlight. He knew this because he literally—through his stomach, with his hands and muscle, but also through his aesthetic enjoyment—drew his own life from them. The fact of the matter is that we too inescapably live within these connections, most basically through our eating, but we don't really appreciate or understand them because we do not have sustained or practical engagements with the variety of geological and biological elements that constitute our natural homes and food sheds.

---

3. The development of local economies will be crucial to this effort because in a local economy the distance between production and consumption decreases, while the awareness of the effects of what we do increases. For a development of these ideas, see Berry 2002 and Wirzba 2007.

Another way to put this is to say that my grandfather understood with an uncommon measure of sensitivity and sympathy the requirements for a creaturely (as distinguished from a godly) human life, a life that is embodied and therefore necessarily and beneficially enfolded within broad geological and biological patterns. Our life, if it is to be true to its own nature, must be lived in response to these patterns. He understood that his own health and well-being depended on the health and well-being of his land and animals, and that he could not flourish alone or at the expense of his non-human neighborhood. Cruelty to or disregard of his animals was thus strictly forbidden. Considerate kindness, even affection, was expected and modeled. His sympathies and desires, while clearly centered on his family and friends, did not end there but extended to his fields and barns. In a fundamental sense he understood that as one creature among others, his life was characterized by need and interdependence. The first rule of an honest, but also humble, life is to honor our need and those we depend upon with kindly and attentive work, with work that does not abuse others for personal gain.

Agrarian, but also hunter-gatherer, societies have clearly been in a more advantageous position to develop this sort of deep insight and understanding that comes from physical proximity and sustained, practical contact. Of course, farmers have never been perfect and could be as destructive as we are. Owing to intense economic pressure, but also personal obstinacy and communal xenophobia, rural communities have often been places of social and ecological failure. Our task is not to advocate for a "back to the land" movement. What we need to consider is how we today, now mostly urbanites and suburbanites, can develop the sorts of sympathies, understanding, and affection that will lead to a sustainable, healthy world. The future of our natural homes and our communities will depend on the economic and political choices made by urban dwellers that have a richer and deeper appreciation for their dependence on land. As thoughtful consumers they can then make the decisions that will encourage and support good farming, good forestry, and good fishing.[4] But here we must start with the frank admission that for the most part, we are ignorant about the "natural" world surrounding us, not knowing how it works, what its limits and potential are, or what it means.[5]

---

4. An excellent resource documenting urbanization trends, but also offering practical suggestions for social, economic, and political reform, can be found in Starke 2007.

5. Consider here the observation of Aldo Leopold: "One of the penalties of an eco-

My proposal is that we begin by figuring out how to expand the scope of our sympathies and care. What mental, bodily, and practical habits do we need to promote so that the care of our ecological homes comes into free and spontaneous alignment with the care of ourselves? My presupposition is that we will only care *for* what we care *about*. For instance, the reason I care as much as I do about my family and friends is because I see them as valuable. They mean deeply to me because they intersect with my living at many levels, and I see without too much trouble how their living and fate intersect with my own. I have sympathy for them not simply because of how they benefit me but because I understand and appreciate how our lives are enfolded within each other. I recognize that in their harm I too am harmed.

When we perform some cultural analysis it becomes clear rather quickly that the scope of what we care about has been significantly narrowed in the modern world due to social forces like urbanization, industrial/market economies, consumerism, and technology. I am not suggesting here that we have suddenly become unfeeling brutes. Rather, the way we feel, and what we are in a position to have feelings about, has changed. What I mean is this: the character of our contact with the non-human world has become much more indirect and highly mediated by asphalt and concrete, climate-controlled buildings, light switches, mega grocery stores, automobiles, televisions, and computer screens. Lacking direct contact with the natural sources of life we are becoming more and more the victims of mass biological or ecological amnesia. Whether we appreciate it or not, most of us operate from and within a "nature-deficit" condition. We don't understand well enough how our living intersects with the living of non-human others.

The most obvious example here would be food. Few of us grow our own food any longer, even a small portion of it. After all, it is humbling, time-intensive work, and requires a vast knowledge of plant, soil, and animal life. Because food comes to many of us in the form of a readily available package—food is always on the store shelf—it is tempting to think that food bears little relation to geological and biological patterns.

---

logical education is that one lives alone in a world of wounds. Much of the damage inflicted on land is quite invisible to the layman ... One sometimes envies the ignorance of those who rhapsodize about a lovely countryside in process of losing its topsoil, or afflicted with some degenerative disease in its water systems, fauna, or flora" (Callicott 1987: 286).

In fact, Wendell Berry has remarked that we live with one of the greatest of human superstitions, namely that "money brings forth food" (Berry 2003: 48)! Missing out on food production, we at the same time miss out on one of the most intimate and practical ways we know in which to enact our interdependence with ecological realities. Moreover, since food comes from far away (on average 1300 miles), and is processed under conditions largely invisible to us, it is easy to think of it in a cavalier fashion and as little more than a product on a par with other factory-manufactured products (e.g., Pollan 2006, Kingsolver 2007).

When we engage members of the non-human world primarily as products to be purchased and consumed, their integrity and depth are significantly reduced. Commodities come to be seen in isolation, cut off from the web of relationships that make them what they uniquely are. In this context it is much easier for us to forget that when we eat a slice of bacon we are eating a pig that had to be cared for and then eventually killed, that when we eat apple sauce we are benefiting from the fruit of a well-tended orchard and mild enough Spring, and that when we drink water we presuppose a sufficient snow-pack and uncontaminated ground water. The sources of life—oxygen, water, soil, sunlight, plants, and animals—though basically free to us, are not without great cost. We know this because for any of us to eat, others must die.

When we forget the costliness of life we not only eat with profound ignorance, we also eat with ingratitude. I take it that one of the hallmarks of gratitude is that we engage and receive others from the perspective of their integrity and value. When we say thank you for something or someone what we are really saying is that they matter and count on their own terms, and that their being enables and betters our own. It is not necessary that we reduce their value to how they improve narrowly conceived human interests. After all, we can take delight in the fact that members of the natural world contribute to the vitality or flourishing of a biotic community far removed from our own spheres of practical living. In fact, one of the key elements of a grateful mind is that it begins with the recognition that what I need and enjoy is not mine by right or personal might. The expression of gratitude is thus at the same time the acknowledgment and the affirmation that for my own life I depend on another. The sources of life, all gifts that make our living possible and potentially a joy, are occasions for gratitude precisely because they are not extensions of myself and cannot be reduced to the status of a possession.

Their meaning or significance is not exhausted in the fact that I bring them under my own control or consume them. There is, in other words, an irreducible wildness and gratuity at the heart of all life, a wildness that exceeds our comprehension and our powers to calculate and control. It is on this wildness that we depend for life (think here of Thoreau's claims: "In Wildness is the preservation of the World," and "Life consists with wildness." [Thoreau 1991]). Before it we must, if we are honest, pause and acknowledge our dependence.[6]

I suppose that one of the great delusions of the modern or postmodern worlds is the idea that we can live within an entirely domesticated world, a world in which the reach of our control is complete. The hype of biotechnology and genetic engineering can lead us to believe that eventually we will construct a world in which we are dependent on nothing but our own ingenuity and power. I am not a Luddite and do not want to suggest that genetic research should simply stop. What I am arguing, however, is that we be careful not to forget that at the most fundamental level, at the levels of respiration and digestion, we live through multiple patterns of interdependence with wild habitats and organisms that have their own forms of integrity and depth. It is arrogant and dangerous to think that we can bring the vast diversity and complexity of our natural world within our complete control.[7] Arrogant because there is simply too much we don't know about how things relate to each other. Dangerous because our presumed control often leads to unforeseen effects that are destructive.[8]

---

6. The shifting, precarious character of modern and postmodern life makes it much more difficult to acknowledge and embrace our interdependent need because the practical conditions for trust are eroding. Because the bonds we share with others are not deep and always subject to risk, we find it difficult to place our trust in others to be a source of help and nurture to us. This dynamic has been admirably analyzed by Seligman (1997).

7. The danger is that in our desire to control we will reduce the world to manipulatable elements that have the effect of distorting our understanding. For a lucid account of how reductionism had such adverse effects on our understanding of diet, see Michael Pollan (2008). Pollan tells the story of how food was reduced to a set of nutrients and the many adverse health effects that followed. A more complete understanding acknowledges that "even the simplest food is a hopelessly complicated thing to analyze, a virtual wilderness of chemical compounds, many of which exist in intricate and dynamic relation to one another, and all of which together are in the process of changing from one state to another." Food, in short, is more than the sum of its nutrient parts, for "the whole may well be more than, or maybe just different from, the sum of its parts" (62).

8. The arrogance and danger associated with our "management" of habitats and or-

What I have been suggesting is that a disposition of gratitude is a key indicator of ecological intelligence or understanding because it is informed by the wide and deep sensitivity that human life is enfolded within and dependent upon a bewildering array of geological, biological, and cultural memberships. When we are grateful we acknowledge that what we receive is valuable and matters beyond what I may or may not be able to do with it. After all, life does not begin and end with us. The human story, in a sense, is meaningful and possible only because it arises within a dynamic evolutionary story that has an integrity all of its own. Gratitude goes hand in hand with a detailed appreciation for this story of life's complexity and mutual interdependence. It presupposes a refined set of sympathies that have been honed through careful observation and patient practices of engagement. It results in the humble admission that we do not and cannot live alone, but must learn to organize our living so as to be in better alignment with the living of others.

Our alignment should begin with the ground under our feet. Soil, dirt, dust, humus—whatever you want to call it—is simply indispensable. Yet it is easily taken for granted by us today. This was not always the case. Ancient literatures refer frequently to the view that all life, humanity included, comes from the soil and to it all the living will return. It is to be revered because it is so much like a great dispenser of life. Not because it is simply the "container" or receptacle of various mineral and chemical elements (as the nineteenth-century chemist Justus von Liebig argued),[9] but because it is like a transformer that perpetually cycles death into new life. Hans Jenny, one of the great soil scientists of the last century, spent his entire life mesmerized by the complexity and diversity of soils. Though not an organism (soil does not multiply like critters do), it made eminent sense to him to describe dirt as a living system that bridges the biotic and abiotic worlds, because when looking at the root—soil boundary under a powerful microscope Jenny noted that the scientific observer cannot neatly or precisely distinguish where the biotic part ends and the abiotic begins. Soil represents a deeply mysterious bridge between the living and

---

ganisms, not to mention the whole globe, are well described by Botkin (1990).

9. Reducing soil fertility to the elements of nitrogen, potassium, and phosphorous, as Liebig did, made possible (along with Fritz Haber and Carl Bosch's invention of nitrogen production) the age of synthetic fertilizer. For the story of how this has led to a decrease in soil health and fertility, see Howard (2006: 69–72).

non-living without which we, as well as plants and animals, simply could not exist.

We would not know or appreciate any of this if it were not for agrarians or people like Jenny who spent the time to work with soil and see it in its details. One could say that the more he saw the wider his range of sympathies grew, so that at the end of his life he could confess to feelings of reverence for it. This reverence for dirt (!), which is closely tied to the disposition of gratitude, turned him into an advocate on behalf of the soil's preservation (see Stuart 1984). Why? Because the soil, in addition to its indispensable role in the processes of life, has its own integrity deserving of our respect and care. The human story would have been impossible without the story of soil. It is perhaps this agronomic realization that sits behind both the Hebrew (*adam/adamah*) and English (humus/humanity) etymologies that link people to the soil.

Soil is a wonder. Besides containing over a thousand different species of lower animals (ranging from earthworms to ants, amoebas, and nematodes), it is also host to millions of molds, bacteria, and other microorganisms. In one piece of research Jenny estimated that there is more living biomass under the ground than there is above it. Together these living elements transform dead bodies into the compounds or basic building blocks for new life. It thus makes good sense to see, in varying degrees of course, that the development and deterioration of civilizations has something to do with soil quality: healthy soils are the indispensable prerequisite for vibrant food production and water retention and filtration. As soils are compromised—as they were in Sumeria, Mesoamerica, the Mediterranean, and the eastern seaboard of the United States—the cultures that live upon them are also compromised (Hillel 1991, Montgomery 2007, Diamond 2005).

If we are to get into a position where we can be grateful for soil, and thus also take better care of it, we have to stop seeing it as mere inert matter that doesn't matter. Soil is not a thing but a complex web of relationships that succeeds because of multiple, dynamic associations that we have barely begun to understand. It is in terms of these relationships that life's possibilities emerge. As William Bryant Logan likes to point out, soil is a continuous and necessary experiment at the boundary of organic and inorganic life, which means it is more like a living system than a mere collection of inert matter and chemical elements. It is an experiment in hospitality because what we see in dirt is a perpetual "making room" for new life to flourish and grow (Logan 1995: 19).[10] Insofar as we fail to understand soil in this complex manner we are fundamentally ignorant. As ignorant and without understanding, it is difficult for us to be grateful or to see soil as deserving of our concern and care.

At this point one could object to this whole project by saying that nature does not deserve our gratitude. We might want to say, following the evolutionary biologist George Williams, that "Mother Nature is a wicked old witch!" (1993: 217). After all, endemic struggle and massive and seemingly pointless suffering or death greets us at every turn. Though we may like to romanticize Nature as our warm and nurturing mother, the fact of the matter is that for those who really get close to it there are precious few signs of reciprocal care. And so in our more sober moments we are inclined to agree with Annie Dillard when she says, "Evolution loves death more than it loves you and me" (1974:176). Or, less dramatically, we may follow Lawrence Slobodkin, who advises, "Nature is neither wise nor benign nor malicious . . . Let humanity do its worst! Rain will still fall, rivers will still flow, and there will be storms and floods and droughts . . . However, there is no certainty that any particular species or landscape will survive" (2003: 11, 99).

Though it may be going too far to ascribe wickedness to the natural world (since this would be an example of a reverse, and thus equally guilty, personification of the natural world), we do need to take seriously the contention that nature's apparent indifference to us renders our gratitude platitudinous or naively pious. Are evolutionary processes uniformly death-wielding or etched in bloody struggle? Clearly not, for then we would be at a loss to explain the evolutionary development of symbiotic or cooperative relationships that produce mutual benefits (think here of the bacteria that while finding our bodies a suitable home also aid us in gastro-intestinal work). Moreover, evolutionary processes have produced various forms of sociality among higher organisms that in certain instances, most notably in primates, give rise to dispositions of affectionate

---

10. Compare the poetic and theological observation of Wendell Berry, who says: "The most exemplary nature is that of the topsoil. It is very Christ-like in its passivity and beneficence, and in the penetrating energy that issues out of its peaceableness. It increases by experience, by the passage of seasons over it, growth rising out of it and returning to it, not by ambition or aggressiveness. It is enriched by all things that die and enter into it. It keeps the past, not as history or as memory, but as richness, new possibility. Its fertility is always building up out of death into promise. Death is the bridge or the tunnel by which its past enters its future" (1969: 19).

care, love, and altruism. Perhaps even more significantly, however, is the fact that evolutionary processes, in varying ways, times, and places often give rise to greater diversity and increased complexity, something we would not expect if evolution were one vast death machine and nothing else. Though the evolutionary record testifies to a good deal of aimless and painful wandering, it has not been entirely without point or value.

Consider here the words of Holmes Rolston: "Logically and empirically, there must be an interplay of order and disorder if there is to be autonomy, freedom, adventure, success, achievement, emergents, surprise, and idiographic particularity. In a world without chance there can be no creatures taking risks, and the skills of life would be very different, if indeed life—as opposed to mechanism—were possible" (Rolston 2003: 69). What Rolston is pointing to is the fact that the diversity and complexity of life require the interplay of order *and disorder*. Without disorder, unpredictability, risk—the very conditions that give rise to pain and death—we would have only the uniformity and regularity of a dead machine. Life forms develop and grow precisely because they are in biological contexts that challenge and can always potentially defeat them. Noting this is not to say that "Nature" is systematically rigged toward our defeat. There is simply too much "success" to see, too many forms of life that prompt us to stand in awe.

Nature's randomness and chance is thus not sufficient warrant for us to say that it is not deserving of our gratitude. Evolutionary processes have given rise to so many diverse, complex, beautiful forms of life that we would have to be blind not to sense their value. That the biological context for their emergence includes suffering and death ought only to increase their value—and thus also our gratitude—because we now have a deeper appreciation for the fact that they did not need to be. Recognizing the contingency of things ought to help us see that the world comes to us as gift. It is never simply a brute presence but always a *given* presence. There is a fundamental gratuitousness about life which ought to give us pause.

My argument in this essay has been that we do not pause enough and then find in our pausing the opportunity and need for gratitude and care. We are, most of us, too hurried in life, too beset by the worries of our own ambition, too locked within the narrow scope of our own worlds. There are simply too many walls, disciplinary and otherwise, that separate or shield us from the wide non-human world. What, practically speaking, can be done about this? By way of conclusion I will offer some suggestions, particularly in the domain of education, of how dispositions of gratitude can be nurtured or cultivated, recognizing that gratitude can be one of the most salient and powerful contexts for responsible environmental action.

Earlier on I mentioned that ignorance, the inability to see details, complexity, and gratuity, forms a primary obstacle to an appreciation of another's value. If this is so, then it is of the utmost importance that we figure out how to get people informed about ecological realities so that they come to understand how their living depends in multiple ways upon the diversity and health of other living systems. What I have in mind here is not simply the addition of an ecological course here and there, because what we need is more than the transmission of biological information. People will not become ecologically literate because they have learned in an abstract manner that they also happen to be biological beings. The knowledge and understanding we are after should be of the sort that is practical and intimate, that goes to the heart of our identity.

Given this basic ignorance it has been well suggested that we need to revise our educational curricula in fairly dramatic fashion.[11] If at one time we thought the university to be the transmitter of "high culture," the place where we learn the cultural referents (in literature, philosophy, the fine arts and sciences) that enable us to navigate through life with decency and honor, the time is now right to imagine and implement universities that will provide ecological referents that will enable people to see in unmistakable terms the many ways in which human flourishing or success is always premised upon biological flourishing. This means that virtually all the disciplines will need to be grounded in the ground, rooted in the soil, so that we do not take for granted economies without trees and water and sunlight, histories without arable land, God without creation, music without birdsong or the beating heart, philosophy without stomachs, architectural/urban design without renewable resources, or medicine without healthy agriculture.

What I'm suggesting here is not quite like "ecology across the curriculum" but rather ecology *beneath* and *within* the curriculum, ecology that *permeates* the curriculum. The point is that ecology is not an add-on to an otherwise fine course of study. Students need to see that the "course" or "running" that the curriculum itself is (from the Latin *currere*) would

11. On the primary/secondary school level, see Sobel 2004 and for higher education, see especially Orr 1991.

stop dead in its tracks were it not for the life processes that are at work deep within it. If I am correct in this suggestion, that means a greatly expanded role for trained ecologists in virtually all university departments. I don't mean simply that we need a greater number of ecologists or agrarians (though that would not hurt), but that we need ecologists who can bridge disciplines, who can make the connections between soil health and bodily health, habitat resilience and economic sustainability, clean water and social justice. These will be ecologists who, in a practical and detailed manner, will deepen our appreciation for the many layers of human interdependence.[12] In this deepening we will witness the expansion not only of our sensitivities, but also our sympathies and care, for at the very least we will now recognize that there is so much more to care about.

The sort of learning I am talking about, if it is to be successful, cannot merely be a learning of the head. I would argue that we need to bring our hands and our stomachs back into the equation. One of the best ways to do this is to get people involved again in the production of their own food. Here we need to remember that for centuries the overwhelming majority of people did in fact grow their own food. We are the odd ones who have lost this ability and the sensitivities and sympathies that go with it (as a test case, how many of us, given the right equipment and seed stock, fertile land, and ideal growing conditions, could provide for our own nourishment throughout the year?). We do not need to recommend that everyone become a farmer, but we should encourage people to become reacquainted with gardening. For this we do not each need a lot of land, nor do we need to grow all of our own food. What we do need are the sensitivities that come from putting our hands and stomachs directly in touch with soil. The growing popularity and success of urban farms, community gardens, and farmer's markets indicate the sensitivity is already there and simply needs to be cultivated (e.g., Halweil 2004).

Hans Jenny once said that he felt fairly confident that healthy soils make for healthy people. He also wanted to think, though he could not do so with anything more than anecdotal evidence, that good soils make for

---

12. One avenue of approach is for ecologists to highlight "nature's services" to humanity, which is to document the many ways in which natural processes or outcomes directly benefit human activities (Daily 1997). This sort of work needs to be made much more widely available and accessible, particularly in urban contexts where people often lack a rudimentary appreciation for these benefits.

good people.[13] What he meant by this, I think, is that putting our hands into dirt teaches us important things about ourselves: that we really do grow out of the ground, that a properly human life is a humble life (i.e., the connections between humus, humanity, and humility are not merely etymological), and that we live through the gifts of others. It would be a grand thing if our schools and universities could play a more active role in the cultivation of an authentic humanity. They can do this more readily if they bring the arts of soil cultivation back into the university. I mean this quite literally.

When I taught at the University of Saskatchewan (Canada) I often rode my bike past test plots and barns. The sights and smells, besides being a personal comfort to me, were a daily reminder that soil, vegetation, water, and sunlight form the indispensable nexus for whatever else went on in our buildings. Being present with corn, canola, pigs, and dairy cows made it more likely that I would contemplate the aesthetics of dirt or the ontology of milk, or that I would at least not see them as irrelevant to aesthetic or metaphysical inquiry. Could our schools do a better job forging the connections between our minds, bodies, and biological habitats? That they could do so is beyond doubt. The question is whether or not they will. I happen to think that our students, not just the little ones, would welcome the opportunity to touch the earth and to become reacquainted with their biological homes. This is why it would be such an excellent idea for universities and colleges to start planning vegetables along with flowers in the midst of their quads, *and have students and faculty take care of these gardens*. Why should this gardening activity not become a vital part of the curriculum and our daily diet?

At Oberlin College David Orr teaches a class in sustainable agriculture each spring. His students, most of them urbanites or suburbanites, have never seen a farm, yet the class is always full. As part of their experience they go to visit David Kline's Amish farm. While there they smell, many of them for the first time, the aroma of freshly plowed soil. They see and stroke his dairy cows, and walk among freshly sprouted vegetables. When they enter the bus to go back home, often with considerable reluctance, many of them simply remark, "This has been the

---

13. We should observe that in its earliest, middle English usage, the word "culture" referred to a cultivated piece of land and, presumably, the skills needed for people to secure their livelihood on it. A "cultured" person thus referred to a husband of the soil (Bate 2000: 13–14).

sanest day of my life." Some of them even vow to pursue careers in agriculture! What this example shows is that more people than we might think are ready to immerse themselves in the natural world and find there their sanity and joy. Should not we as educators do everything we can to facilitate that desire?

The task before us, as I see it, is for ecological intelligence or literacy to become an intimate and vital part of our self-understanding as humans. We need to imagine and implement ways that will foster a detailed and complex appreciation for the many ways in which human life is enfolded within broad geo-chemical and biological processes. With this appreciation will come a sense for the value and wonder of our world, and with that, hopefully, the response of gratitude. I can't think of a better or more inspirational way for environmental concerns to register and take root in our public consciousness than from out of a context and disposition of gratitude.

Response

Biogeochemistry on the Farm

WILLIAM H. SCHLESINGER

HUMANS SEEM TO HAVE spent the first 2 million years of their evolution figuring out how to live apart from nature—first in caves, then in castles, and finally in modern cities. Each step has led to a progressive segregation of a large fraction of our population from nature, where we are sustained by agriculture, trade, currency, and other laudable human constructs that allow the bounty of nature to be carried to the urban sphere. Just as my lack of talent has encouraged my absence from the basketball court and thus any hope of understanding the nuances of the game, so too has the average citizen given up on farming in favor of knowing that a bag of apples is always to be found at Kroger food stores. We have lost the knowledge of nature that might tell us that a particularly tart apple comes with an early cold spell in autumn.

Wirzba asks us to look more deeply, to think about how we might react if the bag of apples was not at Kroger and hadn't been there for weeks. Or suppose a drought on the prairie made it impossible for Kellogg's to produce cornflakes. Or a pandemic disease of cattle meant that Burger King was not able to find beef for its hamburgers. This is beyond the plight of the hungry homeless; consider a day when every citizen is hungry. How many of us would be capable of growing our own food? Where is the once widespread knowledge of the land?

Separation from watching our food grow represents only one of many ways in which humans have separated themselves from nature and lost track of the services that nature provides. Abundant, cheap fossil energy has allowed us to substitute pesticides for predators, irrigation for natural rainfall, and fertilizers for composting. Our water is purified in industrial plants rather than aerating streams, our clothes are dominated by synthetics vs. natural fiber, and our transportation is by jet airplanes and private motor vehicles versus wind and animals. Our food is distributed over vast distances, and we find summer produce, like strawberries, in our grocery store in February. Perhaps this is what we should expect when we invite 6.8 billion people to dinner every night.

Many of Wirzba's arguments echo those of Michael Pollan in his best-selling book, *The Omnivore's Dilemma* (2006). Pollan and Wirzba both argue for a return to biogeochemistry on the farm—that is, to realize that nature is remarkably effective at recycling nitrogen, phosphorus, and other essential nutrients between the soil, plants, animals, and our food. Wirzba focuses our attention on the soil, where a vast community of microbes transforms wastes into resources, producing a closed biogeochemical cycle that neither loses important nutrients nor requires new inputs from outside. Pollan argues in favor of polyculture farming, where crops and animals are carefully planned to cohabit the landscape and recycle wastes. Along with lesser environmental impact, Pollan says that the food tastes better.

Wirzba does not want us to grow our own food, necessarily. He believes that the separation of everyday human life and thought from our dependence on nature explains our indifference to a wide variety of environmental issues, such as ozone depletion, climate change, and overfishing, that should warn us of unsustainable human impact on the global biosphere. Not suggesting that it is in our spirit to return to the Earth, he recommends that we must reinvigorate a gratitude for nature in our voting citizenship. Youngsters playing in a local stream, teenagers on a weekend camping trip, and adults in their backyard garden will be reconnected to the Earth and the species that share the planet with us. We may be happy that we sleep in a cozy bed at night; nevertheless, we will appreciate what nature does for us, "out there."

Of course, he is right, and his ambition is a small first step to reversing the behavioral evolution of the genus Homo before it is too late. We will not grow our own food—at least not 6.8 billion of us, but to know nature and her soil is to respect her, so she can sustain us all.

Five

The Dominion Lie
How Millennial Theology Erodes Creation Care

MICHAEL S. NORTHCOTT

FOR MORE THAN FORTY years environmentalists have sustained an "ecological complaint" against Christianity, a complaint classically articulated by Lynn White and repeated by many others (e.g., Nash 1992). Theologians who resist Lynn White's ecological complaint against Christianity argue that it is unjust when the historic teaching of Christianity about respect and care for creation is properly understood. And they also point out that Christian theologians such as Joseph Sittler (1961) and Francis Schaeffer (1970) were among the earliest ecological prophets, drawing the attention of the churches and the wider society to the ecological crisis in the 1960s (e.g., Northcott 1996: 149–51). However the ecological complaint against Christianity acquires new force in a context in which conservative Christians who voted in 2000 and 2004 in such overwhelming numbers for an administration in Washington DC that for two terms expressed such a callous disregard for environmental law and regulation, and so open to a partiality for polluting corporations. The United States is responsible for more than a quarter of global natural resource use, more than 30 percent of global greenhouse gas emissions, and the lion's share of many other forms of pollution including such long-lived threats to life as depleted uranium, dioxin, mercury, and MTBE.

One of the ways in which these threats to life are visited on the planet and not just on the United States is through the military. The wars initiated by Bush-Cheney created an appalling ecological as well as social legacy even as their primary purpose is to leverage access to fossil fuel in the Middle East and Central Asia (e.g., Northcott 2004). Ironically the amount of oil that would have been saved had the motor corporations not decreased the fuel efficiency of American private vehicles by 40 percent in the last fifteen years would mean that presently America need import no oil at all from the Persian Gulf and could save the billions spent every month on war and other geopolitical initiatives in that region in efforts to secure a continuing flow of oil to the United States (Kennedy 2004).

Besides the behavior of the most avowedly Christian of recent American administrations, international opinion polls and surveys of environmental attitudes and behaviors also reveal that empirical evidence for the ecological friendliness of Christianity is at best ambiguous. The Gallup "Health of the Planet" Survey provides clear evidence that Christian or post-Christian nations are more concerned with environmental problems than non-Christian ones, while nations with little premodern Christian influence, such as Japan and Korea, are at the bottom of any table of wealthier nations in terms of levels of environmental concern (Dunlap et al. 1992). Similarly the evidence shows that among developing nations, Roman Catholic countries such as Brazil and Chile show much higher levels of environmental concern than Turkey or India (Dunlap 1994: 121). But against this the wealthiest and avowedly most Christian nation—the U.S.—shows significantly lower levels of environmental concern on a number of measures than less religiously active wealthy nations (Franzen 2003).

THE ECOLOGICAL POLITICS OF THE CHRISTIAN RIGHT

That regular churchgoing Christians are politically influential in countries where they form a majority of the population is not in doubt. In the United States, Catholics and conservative evangelicals are a political force. Around 40 percent of Americans describe themselves as born again Christians and of those who vote the vast majority vote Republican (Parker 2004). President George W. Bush attracted the Catholic and conservative evangelical vote because he was Republican, and because the party adopted a traditional conservative Christian ethic that is purportedly "pro-life," opposed to such liberal ideas as homosexual marriage, and because it is uncritical in its support of the State of Israel, another litmus test for conservative Christian voters. The Bush administration sponsored anti-environmental policies on a number of fronts under such duplicitous and eco-friendly sounding headings as the "Clear Skies Policy" and the

"Healthy Forests Initiative" (Scherer 2003). Under the Clear Skies Policy the administration undermined the 1970 Clean Air Act by exempting new industrial facilities from the requirement that they fit available anti-pollution technologies, and by lowering federal emission standards on a whole range of pollutants from mercury and particulates to sulfur and nitrogen oxides. It also declared that carbon dioxide, the most important of the climate change pollutants, is not a pollutant at all. Similarly, under the "Healthy Forests Initiative," 58 million acres of previously protected federal land have been opened up to logging, oil drilling, and road building. And the administration pushed for drilling on the Arctic National Wildlife Refuge, an area of land whose quantity of oil will make far less impact on America's oil dependence than the reinstitution of President Carter's 1975 Corporate Average Fuel Economy standards which were struck down by America's last apocalyptic oil friendly President, Ronald Reagan (NRDC 2003).

The naming of these anti-environmental policies is deeply Orwellian and reflects the mendacity of the Bush-Cheney administration. Reagan's administration tore through environmental regulation and increased subsidies and tax breaks for energy corporations. But his Secretary of the Interior James Watt made no secret of their intentions, and there was eventually a backlash among the public that forced Watt's resignation. Bush-Cheney learned from this, and no administration has been better at the business of marketing policy otherwise known as public relations. Among the more infamous applications of PR that the administration pursued was its decision to hire the woman who sold America Uncle Ben's Rice to invent and sell the brand of the "war on terror," in the name of which all manner of evils were visited on the world (Northcott 2004).

POLITICAL LYING

Saint Augustine held that all sin could be understood as lying—for in essence sin is the denial of the truth that God has given us life—as may be seen from his definition of sin: "Sin is the will to keep or to get what one can freely leave alone that justice forbids" (cited in Griffiths 2004). This understanding of sin involves lying, for it is necessary to designate those creatures which we unjustly expropriate as "ours" rather than God's. Publicly Bush-Cheney claimed to be "pro-life," which was among the reasons Catholic and evangelicals voted for them in such large numbers in

2004. However the only kind of lives their policies seemed to be "pro" are those of the corporations who funded their campaign. While they claimed to be on the side of the unborn children of the poor who use public hospitals and publicly funded clinics to terminate their unwanted progeny, in reality their social policies and tax cuts will help foster the kinds of moral and cultural conditions in which more unwanted children are conceived and aborted. Equally, Bush-Cheney policies that allowed energy and mining corporations to pollute the skies and waterways, log the forests, and drill in the wild lands and coastlands are creating a terrible legacy for the children who are born, especially those in poor communities and communities of color who live downwind of power utilities or who must drink the water they poison from polluted public wells (Kennedy 2004). And this is to say nothing of the millions of unborn whose lives will be foreshortened by the ecological impacts that Bush-Cheney visited on the earth's climate, as well as on the environment of the United States.

Political lying is of course as old as Plato. Though he did not commend it, Machiavelli certainly did, and Jonathan Swift wrote a satirical essay in the eighteenth century "On Political Lying" in which he first reminds his readers that the devil is the father of lies. But of the old established maxim "truth will prevail," he is more doubtful:

> Here has this island of ours, for the greatest part of twenty years, lain under the influence of such counsels and persons, whose principle and interest is to corrupt our manners, blind our understanding, drain our wealth, and in time destroy our constitution both in church and state, and we at last were brought to the very brink of ruin. Yet by the means of perpetual misrepresentations, have never been able to distinguish between our enemies and our friends. We have seen a great part of the nation's money got into the hands of those who, by their birth, education, and merit, could pretend no higher than to wear our liveries; while others, who, by their credit, quality, and fortune, were only able to give reputation and success to the Revolution, were not only laid aside as dangerous and useless, but were loaded with the scandal of Jacobites, men of arbitrary principles, and pensioners to France. (Swift 1710)

In her "Reflections on the Pentagon Papers" Hannah Arendt suggests that at the core of modern American politics lies the art of lying (Newey 1997). And some even suggest that political lying is actually a necessary part of running for and holding elective office in a large and complex nation state such as that of the United States. Christians however have conventionally demurred from such cynicism about the possibility of speaking the truth in public, for at the heart of the Christian story is the claim that what was hidden from before the foundations of the world has been made known in the coming of Jesus Christ. Public truth-telling is central to the Christian practices of confession, prophetic utterance, and witness, for Christians know that they continue to live in a world marked by sin even though they also know that even the most secret of sins will one day be shouted from the rooftops. As Stanley Hauerwas argues, politicians lie because they collude with their constituencies in the refusal to acknowledge the continuing sinful character of the society they inhabit. This is because they and we "have not the skill to know how to live truthfully with such sin" and because "we do not want to pay the price that forgiveness requires" (Hauerwas 2001a). Deception also arises from the narrative of individual freedom of the kind advanced by Bush and others, for in order to live without concern for other people, and to deny that we belong to one another, it is necessary to lie; to refuse to acknowledge that we even know of any who suffer from our appropriation of more of God's creation than is our due, means that like Cain, we prefer the lie "am I my brother's keeper?" (Hauerwas 2001b).

The desire to lie is also closely connected with the belief that the political leader governs not with the people but on their behalf. The individual who believes that it is his or her job to lie for the federal government has come to understand political office less as representation and more as rule. However Bush-Cheney clearly understood that if they shouted from the roof tops what they were doing to America's natural resources they might not win public support, and they might face a more difficult time in Congress with their policies. And so they did not shout. They hardly even whispered. But this was not for any lack of conviction on their part that what they did was right. The administration's position on the environment was closely tied to narratives of individual freedom, limited government, the sovereignty of property rights, and perhaps above all the idea that America prospers when its most powerful corporations can create wealth without let or hindrance from the state, and even better with tax breaks and public deficit and tax-funded subsidies. These narratives are clearly not secretive—they were central to Bush's rhetoric, and it was in response to such rhetoric that he attracted the extensive support that he did amongst conservative Christians. The question then is why do conservative Christians put the priorities of big business and property rights above concern for the environment or threats to future generations who will be affected by climate change and other long-term forms of ecological damage?

THE RAPTURE AND THE FATE OF THE EARTH

The most common answer to the problem, advanced in articles by Glen Scherer and Bill Moyers, is that the majority of American Christians believe that they are quite literally living in the end times, that doomsday will involve the collapse and complete corruption of all worldly political and social institutions and widespread apostasy among Christians, and that the earth itself will also begin to break down and ultimately be destroyed in the last judgment (Scherer 2004, Moyers 2005a, 2005b). Christians who have adopted this apocalyptic view of current history have been educated by the *Left Behind* novels and films of Timothy LaHaye and by numerous sermons, tracts, and treatises in the tradition of premillenial dispensationalism whose origins can be traced to the writings of a seventeenth-century Jesuit, but which was popularized in this country and in the United Kingdom by James Nelson Darby, Charles Schofield, and latterly Hal Lindsay, Billy Graham, and Timothy LaHaye. Millions of conservative evangelicals adhere to this belief system in the United States and dispensationalism is also a powerful missionary credo that has spread to many other countries as its adherents seek to reach "every tribe and nation" before the end comes. The dark portrait that their informants paint of the end of the world is made bearable by the belief in what is called the "rapture." This idea arises from a misreading of a passage in St Paul's second letter to the Thessalonians which is said to indicate that, before what dispensationalists believe will be a "great tribulation" that will afflict those who remain on earth at the end times, righteous Christians will disappear from their homes and workplaces, cars and airplane seats and ascend to heaven. This bizarre belief is widely disseminated among the more conservative Christian denominations, including not only Southern Baptists, but holiness and Pentecostal churches, Covenant and Nazarene churches, and most of the really large non-denominational mega-churches that are now common throughout the suburban heartlands of America from coast to coast.

Premillenial pessimism about the end of the world is influential in evangelical disregard for the need to conserve nature. There is no point in working to conserve the earth when it is destined for destruction in the end times, as indicated by the tide of environmental disasters that are the fate of the earth according to dispensationalist interpretation of the Book of Revelation (Northcott 2008). The influence of such beliefs are also illustrated by the experience of a Portland Pentecostal pastor who was converted to the environmental cause by a 1,000 mile sabbatical hike in the Rockies. He does outreach for the Christian Society of the Green Cross and in one such visit to a Baptist church in Portland he argued that God requires Christians to steward the environment for future generations. In response a member of the congregation challenged him with the question "Do you worship God or nature?", the implication being that inter-generational ecological concern was inspired by nature worship and not the Bible (Smith 1997). Another asked, "Why should we worry about the earth when the Bible says it'll all be destroyed in the end times, when God will make a new heaven and a new earth?" Here the time frame of dispensationalist eschatology is crucial to understanding the unwillingness of many conservative evangelicals to embracing the challenge of ecological responsibility.

This foreshortening of the earth's future connects with a larger cultural problem concerning time and the future in contemporary society. The consumer economy not only encourages us to want stuff, and to get it now, as witness the extraordinary levels of consumer debt in the U.S. and the UK. It also undermines the virtues of patience and temperance that might allow us to moderate desire by waiting for what we want, and so clarifying whether or not what we think we want, and the desire to want it, are really wise and will really be to our good. There is I suspect a deeper collusion here between the kind of impatience that is fostered by the debt-driven consumer economy of infinite desire and the impatience manifest in Christian belief that the end of the world is right around the corner.

St Paul in writing to first-century Christians at Thessalonica who had gotten over-excited about the end of the world, advised those who were becoming imprudent in their daily lives—giving up their jobs and their marriages because of their impatient expectation of the return of the Lord—to relearn patience and the art of waiting on God, for the Lord comes when he is not expected "like a thief in the night" and "no one knows the day of his coming."

In addition to a foreshortened attitude to time among end timers there is the problem that those who believe they know the conditions of the end also come to imagine that they can help bring it about, and that consequently human destiny and history are somehow in their power. This desire to get a handle on history's outcome is nowhere more evident than in the attitude of end-time dispensationalists to the State of Israel, and in particular to the designs of some in Israel to rebuild the Temple of Solomon on the Temple Mount in Jerusalem. From James Darby to Timothy LaHaye, the rebuilding of the Temple is viewed by dispensationalists as the key condition for the beginning of the Great Tribulation and the return of Christ to the earth and from the early-nineteenth century this view of Israel's place in end-time history influenced first British and now American foreign policy in Palestine. The influence of this kind of controlling view of history on the Bush administration is most clearly evident in its close and uncritical relationship with the administration of Ariel Sharon, who more than any other Israeli leader has talked publicly about the Temple site in Jerusalem.

RIGHTEOUS EMPIRE AND THE NEW DOMINIONISM

On the attitude of the Bush administration, and of many conservative evangelicals, to big business, environmental law, and nature conservation there is however a different logic at work than that of end-time speculation, or a desire to bring in the end of history. Far from imagining that the end is close, the Bush administration in both foreign and domestic policies appeared to be involved in empire building for the long haul. It did not seem to be acting as though it believes the end is nigh or that the judgment is near. If there is a strain of millennialism that provides ideological backing for the imperial tenor of this administration, and its fire-sale approach to natural resources, it is the more traditional style of American postmillennialism that is at work. Jonathan Edwards and Woodrow Wilson were both postmillennialists. They believed that on these shores, in this "new world," God had begun a work which presaged the beginning of the thousand-year reign of the saints on earth. The Kingdom was coming in when the Puritans founded their righteous colonies on these eastern shores and the Union of States after the Revolution, and the Civil War, were both interpreted by postmillennialist preachers as the violent birth pangs of this new millennium. And if a righteous empire had been founded here in the New World then it was the responsibility of its leaders to spread this vision of righteousness through the influence of America's corporations and its military, around the world. Wilsonian foreign policy mobilized the language of "redeemer nation" in this regard, and it is this same kind of postmillennial rhetoric which was manifest in the second inaugural speech of George W. Bush with its constant repetitions of the words freedom and democracy, and their counterpoise with the claim that America is acting on the world stage to defeat tyranny (e.g., Northcott 2004).

The particular form of postmillennialism that was on the rise in the Bush-Cheney era is more overtly theological than that of Wilsonianism and is known variously as dominionism or theonomic reconstructionism. Among its key ideologues are Cornelius van Til, Rousas Rushdoony, Francis Schaeffer, and Gary North. Together they promote the belief that Christians are given dominion over the earth and over human society in the present era, and are to seek in every way possible to impose the terms of Christian dominion, namely the laws of God revealed in the Bible, on the societies in which they reside. Hence there have been a number of moves in recent years both in Congress and in local state legislative assemblies and courts to defend and uphold the Ten Commandments as the divine law that underlies the laws of the United States and the institutions that uphold and adjudicate them. At the heart of the reconstructionist message is the belief that America was once, and can be again, a Christian nation and that what stands in the way of achieving this is secular humanism, and the unrighteous lives of those who hold office in American institutions. Starving state education and welfare services of funds and transferring services to Christian institutions and private businesses are key elements in the Religious Right's program to re-Christianize American institutions (Belise and McDowell 1989). The other key elements in the Bush-Cheney administration's program—ending measures to redistribute wealth through taxes and welfare, reducing regulation of private businesses, and freeing up natural resources for private use—are also central themes in Belise's and McDowell's book. They suggest that "Scripture makes it clear that God is the provider, not the state, and that needy individuals are to be cared for by private acts of charity" (187). They argue for the abolition of agencies such as the EPA as a hindrance to a healthy economy because such agencies manifest a secular lack of faith in divine providence to supply all the natural resources that humanity needs, for "the Christian knows that the potential in God is unlimited and that there is no shortage of resources in God's earth" for "God has made the earth sufficiently large with plenty of resources to accommodate all the people" (197).

At the heart of the dominionist attack on environmentalism is the idea that it emanates from a secular humanist agenda that acquired power in America as a result of a number of significant judgments of the Supreme Court in the 1960s concerning such matters as public prayer and abortion. David Barton of WallBuilders Inc. argues that the Supreme Court decision to ban public prayer in public schools in 1961 led to a direct decline in standards of education and morality in America in the 1960s, and that the road to moral and educational recovery involves precisely turning around the legislature in favor of the centrality of Christian law and prayer in public institutions in America, and furthermore, replacing secular humanists with Christians in public office. Dominion is the key here. As reconstructionist preacher James Kennedy suggested in an address to a convention of the Christian Coalition in 1995, "true Christian citizenship" means that Christians are "to take dominion over all things as vice-regents of God" (Diamond 1995). We find these same claims and sentiments in the writings of prolific reconstructionist author and founder of the Christian Institute for Economics Gary North:

> Christian people are required to take dominion over the earth by means of all three God-ordained institutions, not just the church, or just the State, or just the family. The kingdom of God includes every human institution, and every aspect of life for all of life is under God and is governed by His unchanging principles. All of life is under God and God's law because God intends to judge all of life in terms of His law. (1990: 52)

It is in the seemingly obscure writings of Christian reconstructionists that we can see clearly the theological underpinnings of many of the actions, policies, and rhetorics of the Bush administration with regard to the environment. Reconstructionists believe that the biblically mandated institutions through which dominion should be exercised over natural resources are those of the family and private property, whereas the state is an interloper in natural resource allocation and use that has no place in biblical law (Alvarado 1987). Private property is the preferred form of ownership because only when all common resources belong to individuals will they be stewarded in the interests of their owners, whereas common resources are always subject to the overuse of individuals who have no vested property interest in preserving them (North 1990). Consequently anything that reduces the holding by the state of public land, and that reduces the power of the state over natural resource allocation and use is viewed by reconstructionists as pursuant to re-inaugurating biblical law with regard to the environment. The conservative theocrat Rousas Rushdoony, whose writings played a key role in the emergence and growth of the Christian Right as a political force in America, similarly argues that the Bible places property in the hands of the family, not the state. It gives property to man as an aspect of his dominion, as a part of his godly subduing of the earth. The stewardship of resources should be supervised by the most intensely committed social unit, the family (1984).

Gary North argues that the family, while not the only legitimate form of ownership "is unquestionably the most universally recognized ownership institution historically, and it is the social unit to which God originally announced the dominion covenant" (North 1987). Moreover over-zealous efforts to reduce pollution from business activities are evidence of the false messianism of the secular state:

> The rise of the messianic State is a greater threat to liberty than pollution is. Pollution is a recognized evil; the messianic State is the agent of a rival religion. A whole system of incentives and sanctions is available: fines, tax credits, pollution control standards, and even outright prohibition. What must be recognized is that the quest for zero pollution is messianic. It is a program that covers the real intent of its promoters: salvation by legislation. If men do not restrain themselves voluntarily as both polluters and pollution-fighters, the social order will be torn apart by the messianic quest for the perfect environment. Such an environment is available only after the final judgment, when the curse is removed. (1990: 360)

Pollution in other words may be life-shortening but its presence is simply evidence that Christians continue to live in a fallen world, marred by sin. Biblical law is designed to restrain sin and promote dominion, but not to achieve the promised redemption that only God will ultimately bring about at the end of all things. For fundamentalist Christians the state, when it works to preserve a pristine environment, is setting itself up as a false savior.

There is collusion in this anti-state position between conservative Christianity, the Bush-Cheney administration, and the corporations. For while the energy corporations say that they hate the federal government, and Bush-Cheney systematically gutted the Environmental Protection Agency and the Department of the Interior of independent scientists and of enough funds or even legal rights to actively pursue polluters or prevent the destruction of America's natural resources by corporations, they at the same time oversaw a vast transfer of resources free, gratis, to private corporations including coal, oil, and nuclear energy companies. The contradiction at the heart of conservative Christian and conservative political thought is that while the nation-state, and especially the federal government, is represented as a collectivity that undermines the capacity of individuals and small communities to show compassion and to carry responsibility for the moral project of stewarding God's good earth, at the same time the powers of the federal government vastly increased under Bush-Cheney, and the federal deficit grew dramatically. Big government in reality is precisely what big business likes the most. Conservative Christians, inasmuch as they back the corporate and big business agenda of wealth creation unfettered by environmental or social regulation, are in reality backing big government, though they may claim that they are voting for the little guy or family values.

THE POST-SECULAR AGENDA OF DOMINIONISM

The strange alliance between big business and conservative Christianity is at first hard to explain. Why would conservative evangelicals associate the gospel of Jesus Christ with the capacity of giant corporations to exploit and pollute God's creation with little or no hindrance from the federal government? Or why would the holiness Pentecostal movement become associated with something as evidently unbiblical as the prosperity gospel? Michael Lind is partly right when he suggests that the alliance of the Christian Religious Right with the Republican Party results in a "Frankenstein operation" which stitches "the bodiless head of Northeastern neo-conservatism onto the headless body of Southern fundamentalism" (Zaitchik 2004). But this is by no means the whole answer, for there are deeper and longer standing currents at work here that go back to the evangelical movement in eighteenth- and nineteenth-century America, which I have reviewed elsewhere at greater length (2004). As Charles Sellers suggests American Calvinism provided the "spiritual medium" of the transformation of America into a capitalist society "sanctifying worldly work as religious duty and wealth as fruit of grace" (1991: 29–30). Despite initial resistance especially among rural and blue collar Protestant evangelicals, by the late-nineteenth century Protestants had almost universally embraced the new market economy and its corporate actors, which included the national Bank, many smaller regional banks, stock holding corporations, stock markets, and the new retail sectors of American cities, and the related development of the mail order company (Zinn 1980). Indeed many features of evangelical religion were associated with market activity. Thus evangelical tracts and books were to form the first large-scale market in printed media, anticipating the emergence of consumer culture, while evangelical missionaries and preachers saw the development of a market both within and beyond America as a God-given device for the rapid spread of the gospel to all regions of America and beyond its shores to the South and across the Pacific (Knord 2001, Long 2001).

At the heart of the emergent marriage between Protestant evangelicalism and American capitalism was the centrality of individual choice to the evangelical identity (Noll 2001: 267). Evangelicalism grew rapidly as the religion of choice in America in the aftermath of the American Revolution because it offered a more flexible and dynamic style of religion to people whose lives were caught up in revolutionary change. It was "better able to meet the needs of rootless egalitarian-minded men and women than were the static churchly institutions based on eighteenth century standards of deference and elite monopolies of orthodoxy" (167). Evangelical religious experience offered the individual a sense of "enduring personal stability" and the "dignity of the self" in the midst of the rapid transformations of the political, industrial, and economic revolutions of the eighteenth and nineteenth centuries: individuals so empowered were also empowered socially and politically to affirm the sovereignty of the common people, and to shape the culture in their own interests (267). Consequently evangelicals by the nineteenth century were consistently opposed to the establishment of religion, and in favor both of a republic and a marketplace unfettered by the traditional hierarchy of church and state. Religious disestablishment in other words had both political and economic consequences for there was an intrinsic link between the embrace of political disestablishment and freedom in religion and the embrace of the market economy by the new nation (269). Having rejected hierarchical ecclesiastical regulation of their worship and beliefs and reading of Scripture, evangelicals were equally opposed to government regulation of the "public spaces in which they hoped to promote their religion and they were predisposed in favor of situations in which individuals could make the choice for God freely" (269). Analogously, if the Spirit could guide the individual to make the right choice for God, then surely similar processes were at work in the new alchemy of the market economy (270). Consumer choice thus became an article of evangelical faith.

This evangelical combination of individualism, trust in the alchemy of the market of private choices, and suspicion of the state is taken up but also significantly modified in the current Christian reconstructionist and dominionist agenda by the extent to which it is a Christian America that is sought. The logic of this project is that in a secular democracy it is not possible for long for the individual to experience freedom because, as Rushdoony argues, the source of law moves from God to the state. It is impossible for the individual to maintain his liberty very long in a democracy, because power is delegated to the state, to the general will of the democratic mass as it expresses itself in the state.

A fundamental axiom of political life is this, that *power allies itself with power.* A power group is not interested in charity; it is not in existence to subsidize weak and struggling groups who need but cannot give help. Unless firmly restrained, power always grasps for more power, and hence it allies itself with other powers, and a struggle for power between cooperating yet competing power groups follows. Thus, as a democracy develops, the powers of the state, and the powers of big business, big finance, big labor, criminal syndicates, big pressure groups, powerful minority groups, all now unchecked by the higher law of God, these powers all prosper at the expense of the individual (Rushdoony 1984).

As Rushdoony goes on to argue, the power grab extends past the borders of the individual state or region. Multinational unions are created in a search for more power and "this leads either to irresponsible warfare as a result of meddling in foreign affairs, or to irresponsible alliances." Consequently, as Christian economist Timothy Terrell argues, "Christians must stand against the aggrandizement of the state, wherever it appears. This means protesting not only where Christians are prevented from assembling for worship, or where a Christian family's educational choices are limited by the state, but at any point at which the state has overstepped its bounds. Our evangelism must challenge the idolatry of statism as it would any pagan image-worship" (2003).

ENVIRONMENTALISM AS THE NEW PAGANISM

For reconstructionists and dominionists, the really objectionable thing about environmentalism is that it is a form of idolatry or paganism and represents a return to the worship of the earth of the kind practiced by the native Americans who inhabited the lands of America before the Puritans (Wright 1995). This anti-environmental apologetic was first proposed not by an American but by the French Protestant philosopher Jacques Ellul, who in his *The Subversion of Christianity* argued that environmentalism was essentially a pagan philosophy that involved a pantheist worship of nature (1986). This is the main line of anti-ecological argument at the Acton Institute, a conservative Christian think-tank that has sponsored a whole raft of publications and reports that call into question mainstream environmental thinking. In *The Cross and the Rainforest*, one of the principal targets for critique is the perceived paganism and earth worship of many green thinkers and environmentalists. Bill McKibben is criticized for substituting nature for the Christian God (Whelan 1996). Similarly L. Russ Bush argues that humanistic concern for ecological issues is bound up with a cultural shift toward "new age" religion, and that this shift is sustained by scientific naturalism—the belief that the universe birthed the earth and the human species without divine power—and with spiritual monism, the belief that ultimately all beings, all life, is spiritually one (Bush 1992). Bush and Whelan are prepared to acknowledge that there is an environmental crisis but its origin they argue is a spiritual rather than a material one; it is the failure of modern men and women to worship God as Trinity, and to acknowledge the Lordship of Christ that is really what lies behind the environmental crisis, which may best be seen as divine punishment for human idolatry (Whelan 1996). Love of trees, or a concern that the sheer weight of human numbers is leading to the extinction of wildlife, are both evidences of idolatry for Whelan and his ilk; there can be no better thing for the environment of the earth in their perspective than that humanity should have so multiplied that it is now possible for humans in every place to subdue the forest and drain the swamp and hence put God's creation in service of human wealth.

At the heart of the anti-environmental rhetoric of conservative Christians of both pre- and post-millennial guise is the belief that environmentalism is interfering with the God-given right to dominion, the human mandate as given in Genesis to be fruitful and multiply, to inhabit and enjoy the fruits of the land. This account of dominion argues for the right of private enjoyment of property and land without interference from the state. Environmentalism is seen as an attack on farmers, miners, and wealth creators who would use the natural resources they own, or work on, to make a living for themselves and their families (Arnold and Gottlieb 1996). Environmentalism is also said to subvert the Protestant work ethic and the Lockean and Republican ideal of minimalist government according to which the prime duty of the state is the maintenance of civil order so that individuals can enjoy their own property (Arneil 1996). As the conservative libertarian lobby organization the American Policy Center puts it "the moral values that the environmentalists are trying to change are those at the very foundation of Christianity—the root of Western Culture. In particular, they want Americans to turn away from the idea of private property ownership, individual liberty, elected representative government and man's God-given dominion over the earth" (DeWeese 2003).

DOMINION AND FALL

Conservative evangelicals hang a great deal of their beliefs about appropriate attitudes to the environment on the interpretation of the two words "dominion" and "subdue" in Gen 1:26–28. Richard Land of the Southern Baptist convention suggests that God tells humans that we are to have dominion (Hebrew *radah* meaning "to rule") over the creation and to subdue it (Hebrew *kabash* "to bring into bondage"). These are strong dominant words in the biblical text and leave no room for doubt that God has placed human beings first in creation. This human preeminence in the created order is extended when God tells Noah, "Everything that lives and moves will be food for you. Just as I gave you the green plants, I now give you everything" (Gen 9:3, NIV). Thus while God gives human being authority for ruling and superintending nature, he remains Lord of the creation. He is the Lord of the earth. We merely are vicars and vice-regents (Land 1992: 23). However Land is prepared to concede that there are restraints on what we may do with plants and animals; so for example while we are supposed to domesticate them, and while it is legitimate to experiment on them for "better human health," it is wrong to cause animal suffering "merely to improve cosmetics."

When we look at the other uses of the word dominion in the Hebrew Bible we find that the overwhelming use of the word is not to describe human rule, but human misrule over society and the earth. The word occurs a number of times in the Book of Daniel and its usage is quite clear—the empires and kingdoms of the world have usurped the rule of Yahweh over the earth and over the people of God and their misrule will eventually be brought to an end (e.g., Van Houtan and Northcott 2010). In the New Testament we find an even greater challenge to the conventional evangelical dominion narrative, for just as before the Fall dominion is said to have been lost so the Second Adam, Jesus Christ is the only one who according to the Gospel writers, and the letters of St Paul, is to exercise dominion in the time between his first coming and his coming again.

Both prophets and apostles in the Bible resist claims to human dominion on earth because when human empires and kings, and even Israel herself, claimed to exercise dominion, it produced not a more fruitful earth or a more righteous society but quite the opposite—misrule, unrighteousness, corruption, and idolatry. In this perspective the problem with the dominionist version of millennialism is the same as that of pre-millennialism; it sustains an attitude of control over history and manifests an imperial desire to determine the destiny of the earth itself, which is directly contrary to the claim of the New Testament that Jesus Christ alone is Lord of all. As Karl Barth suggested in the posthumously published final fragments of his *Church Dogmatics*, the problems that humanity faces in the modern world are precisely a result of the human claim to lordship. The disorder of human society, and I would add of ecological destruction, have their root in the claim of man to be his own master, and consequently to "live a lordless life".

When man, alienated from God, tries to live a lordless life, in no case does this result in his becoming the lord and master of the possibilities of his own life. The "You will be like God" (Gen 3:5) "you will be your own lords and masters," was from the very first the promise he thought he should grasp when he started on this path. In fact, however, there never has been, is, or will be any fulfillment of this promise. In the foolish and hopeless attempt to escape from the sphere of God's lordship, it is not so simple for man to become even a little God and Lord with the implied approximation to God's supremacy and controlling power in the fashioning of human existence. Even a partially free control has always been everywhere the myth, but only the myth and illusion, of the person who thinks and claims that he has come of age and is now sovereign and autonomous. In thinking this—and the more self-consciously and emphatically he does so—the more he is overtaken by the opposite. He ceases to be the free lord and master he could and should have been in the sphere of God's lordship if, instead of fleeing from God, he had oriented himself to him. Parallel to the history of his emancipation from God runs the emancipation of his own possibilities of life from himself: the history of the overpowering of his desires, aspirations, and will by the power, the superpower, of his ability. His capacities when he uses them, as Goethe describes so vividly and with such frightening profundity in his poem "The Sorcerer's Apprentice," become spirits with a life and activity of their own, lordless indwelling forces (Barth 1981: 214).

Barth here is suggesting that it is possible for humans to rule in a proper way. But such is the modern human revolt against the righteous command of God that Christians cannot help but protest and refuse the disorder of modern civilization (Barth 1981: 205ff). At the heart of what Barth calls the lordless powers of the modern age are Leviathan and Mammon, the technological powers and enhanced economic wealth, which make their suasion possible over the great multitude of human beings (229). The dominion of leviathan and mammon "reveals, though it does not constitute, the plight of man, the profound unrighteousness in which we people exist—each alone and in mutual relation—because of the basic unrighteousness of our relationship to God, the unrighteousness in which each for himself and all for all others we inevitably make life more or less difficult" (233).

ECOLOGICAL EVANGELICALISM

Despite the anti-environmental agenda of many creationists and Christian libertarians, there are strong and active voices among conservative evangelicals in America who read Barth in preference to Darby or LaHaye and who have not been tardy in attempting to draw the attention of American Christians to the ecological crisis. The first was Francis

Schaeffer, who penned a powerful indictment of industrial civilization and its disrespect for creation entitled *Pollution and the Death of Man* just a few years after Rachel Carson's epoch making book *Silent Spring* (Schaeffer and Middleman 1992). Calvin de Witt of the Au Sable Institute of Environmental Studies has been a significant voice, making the case for a biblically based conservation theology in a range of powerful and original essays, sermons, and monographs (DeWitt 1991). The Evangelical Environmental Network, which authored the Evangelical Declaration on the Care of Creation, represents a nationwide attempt to shift evangelical consciousness towards greater respect and care for the environment, and to ground this shift in core evangelical beliefs, and in the interpretation of Scripture.[1] But Christian critics of the Evangelical Environmental Network and its Declaration on Creation accuse it of implicit socialism when it adopts environmentalist arguments that ecological costs should be visited on those who create them through state regulation. For dominionists and dispensationalists alike, state environmental regulation is an unwarranted interference in the biblically mandated regimen of private property and the free market system (Terrell 2002).

Evangelical Protestantism remains divided in the United States at the present time on the ethics of the environment. Evangelical leaders issued a statement on climate change in 2005 in which they sought to persuade Congress and the White House that their constituency of 30 million evangelicals are concerned about climate change and environmental problems and want to see the United States develop a proper response to them is a powerful example of the potential of environmentally responsible evangelicals to speak publicly to an administration and to many congressional representatives who rely on the Christian constituency for support (Goodstein 2005). But given that according to the Pew Research Center four out of five evangelicals voted for Bush in 2004, the political impact of evangelicalism on environmental issues remains pretty negative (Page 2004). Evangelical lobby groups such as the Christian Coalition see the primary moral issues in the political realm as being concerned with the "pro-life" agenda already mentioned, as was particularly evident in the 2004 Presidential election. But tragically this conception of a pro-life agenda excludes other-than-human life. At time of writing the envi-

---

1. The Declaration is available online at http://www.creationcare.org/resources/declaration.php and is reprinted with commentaries by a number of authors including DeWitt and Northcott in R. J. Berry 2000.

ronment does not appear to figure high on the agenda of those making decisions about candidates for the next presidential election. Given the power of the evangelical constituency in American politics it could make a significant difference but the evidence is not strong that the leadership on these issues that Cal de Witt and others have given is yet being taken up by the conservative Christian constituency. If conservative Christian Americans continue to believe in Timothy LaHaye's vision of an earth that awaits eventual destruction by a divine judge, then it may be that the only hope for an ecological awakening among American Christians is a downturn in evangelical influence. The sociological evidence is however moving in the opposite direction. Mainline churches continue to lose members to the nondenominational mega-churches that have sprung up all over the United States. These churches meet in buildings that are designed like shopping malls, and their sanctuaries typically completely exclude daylight or any other hint of the presence of God's creation beyond the large encircling car park that surrounds these buildings. And no matter how many droughts and storms plague the American South as the planet gradually warms up dispensationalist Christians will continue to believe that these are not evidence of civilizational collapse but signs foretold in Scripture of the end of the world.

Response

A False Dominion of Control

ROBERT B. JACKSON

RECENTLY, TWO AUTHORS, GLEN Scherer in *Grist* (2004) and Bill Moyers in the *New York Review of Books* (2005), published influential articles on dominionism, the notion that biblical law was the cornerstone of a new American theocracy. For the believers they described, environmental protection is a waste of time. Why bother to save the Earth when life is ending in our generation? Why so much effort devoted to a doomed cause?

It's not that I think Moyers and Scherer were wrong, it's just that I think there is a more common aspect of dominionism than the extreme form they describe. Yes, there are people who believe that bringing an end to the earth would be a good thing. I just don't think there are as many of them as Moyers and Scherer purport.

Why this matters is because such an extreme perspective allows us to marginalize people of faith, to strengthen our own form of dominionism, our scientific superiority that suggests the world would be a better place if we could just grow up and leave religion behind.

With this chapter I would like to follow-up Michael Northcott's comments briefly by addressing a different form of dominionism, one that I believe is more important—the dominion of control. It is a form of dominionism that most of us subscribe to, at least tacitly. Without question, the most famous environmental passage in the Bible is the first chapter of Genesis, verse 28:

> And God blessed them, and God said to them, "Be fruitful and multiply, and fill the earth and subdue it; and have dominion over the fish of the sea and over the birds of the air and over every living thing that moves upon the earth."

We've been doing our best imitation of dominion ever since. Here in the United States, perhaps the group of people who best put these words to work was the Mormons. They subdued the land, building what Donald Worster calls a "hydraulic society" (1986). A century ago, John Widtsoe, a Mormon hierarch and church Apostle, defended the irrigation society they created, extending the Genesis view:

> The destiny of man is to possess the whole earth; the destiny of the earth is to be subject to man. There can be no full conquest of the earth, and no real satisfaction to humanity, if large portions of the earth remain beyond his highest control. (Quoted in Stegner 1988)

For the first time, we hear the antiquated term "dominion" replaced by its modern equivalent, "control." I'd like to illustrate the thread of dominion and environmental control briefly through the story of the Exodus. If we follow Moses on his journey, we see a new kind of dominion. "Come with me," Moses said to the Israelites, as they prepared to leave Ramses and Egypt after four centuries of captivity (Exod 14–16). Three environmental miracles mark this exodus. First, with the Egyptians approaching, Moses stretched his hand over the sea and divided it, allowing the Israelites to pass between the water. When the Egyptians followed, Moses again stretched out his hand and they drowned. In the second month of their journey, the Israelites began to starve in the desert. The second miracle then occurred:

> Then the Lord said to Moses, "Behold, I will rain bread from heaven for you; and the people shall go out and gather a day's portion every day, that I may prove them, whether they will walk in my law or not." (Exod 16:4)

And they harvested manna from the desert, they turned the desert to their purpose.

Finally, they continue to Rephidim, but there was no water to drink. They murmured against Moses once again. Moses asked God for direction:

> "You shall strike the rock, and water shall come out of it, that the people may drink." And Moses did so in the site of the elders. (Exod 17:6b)

These three miracles frame the narrative of the Israelites' escape from Egypt.

I'd like to examine this narrative in light of today's dominion, to examine each miracle in turn, working backwards through the Israelites' journey, comparing those miracles to our dominion over nature today.

When Moses struck the rock at Rephidim, he brought forth water. What was miraculous in God's hands is today commonplace. In the U.S. alone, almost a million new wells are drilled every year. Three thousand times a day, people strike rocks all over our country and bring forth water, 75 billion gallons a day. What was miraculous is now a routine engineering task.

The second miracle of the Israelites' escape was their ability to harvest the desert. "Now the house of Israel called its name manna; it was like coriander seed, white, and the taste of it was like wafers made with honey." They made the desert bloom and turned it to their purpose. However, God put limits on what they were to take, only as much as they could eat in one day.

Today we have no limits on what we harvest from the desert. We combine our miraculous ability to strike the rock, to draw water that may have been laid down ten thousand years ago, and use it to make the desert green. Manna? How quaint. How about strawberries and oranges and tomatoes and olives and wine? Fly across the United States and see the bounty of our ability to strike the rock and harvest the desert. What was miraculous is now routine agricultural practice.

Finally, the Israelites escaped because they controlled water, or called on God to do so. Moses parted the sea for their escape. Today, we don't part seas, we make them. We store more water behind our largest dams than is held in the Great Lakes of Michigan, Erie, and Ontario combined. The scale of our dominion—our control—dwarfs the Old Testament miracles of the environment. Environmentally and technologically speaking, we are God.

That recognition, the extent of our environmental control today, is what should link atheists, agnostics, and people of faith together. We control the environment in ways that were unthinkable in biblical times. We possess the power of unlimited exploitation. That power concerns me more than the extremists Moyers and Scherer describe who would like to bring about the end of the earth.

I'd like to close with a quote from Wallace Stegner. Stegner spent much of his career writing about dominion, space, and limits in the U.S. In a series of lectures at the University of Michigan in 1986, Stegner presented a vision at odds with the supreme control of Widtsoe I described earlier:

> The Garden of the World has been a glittering dream, and many find its fulfillment exhilarating. I do not. I have already said that I think of the main-stem dams that made it possible as original sin, but there is neither a serpent nor a guilty first couple in the story. In Adam's fall we sinned all. Our very virtues as a pioneering people, the very genius of our industrial civilization, drove us to act as we did. God and Manifest Destiny spoke with one voice urging us to "conquer" or "win" the West; and there was no voice of comparable authority to remind us of Mary Austin's quiet but profound truth, that the manner of the country makes the usage of life there, and that the land will not be lived in except in its own fashion. (Stegner 1988: 46)

As we reflect on what Michael Northcott writes, his words remind us of our biblical power over the environment. My hope is that this forum will also remind us to wield that power with intelligence and humility.

Six

Anti-Imperial Themes and Care for Living Nature in Early Christian Art

The Good Shepherd as a Model for Christian Environmental Ethics

SUSAN P. BRATTON

CHRISTIANITY IN AN IMPERIAL WORLD

ONE OF THE ODDITIES of environmental critiques of Christianity is the repeated attack on the King James translation of Gen 1:26, that humans are to "take dominion" of the earth. These criticisms dismiss the Christian life before King James, some 1600 years, and never ask if the early Christians were concerned about the "dominion" passage or interpreted it as some moderns. Francis Bacon and his contemporaries, for example, used the King James account to justify a rational study of nature, the inductive method, and using scientific results to improve human welfare (e.g., Merchant 1989, Barbour 1997). The Christian Scriptures substantially reinterpret the Torah and ancient Hebrew cosmology, as well as focusing more on some texts than others. The Book of Hebrews, for example, replaces the ancient Hebrew system of sacrifice with the death of Christ, while John 1 identifies the Messiah with the creative Word of Genesis 1. The Hellenized and Roman cultural environment influenced early Christian cosmology, and Christians clearly drew on or addressed a variety of political and ethical sources, including Stoic and Platonic philosophy.

Excessive ecotheological focus on a handful of explicitly cosmological biblical passages also ignores Christianity's origin as a religion based on reform. Jesus of Nazareth initially addressed conflicts within Judaism, such as the relationship of Jewish law to the demands of the Roman occupation of Palestine. After Jesus's death, the apostles confronted Hellenized urban lifestyles, and the cults of Greco-Roman deities. Rodney Stark has convincingly argued the early church was successful in attracting members because it consciously addressed major social problems in the economically and ethnically dispersed and oft-mismanaged empire (Stark 1997). The first Christians were deeply concerned about the meaning of kingship and government in a political sense, and the New Testament repeatedly addresses the stressful interactions of a minority religion with the suspicious state.

The purpose of this essay is to explore an underutilized source, religious art, and to ask how the early Christians approached issues of "dominion" and "kingship," particularly relative to nature. I will focus on frescos, mosaics, and sarcophagi from the Roman catacombs and late ancient mausoleums. Although the earliest possible date for compositions with Christian symbols or themes is about 180 CE, a majority of art historians identify the oldest works as early third century. The art thus first appears a few decades to a century or so after the first collections of Christian texts, which are also difficult to absolutely date. The earliest art documents the socially formative period of the house churches and Christian burial grounds, followed by the establishment of public places of worship.

Since the question of human dominion is intimately linked to concepts of kingship, lordship, and rule, as well as to human rights to exploit nature, we can ask how frequently Roman Christian art invokes themes of royalty, military dominance, and political control of natural resources, as well as whether the art displays Christians harvesting environmental resources or conquering the wild. Early Christian art does depict scenes from Genesis, including Noah's ark and Eden. Is dominion incorporated? And of course, if Christianity is the ultimate source of Western hubris toward nature, are Christian paintings more violent towards animals and plants, or perhaps more indifferent towards them, than non-Christian Roman works of similar age? Since Christians established their own catacombs during the age of the martyrs, we should suspect that motifs of kingship are nuanced and potentially counter-cultural. From reading the New Testament, we can also guess that care-giving and ministry are important themes, and that natural settings and objects serve as allegory or metaphor. Late ancient Christian art is predominantly funerary. It borrows motifs from non-Christian sarcophagi and catacomb paintings, some of which, such as evergreen funeral wreaths, still mark our twenty-first century sympathy cards and tombstones. The sculptors and painters taking commissions from Christians were familiar with conventions concerning the depiction of deities and the emperor, and some probably executed commissions for Jewish clients. Early Christian art thus incorporates, edits, and interprets themes from pre-Christian and non-Christian artistic models. The profusion of grapes in the Christian catacombs is similar to those from Dionysus's vineyards, and Noah's ark looks much like the earliest known Jewish representation of the ark as box-like.[1]

CONCEPTS OF PARADISE

The first question is to what extent did ancient Christians utilize biodiversity and living nature as metaphors (e.g., Bratton 2007)? Even a casual visit to the Roman catacombs will demonstrate that early Christians happily adopted Roman Homeric motifs, such as pastoral scenes, and copied stock Roman funerary designs suggesting natural productivity, including the Four Seasons, evergreen vegetation, fruiting vineyards, colorful peacocks, and blooming flowers. On the ceilings of the typical subterranean burial chamber, or *cubiculum*, vines twine around the borders and cheerful songbirds in flight decorate the corners. Ever-renewing nature is a symbol of the resurrection and of the best of human existence. Early Christians did, however, subtly edit pagan images. The Christian phoenix "was adjusted to depict not the moment of its dramatic death, but rather the positive, triumphal aspect of its rebirth from the ashes, more appropriate to the Resurrection of the flesh" (Bisconti 2002: 103).

Relative to the small size of the chambers, the diversity of natural images is high. Although the emphasis remains on species with key symbolic meaning, such as sheep and grapes, or peacocks with their supposedly decay-resistant flesh, the artists varied the types of organism or placed birds in scenes with plants to give the impression of an integrated living environment. The deceased would rise in a realm of both physical sustenance and of natural beauty, much like the fertile fields carpeting the hills over the catacombs, which were, by legislation concerning all cemeteries, outside the walls of Rome. According to art historian Fabrizio Bisconti:

1. The earliest known image of the ark is on a coin from Apamea (now in Turkey) in 217–18 CE. The coin is almost certainly from a Jewish source, as Christians at the time would not have been socially influential enough to have been producing currency. A photograph may be viewed in Spier (2007: 171).

> The leitmotif [recurring theme] of floral tapestry also appears in Jewish catacombs, as well as, significantly, in the double *cubiculum* of the Catacomb of Vigna Randinini that displays this theme alternating with images and signs of the more popular cosmic repertoire. Thus, this decoration provides a useful indication of how much the common significance of the floral motif was relevant to different religious cultures. It could suggest a fertile and happy world, a vegetable garden, the Garden of Eden inspired by Gen. 2.8–10, understood as a park, perfumed by an everlasting spring. (2002: 99)

The eternal life of the catacombs is neither streets of gold, nor an ethereal heaven lifted away from things of the earth, but a viable environment, where the wild and the cultivated co-exist. Eden is far more destination than origin in a majority of the surviving early Christian art. Christians die to rise again in a lush flowering and fruiting landscape, graced by the music of colorful songbirds, rather than in a abstract sky of fleecy clouds (e.g., Wright 2008).

The most common image of Jesus or of idealized Christian leadership is the Good Shepherd (see Fig. 1). Although the artistic model for the Good Shepherd is pagan representation of the divine messenger Hermes, the Good Shepherd of the Christian catacombs invokes associations with the youthful and courageous biblical David, and of texts, such as John 10, where Christ declares himself to be the Good Shepherd and his followers to be his flock. In John 10:11, Jesus of Nazareth states: "I am the good shepherd. The good shepherd lays down his lie for his sheep" (NRSV). Art historians do not universally agree there is adequate evidence the Good Shepherd is Christ, although the portrait of the humble youth with a sheep on his shoulders is certainly an icon of proper behavior (Jenson 2000: 38), and its central position in ceiling after ceiling implies theophany. The Good Shepherd borrows from Homeric philosophers in bucolic settings and from Virgil's agriculturally conscious landsman. His posture and dress replicates earlier depictions of Hermes with his staff. The figure therefore projects an array of virtues, including philanthropy, conscientious citizenship, rationale pursuit of ethics, and care of others. The biblical parallels, such as the parable of the shepherd struggling to find his lost sheep, are statements, not just of salvation, but of penance, faith, ministry to each creature, and persistence in the face of difficulty (Bisconti 2002: 120).

The Good Shepherd is hardly the Roman notion of an emperor or worldly ruler. Although much Roman funerary art depicts the deceased in full armor or astride a noble warhorse, weapons are rare, while not completely absent, from the Christian catacombs. The oldest images of the Good Shepherd display a boyish beardless face, with its implicit innocence, and lack of malice and worldly cynicism. Aside from adoring sheep, his loyal dog often accompanies him. He wears the clothes of a simple farmer or even a slave. He carries the tools of his trade, including a purse, pipes, or a bucket of sheep's milk, instead or a scepter or sword. He wears none of the clothes of Caesar, not even the toga of a Roman citizen. The Good Shepherd is a reversal of the realms of earthly and, particularly, military power and authority. The depiction of Christ as King thus evolves and becomes more prevalent through Christian history. In the earliest art, Christ, in his various personae, is dressed as landsman, citizen, or philosopher. By the construction of the early-Byzantine churches in Ravenna, Italy, however, Christ appears wearing purple, which identifies him as regent. By the Gothic, a regal Christ wearing a golden crown or nimbus, and sitting on a jeweled throne, is a common figure in the stunning stained glass of European cathedrals.

The Good Shepherd, in contrast, is most frequently surrounded by trees, herbs, and birds, rather than by angelic retainers, as is the norm for Christ in medieval altarpieces. In the "Good Shepherd Cubiculum" at the Catacomb of Domitilla, the Good Shepherd carries a lamb in the central roundel of the white ceiling. Four trees (cedars or junipers) with their narrow crowns pointing towards him, alternating with four birds standing among flowers, encircle him and mark the cardinal directions. The four corners of the ceiling consist of birds in vegetation topped by floral borders. Below on the facing diagonal frames, the painter has positioned frontal views of peacocks (Fasola 2002: 61). The Shepherd's power is expressed by his ability to sustain life and to generate peace and tranquility, or the ideal states for both terra and for humanity.

A similar composition graces the Cubiculum of the Velatio (Veiling) at the Catacomb of Priscilla. A central Good Shepherd carries a sheep, while two others stand undisturbed and confident at his feet. On either side of him are two trees, each with a dove holding an olive branch in its beak. The doves top leafy trees, not much taller than the Shepherd (Carletti 2001: 20–23). Immediately below and above the central roundel, aligned with the Shepherd's head and feet, are two celestial peacocks with magnificent, colorful tails. To the right and the left are two recognizable quails, a species grounded in the earth. This elementary cosmic sequence rotates "around the driving force of the Good Shepherd" (Bisconti 2002: 95). Beyond them are song birds carrying sprouts in their mouths. Noah's dove is a frequent motif in the catacombs, and the olive branch in her beak symbolizes peace, divine blessing, and the ability to construct a nest and to reestablish life after the flood. The song birds, similarly, are preparing to nurture a renewed generation. The images in the arches radiating out from the central dome include the three Hebrew children in the fiery furnace, a praying figure (orante), Abraham preparing to sacrifice Isaac, and Jonah spewed forth from the sea monster. These salvic narrative scenes concern faith during trial, obedience to God, and proper forms of worship and sacrifice (both offerings to God). One of the most remarkable features of these paintings is the degree to which realistic living creatures mediate and maintain the bonds between the heavenly and earthly realms. Heaven is not a distant and imagined realm, but an eternally providential version of God's original and already familiar Creation.

A number of third- and fourth-century Christian frescos and sarcophagi present Orpheus wearing shepherds or Oriental garb and a Phrygian cap, the later an indication he is a foreigner from the east. Critics again differ as to whether one can prove the figure is Christ, or perhaps David. Orpheus does appear with a representation of David in the Catacomb of Domitilla (Bisconti 2002: 103), and ancient writers, such as Clement of Alexandria, present Orpheus as a metaphor for Christ, since Christ can tame the wildest of beasts—the human (Jenson 2000: 41). Christ/Orpheus appears "depicted with a lyre in his hand, surrounded by the animals he tames through the sweetness of his melody" (Fasola 2002: 65). Bisconti documents one arrangement where "the figure of Orpheus amongst the animals represents the unifying junction of a group of four New and Old Testament scenes that alternate in a criss-cross fashion" (Bisconti 2002: 103), perhaps unifying the association with Jesus and David. In the best known example of the theme, from the Catacomb of Sts. Pietro and Marcellino, Orpheus holds a lyre while an eagle looks across at him from a tree (103–4). Although the eagle could have a biblical basis, it is also an obvious symbol of the Roman state and legion battle standards. The composition thus implies the submission of the governing powers to the ethical and spiritual message of the early church.

The early Christian frescos and mosaics capture sacred time through portraits of the Four Seasons. Branches simultaneously fruiting and flowering also represent the timeless and eternal. The heads of the Seasons personified may appear around the Good Shepherd. The Seasons as boys holding the fruits of the land and air appear on Christian sarcophagi, just as they do on sarcophagi featuring Dionysus. "The succession of the seasons, and precisely nature's coming into flower after winter, was considered the symbol of the Resurrection" (Carletti 2000: 27–28). Another marker of time, birth, is not as prevalent a theme as it is in later Christian art. In the catacomb of Priscilla, the oldest known painting of the Madonna and child without the Magi, dating from the second half of the second century or early third century, is positioned near a fresco of the Good Shepherd. Yet the emphasis of a majority of the frescos is on rebirth, rather than on human reproduction, family lineage, or child-rearing (24–25). The Shepherd milking a sheep or carrying a bucket of milk, food for the new born or the new Christian, is a common early metaphor for the provision of spiritual needs and of eternal life.

Adam and Eve with the serpent twined around the Tree of Life do appear in the catacombs frescoes. The context is typically a separate frame from the profuse pattern of vegetation and animal life dominating so many walls and ceilings. In later Christian art, Adam and Eve often appear in Eden with a full array of animals and plants, in some exemplars at the moment of the Fall. Such compositions associate sin more completely with the diversity of nature than is typical in the Christian art of late antiquity, where natural objects are predominantly symbols of the holy. The first catacombs painters did not record the Genesis sequences of cosmic creation, or consider the first moments of time. A visitor does not observe God brooding over the chaos of the waters or raising a hand to generate the fishes. The earliest art lacks historic sequences of the seven days of Creation, which do become an important subject in illustrated Bibles, but the oldest extant examples are probably fifth to sixth century (Kessler 2007). Adam in Paradise and Adam naming the animals are also established subjects by the fifth century, with the implication Christ is the new Adam. An exceptional example is a fifth-century ivory diptych (probably of Roman origin) with Adam naming the animals, where the opposing panel records scenes from the life of St Paul, including the serpent ineffectually biting the traveling apostle. Adam relaxes with an eagle, a songbird, a bear, a bull, sheep, a boar, an elephant, a horse, a goat, a stag, and a doe. Here the animals are allegorical and signify "the passions that must be overcome by the virtuous man (as noted by the Jewish author Philo and frequently by Christian theologians) and in a broad sense, sin and danger.... While in paradise, man has no need to fear wild beasts, but after his expulsion from Eden, the beasts were a greater threat." Paul, as a virtuous Christian, shares the characteristics of Adam in Eden, so "the viper's bite had no effect" (Spier 2007: 264–66).

The earliest artistic arguments for God's saving authority rest not in the construction of a complex universe, but in the on-going process of reproduction and survival. The dominant metaphors are often based in horticulture or animal husbandry. This has a parallel in the New Testament parables of ever-lasting life, where the imagery reflects agricultural practice or fruitfulness, such as the wheat and the tares, Christ as the true vine, or the shepherd rescuing lost sheep. Christ as Creator who started it all is not as prominent, as Christ as a providential font of life who keeps all that exists going forever, reflecting Classical culture's "concept of cyclical and continuous recurrence of time" (Bisconti 2002: 97). The prevalence of wheat, grapes, sheep, and fruiting trees accentuates the divine as care-giving and immediately accessible, rather than as transcendent, mighty, and beyond time. As Christian artistic expression develops, it incorporates more complete sequences from Genesis, and is more likely to depict nature as fallen, and therefore as a potential spiritual danger or temptation, perhaps due to a switch in emphasis from a strictly funerary to a more openly instructional context, or as a response to growing ascetic influence.

NATURAL METAPHORS FOR CHRIST

To avoid treating animals and plants as mere objects, we might ask what they are doing in the layouts, and how they interact with other figures. Although backgrounds are sparse, including those associated with people, and the art tends towards the representational, the peacocks and partridges of the Cubiculum of the Velatio are standing on the ground among trees and other plants (see Fig. 1). The peacock is in its proper habitat at the forest edge, despite its celestial associations. Frequently, peacocks and other birds feast on grapes gathered in vessels or consume larger fruits. Birds carry twigs and branches, an activity associated with nesting and nurturing new life. Two flying song birds holding branch tips in their beaks frame and face toward the ornant (praying female figure with up turned hands) in the lunette on the rear wall in the Cubiculum of the Velatio, an alignment relating prayer with nest construction, and therefore the nurturing of others. In the fourth-century Mausoleum of Constanza (a Christian daughter of the emperor Constantine), ceiling mosaics incorporate birds drinking from silver vessels. Birds represent human souls, so it is no coincidence one is drinking from a decorated, two-handled vessel, probably containing wine, while two songbirds take liquid from an open cup. The flora in this mosaic includes pines with cones, palms, olives, and laurels—species equally representing eternal renewal of life. Sheep on Christian sarcophagi similarly drink from running streams.

Natural features and processes serve as metaphors for Christ. The catacombs frescos and carvings on early sarcophagi frequently display Moses striking the rock in the Wilderness of Sin. The typical painting presents the water as a bright blue flood pouring across a rough rock face, suggesting unending provision of the substance necessary to all life. Exodus 17:5–6 reports: "The Lord said to Moses, 'Go on ahead of the people, and take some of the elders of Israel with you; take in your hand the staff with which you struck the Nile, and go. I will be standing there in front of you on the rock at Horeb. Strike the rock and water will come out of it, so that the people may drink.' Moses did so, in the sight of the elders of Israel." The Hebrew text does not call God the rock, but reports God is standing with Moses at the miraculous spring. First Corinthians 10:1–4 provides the analogy between Christ and the water from the rock: "I do not want you to be unaware, brothers and sisters, that our ancestors were all under the cloud, and all passed through the sea, and all were baptized into Moses into the cloud and the sea, and all ate the same spiritual food and all drank the same spiritual drink. For they drank from the spiritual rock that followed them, and that rock was Christ." The paintings imply both baptism as a source of everlasting life, and Christ as the rock and as the water assuaging spiritual thirst. As the Apostolic succession and the primacy of Peter become a greater concern for the church in Rome, this image is replaced by the jailed Peter miraculously either touching or striking a wall with a wand in his prison, which becomes a rocky hill or mountain side bursting forth with water splashing down across boulders (see Fig. 3). The jailors, whom Peter baptized, hold out their cupped hands or lean down to drink. In an example from the Catacomb of Callixtus, Moses, in humility untying his shoes as an indication of the presence of the One God, stands behind Peter as he touches his wand to a large rock completely coated in flowing water (Spier 2007). The portrayals award Peter the authority of both Moses and Christ, which is transferred to the Bishop of Rome. This authority, however, does not claim the authority of the emperor, but emphasizes government interference with Peter's mission, and the importance of the church in guiding and replenishing the state. Christ is simultaneously Peter, the rock and the refreshing spring.

Christ may also appear standing on a rock form which the Four Rivers of Paradise originate, again implying Jesus is both the rock and the sweet flow. An example is a Sarcophagus with the *Tradito Legis* where Christ stands on the water producing rock and gives the open scroll of the law to Peter, while St Paul looks on. Moses and the rock appear on one end of the sarcophagus and Peter and the thirsty jailors on the other, linking the water that feed Creation with baptism and Christian instruction (Spier 2007). Once basilicas are established, deer lapping clean water from the Rivers of Paradise become a frequent component of apse and ceiling mosaics. The emphasis is on the continuing expression of God's love through the subtle and quiet flow of Providence. Christ is the fruiting vine, the pure water, and the flowering branch. The activities of living creatures reinforce the basic natural process of regeneration as a dominant metaphor for spiritual renewal, salvation, and human fulfillment in resurrection.

Late antique painters and sculptors oriented animals and plants towards holy persona and sacred events. One of the ironies of the Good Shepherd, as the most prevalent figure conveying Christian leadership, is he interacts not with the human, but with the greater Creation. By classical convention companion animals reflect the characteristics of the master they serve. Their affection and attention recognizes the exceptional expression of these virtues in a human or a deity. A romping, muscular panther often follows Dionysus, for example. The Good Shepherd's dog looks up expectantly toward his master's face, as if awaiting a command. The Shepherd shares the best characteristics of his animal helper, who is patient, protective, loyal, gentle, and courageous. The dog symbolizes the behavior of the disciplined Christian, who assists Christ in caring for the sheep. The Good Shepherd is also his sheep and becomes the cosmic sacrifice of the meek.

The Nativity in the stable appears in the fourth century, and from the beginning, friendly adoring animals look down on the infant Jesus. On a sarcophagus lid from the Vatican Pio Christiano Museum, the lumbering, bulky beasts touch the child's swaddling clothes with their muzzles. A similar carving sets the ox and ass so close to the baby, that the ass could easily nuzzle his face (Mancenelli 1981: 62). We are so accustomed to the benign, protective ox and ass that we no longer ask, why would anyone portray a divine figure in this setting? The depiction is a reversal on earthly kingship where human retainers would stand guard, yet invokes Christ as the beloved author of the cosmos. The animals willingly join the sacred birth, substituting for palace nursemaids. The birth of the Savior is the birth of all living. The adoring ox and ass welcome the humble of humanity to come and believe.

Aside from the dog, the donkey is the most frequent "working" associate of Christ. Thomas F. Matthews in *The Clash of the Gods* points out Christian carvings of Christ's entry into Jerusalem were a purposeful contrast to depictions of the *adventus* or parade ceremony, where the Roman emperor enters a city on a tall, magnificent warhorse, surrounded by an armed escort. On early Christian sarcophagi, in an inversion of worldly order, Christ enters Jerusalem on a struggling donkey, bending under his weight. Her colt accompanies her, identifying her as servant and caretaker. Matthews concludes the lowly equine subverts Roman political values:

> In all of these manifold appearances of the ass one detects something of the special pleasure that Christians took in believing Christ had led them into a kind of looking-glass world in which all the traditional values were turned upside-down ... Symbol of stubborn stupidity, the ass recognized the divine Logos; Baalam's ass was thought by Irenaeus to have recognized the Christ, the Divine Word himself, in the angel that confronted him. The ass that looks over the crib practically kisses the Christ child, so intimate he has become with the Word. (1999: 48)

On the sarcophagus of Junius Bassus in the Vatican collection, Christ's donkey, with her head up, approaches two figures, one of whom has climbed a tree. The two welcoming youths, one over and the other next to the donkey, create an image of intimate and safe space around the triumphant Jesus. This is not the mount of a warrior to be feared, but the friendly partner of a gentle master. The ass and dog as symbols do not convey a message of kingly and perhaps brutal and unthinking dominion, or of Jesus's earthly rule as conquest. The battles of a royal or armored Christ or his angels against the minions of evil, including vicious beasts of the earth, are absent from the earliest art, and slowly emerge during the early medieval period to become widespread by the Gothic.

DANGEROUS BEASTS AND THE ABSENCE OF HUNTING

Catacombs frescos and carvings do present encounters with dangerous wild beasts, but these adventures are predominantly unarmed. Sampson wrestles a lion, a rare Christian declaration of human strength defeating the wild. More common is Daniel in the lion's den, with its implications of wrong-doing and indifference to divine will on the part of an earthly empire. The lion was already a symbol of kingly authority, so supernatural authority shutting the lion's jaws implies God's power as Creator supersedes that of the emperor. In the earliest art, the angels of the biblical narrative are not necessarily present, and Daniel stands alone with predators, stilled by God. Today's children's Bible storybooks tend to feature David slaying the lion and the bear equally with the trials of Daniel. Although the early art depicts David, and he may hold a sling (Bisconti 2002: 103), he is not standing over dead wildlife.

Late antique Roman art is profuse with hunting (see Fig. 4). Floor mosaics in the homes of the wealthy idealize the capture and killing of game of all sorts. Military leaders were interred in sarcophagi glorifying boar or lion hunts, as metaphors for masculine honor actualized in dedicated service to Roman military and colonial ventures. Household mosaics and frescos document the Roman games, including grandiose events dispatching exotic species, such as tigers. Early Christian art, preferring Christ as Orpheus, edits out much of this violence towards nature. Fabrizio Bisconti finds hunting appears only twice in painting in the Christian catacombs (2002: 107). Christian sarcophagi do incorporate an occasional hunting scene on a recycled lid. Yet, the spears and swords have largely disappeared. The reasons for this are complex and may never be completely known. Christian pacifism and resistance to state religion, as well as the reality of persecution, are obvious potential roots. In "civilized" societies, hunting is a privilege of the elite. When conducted by military officers in the colonies and owners of large estates, it can serve as a form of re-conquest and a reminder of territorial control.

Christian indifference to hunting and to symbolic slaughter of wildlife may also lie in rejection of the Roman games, which were both a remnant of an offering to the old pantheon, and an open expression of Rome's colonial might. The games arose from funerals to pay "duty or tribute to dead ancestors," particularly prominent men (Kyle 2001), and were historically organized to propitiate the supernatural protectors of Rome. The celebration of the festival of Jupiter of Latium probably began without games in the fourth century BCE, but had acquired them by the first century CE (Kyle 2001: 39–40). Since Romans staged games as an ex-votive ritual, the early Christians attacked the games as a form of human sacrifice, where prisoners taken in battle died for public entertainment. After his conversion, Constantine terminated the Secular Games in 314 (Turcan 2000: 155). The theologian Tertullian denounced the festival of Jupiter Latium as human sacrifice and rejected Jupiter as a deity "whom they drench with human blood at his own games" (Kyle 2001: 40).

Staged battles with animals were competitive symbols of Rome's expansive dominions. Although the early funerary versions utilized indigenous animals, politicians and generals began adding elephants, lions, and leopards, prior to the second century BCE. If the freedom to chase ibex in Palestine served as a demonstration of Roman power, the ability to transport the fierce and the exotic back to Rome was an even more impressive proof of Roman might. As Richard Beacham concludes: "The trend thus established encouraged the spectators to associate military prowess and the geographic expansion of Roman influence with various animals from the distant realms subject to Roman might. Through the display of such exotic booty, power was rendered both graphic and entertaining" (1999: 12). Pompey proved the extent of his foreign conquests by sponsoring events with "six hundred lions . . . four hundred and ten leopards and panthers, and eighteen elephants," as well as displaying a lynx, baboons, and an Indian rhinoceros (64). In the ancient world, conquerors paraded subjected rulers through the city gates, along with the enslaved remnants of their vanquished armies, and recorded the event on stone monuments, as the Triumphal Arch of Constantine in Rome. Gladiatorial battles imitated the acquisition and retention of an empire. Early Christians rejected this concept of rule in general, and their frescos of quiet fields and gardens filled with a diversity of unmolested creatures are, considering New Testament and other early Christian teachings, a subtle, yet demonstrative, counterpoint.

HUMANS AND THE COSMOS

We now should address the broader theological context of nature by asking which rituals and human activities are associated with natural motifs. In the catacombs, scenes from the activities of the church or from biblical narratives of salvation surround or cover the dead interred in the walls, and natural objects dominate the ceiling. The Cubiculum of the Sacraments in the Catacomb of St Callixtus features frescoes of the Eucharist and Baptism. In the middle of one wall, paintings of a paralytic, laying hands on bread, a table with seven Christians participating in a common meal, Abraham ready to sacrifice Isaac, and an agriculturalist with a digging tool span between two layers of the *loculi* or recesses accommodating the dead. At the top of the wall Jonah emerges from the water between two birds, a scene reminiscent of the paralytic healed at the pool of Bethsaida, of baptism, and of the raising of the dead. Above, across the damaged ceiling are the birds and plants of Paradise. In the most basic sense, the wall around the dead is where the Christian has been, and the natural sphere above is where the Christian is going. Jonah, who had returned from death in the belly of the sea monster, is often a transitional figure occupying the ceiling with the Good Shepherd, or appearing in arches over entrance ways, as in the Cubiculum of the Velatio. The Eucharist is the summary of divine providence in the world. The fields of the Good Shepherd receive the faithful in the afterlife and thus are an analog of the table set with loaves and fishes. The sacred feast in the Cubiculum of the Sacraments offers two or three dishes with fishes or loaves in front of the diners, while full wicker baskets, with seven to twelve loaves (shown life sized relative to the human figures) sit at the ends of the table (Baruffa 2000: 79–84). The Eucharist is about sharing commodity; the birds, flying among the figures on the wall and ascending to the ceiling, are about the natural productivity and life giving renewal of God's Creation.

In the Cubiculum of the Sheep, in the Catacomb of Callixtus, the Good Shepherd carrying a lamb appears on a wall with a ram and some sheep. On either side of him, two men are holding their hands out to take water gushing from rocks in the form of forest waterfalls, rather than a well or a constructed fountain. On an adjoining wall, Jesus blesses the loaves and fishes. Large baskets of bread sit on the ground. A third wall captures Moses striking the rock in the desert, with a man also holding his hands into the cascade to capture water to drink (Baruffa 2000: 111–14).

The productivity of the earth itself as shown by the trees, pastures, and freely flowing springs is a metaphor for divine blessing and continuing life in Christ.

EARLY CHRISTIAN VALUES

Early Christian art is not environmental in the twentieth-century sense, as it is not explicitly about the restoration of a degraded earth. The cosmology is one of peacekeeping and egalitarian care. Images of command and control are limited and intentionally edited out. Some of the finest carvings and paintings, in terms of craftsmanship, are a critique of human kingship misapplied. Christ riding on the donkey, coming to bring food and healing to the poor, is the opposite of the triumphal Roman entry, where the spoils taken from other lands, including human captives, parade through the gates. Wanton exploitation and brutal conquest, including the slaughter of exotic wildlife, are unnecessary in a community that can perceive and freely distribute the bounty of God. For the early Christian, dominion is an irony. The increasing presence of these countercultural themes on expensive art objects from the most professional workshops, by the fourth century, is evidence that people of means and elevated social rank were questioning the ethics of the Empire and were contemplating the meaning of proper kingship and "dominion." The founders of Christianity were concerned about their role as witnesses of a righteous life, even in death.

Some of the commonest environmental critiques of Christianity are incongruent with the content and apparent political agenda of early Christian art. The art does not tout well-armed sky gods, and its themes are frequently anti-imperial. Nor does Christian art displace the old supernatural beings, leaving their vineyards, pastures, and woods spiritually unattended. The Good Shepherd and Christ as Orpheus explicitly adopt the roles of natural care-takers. Late antique art does not emphasize God as transcendent and completely other, but rather praises Christ as with us. The Shepherd continues as a predominant persona of Christ into the Byzantine period, when Christ as King becomes far more prominent.

The early church portrayed Christ as not just attractive to sheep and children, but to all creatures. In the true kingdom, peace extends to the entire Creation. Human care for other species, wild and tame, is thus an actualization of divine intent for nature, and a premonition of the *telos*, or the end of sacred time. The bread and wine of the Eucharist have imbedded within them an array of blooming flowers, fruiting trees, and nesting birds. The same providential flow of blessing that breathes life into the deer drinking from the Rivers of Paradise, or the dove carrying a branch to her nest, pours grace into the church and welcomes everyone to a shared table with great baskets of bread. The respect due both the elements and the participants at the table is a potential model for our "taking" from Creation. Sustenance is a blessing, and intended to be enjoyed. Yet, sharing and caring are integral to its nutritive value and to maintaining the workings of providence through the living cosmos.

The Good Shepherd is equally a model of Creation care, if we visualize the sheep resting on his shoulders, not just as the soul of a Christian, but simultaneously as the living biosphere on which we depend. The Shepherd gently bears the entire earth and all humankind. His love is so great he offers himself up as the Lamb and replaces humanity and all Creation on the altar of God. Everything around him is joyful flowering and fruiting. The Shepherd is eternal life. Humankind's slow destruction of the world's diverse ecosystems, progressing as the annihilation of a bird population here and a flowering prairie there, is much like vandalizing a catacombs ceiling. First the flying songbirds are defaced, then the seasons disappear from the margins. Finally, the Good Shepherd is obliterated, along with his sheep. The fragmented frescoes decay into dark stains, dust and flakes of plaster.

The Good Shepherd may, in fact, provide a useful lesson for the modern stewards of biodiversity. Today's response to endangered species and habitats is too often one of lost inventory. Species arrive on the endangered species list long after they have lost their reproductive potential. The red books become catalogs of irreplaceable antiques, which collectors struggle to preserve. The realm of the Good Shepherd is one of continual care and renewal, where any interruption of divine providence is a tragic deviation from divine intent. If we refrain from greed and hubris, and the other indifferent excesses of human control, and, instead, join the Shepherd in gentle care-taking, God's blessings will flow unhindered and the greatest art work of all, the Creation, will retain its beauty and its diversity until the end of days.

FIGURE 1: Good Shepherds (I). Based on statuettes of Hermes, the Good Shepherd is a friend and caretaker for the living earth. Portrayals show him as youthful, wearing the clothes of a simple landsman, and as accompanied by or carrying animals. First half of the fourth century. Location: Museo Pio Cristiano, Vatican Museums, Vatican State. Photo Credit: Scala/Art Resource, NY.

FIGURE 2: Good Shepherds (II). Jesus, in an inversion of the usual Roman triumphal entry on a warhorse, rides a humble donkey. The relationship between the entering "king" and those greeting him is intimate and friendly. Sarcophagus of Junius Bassus. Detail: Entry into Jerusalem. Circa 359 CE. Location: Museum of the Treasury, St Peter's Basilica, Vatican State. Photo Credit: Scala/ Art Resource, NY.

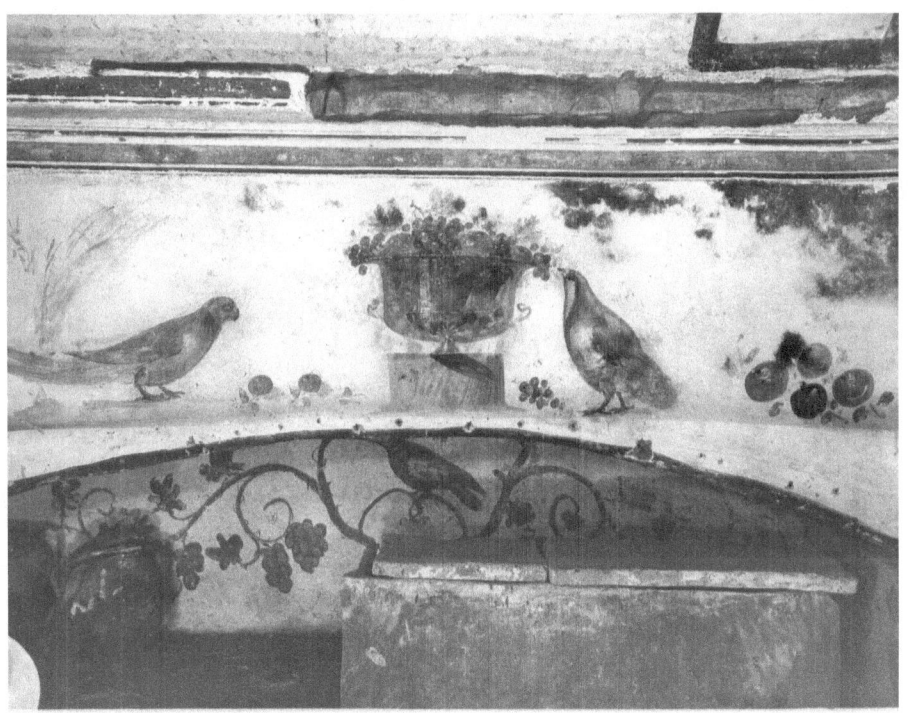

FIGURE 3: Birds feasting on grapes. Fresco from the Christian catacombs depicts a partridge feasting on fruit. Note the other birds and vines in the integrated composition. Location: San Sebastiano, Rome, Italy. Photo Credit: Alinari/Art Resource, NY.

FIGURE 4. Imperial Roman violence towards animals. Men assisted by hunting dogs capture a rhinoceros, with intent to remove it from the wild. Third to fourth century CE. Detail of the Big Game Hunt, mosaic in the ambulatory of the Villa de Piazza Armerina, Sicily, Italy. Location: Villa del Casale, Piazza Armerina, Sicily, Italy. Photo Credit: Eric Lessing/ Art Resource, NY.

FIGURE 5. Armed gladiator slaying a leopard as part of a public display for entertainment. Third century CE, from Smirat, Tunisia. Detail from "The Magerius Mosaic" which displays hunting scenes in celebration of the Venationes offered by Magerius. Location: Museum, Sousse, Tunisia. Photo Credit: Vanni/Art resource, NY.

Response

Seeing through a Columbine Flower

MAKOTO FUJIMURA

> This life's dim windows of the soul
> Distorts the heavens from pole to pole
> And leads you to believe a lie
> When you see with, not through, the eye.
>
> —William Blake

IN 1998, I BEGAN a series of works in response to the Columbine High School incident. In one single day, the sleepy environs of a high school in Littleton, Colorado, became a backdrop to American tragedy, where students, with a cache of automatic weapons, shot peers and teachers. I intuited then a symptom of a larger cultural malaise. I wrote:

> In the aftermath of the Columbine High school shooting, and upon a recommendation by a photographer friend (who covered the tragic event for the New York Post), I walked in the mountains of Colorado, looking for wild columbine flowers. They grow numerous on the sunny mountain faces in summer, white flowers with purple petals and tails like tentacles.

I noticed that there were a few flowers growing in the shade of trees. Instead of purple petals, they were completely white, almost transparent. The delicate flowers symbolized for me perfectly the fragility of lives, so young, haunted by the encroaching darkness of violence. The beauty of them so reminded me of one girl who was reported to have looked in the eyes of the perpetrator who held a gun to her head, taunting her, "Do you still believe in God?" She said, "Yes, I believe" and was shot.[1]

---

1. The account in Bernall 1999, detailing the confession of Cassie Bernall has been

Fujimura: Seeing through a Columbine Flower

FIGURE 6: *Columbine Dream.* 2004, 60.2cm x 72.6cm. Mineral Pigments, Gold, Oyster Shell White on Kumohada. Used with permission of the artist.

Later another friend told me that the columbines were the early church's symbol for the Holy Spirit. When I paint the columbines, they come out almost like angels.

In the "Columbine Dream" painting reproduced in this response paper, Columbine flowers float in the dark, azurite background (Fujimura 2004). The flowers are painted with oyster shell white, and pure gold powder. The white is made by letting Japanese oyster shell decompose in the beaches of southern Japan and then purified. The resulting color is semi-opaque, possessing both transparency and material presence at the same time. Pure gold powder, mixed in refined hide glue, gives the surface extra glimmer and in a proper light will "leap out" of the background. I have pondered, ever since then, why I felt the urgency to paint these images,

disputed. Despite the uncertainty of what was exactly said, Cassie Bernel's testimony, and her willingness to die for her faith, is clearly noted in her diaries.

which were later exhibited in New York and Tokyo. When I would write about the origins of the series so that words can accompany images, galleries often would edit the essay, leaving out the story of the girl being shot (in Japan), or leaving out her extraordinary confession (in New York), to make it more palatable. I would edit it back and say something like "I really need to honor the memory of what happened in order to exhibit this." Later on I wondered "Why did I do that?" Why did I care so much about the actual incident?

It occurred to me, reading Ms. Bratton's paper, that I needed to do this as a mediation, simply to navigate through this period in history, to understand both the magnitude of loss and the violence in the world today. As a "Ground Zero" resident of New York City, my family and I were severely affected by the events of September 11, 2001. Since then, the language of lamentation that I began with the Columbine series has developed to a longer, sustained journey literally via the ashes of 9/11, now resulting in further meditation based on T. S. Eliot's "Four Quartets," as well as Dante's *Divine Comedy*. Ms. Bratton notes that early Christian art was mainly funerary, and that "realistic living creatures mediate and maintain the bonds between the heavenly and earthly realms."

As an artist, I deeply resonated with these statements. My works of late are funerary works, especially after the Columbine incident and September 11, 2001. I need nature's symbols, such as a columbine flower, to help me enter in to the suffering and hope.

Mediation of such a condition is part of "dominion" keeping. A responsible mediation is an integral part of the call to steward nature as well as culture. Artists are to "subdue" the materials, but they cannot do so unless they respect the essence of the materials used. In other words, the artist's way of "subduing" is to collaborate with materials, giving raw materials the breath of life. Dominion then is an art of collaboration, a dance between the maker and her materials.

In my case, I use natural materials in my works—minerals, paper, gold, and silver—and while I do find myself collaborating with materials, I wrestle with them, too. If you are an artist, dancer, writer, or anyone associated with creativity, the reality of creativity is that we need to translate ideas into creative acts, and such focus requires enormous energy, wrestling with the incarnation, and responsible editing. The Nihonga ("Japanese style painting") materials such as azurite, malachite are themselves pulverized, allowing the prismatic refractions in the many layers of the surface of the painting. This process points my journey of faith, the wrestling of my own heart faced with a broken world. I also need to be "pulverized" in order to be used for Divine purposes. The "birth pains" that accompany such generative creativity in the world that is not what it ought to be makes any act of creativity enormously challenging and difficult.

In such a journey, especially in a Christian paradigm, what began as a funerary work can often turn into a celebration of a greater feast. The power of the imaginative act is to anticipate what the eye cannot yet see. Artists have the power to see life through death. This is the tension, at the heart of creation, to see, as William Blake would have it, through, and not with, the eye.

Seven

Nature and the Nation-state
Ambivalence, Evil, and American Environmentalism

KYLE S. VAN HOUTAN *and* MICHAEL S. NORTHCOTT

And they talked of the land behind them. I don' know what it's coming to, they said. The country's spoilt. It'll come back though, on'y we won't be there. Maybe, they thought, maybe we sinned some way we didn't know about. (1951: 271)

—John Steinbeck, *The Grapes of Wrath*

FIGURE 7: *St. Jerome and the Lion.* Roger van der Weyden. Oil on oak panel. Used with permission of The Detroit Institute of Arts.

Diversity and Dominion

Walking through the National Gallery of Art in Washington, DC we were struck by the number of images of Saint Jerome on display. Depicted in various settings, Saint Jerome is seen writing at his desk with a lion coiled at his feet, engaged in prayer at the entrance to a cave, performing acts of self-mortification, or—most notably—in a reference to the classical tale of Androcles, plucking a thorn from a lion's paw. Weyden's painting of Saint Jerome in this chapter shows him in two poses at once. In the upper left corner of the painting he is engaging in an act of penance, using a rock to chastise his flesh. Like the Christian desert fathers before him, Jerome is using the wild to subdue his bodily desires and heal his soul. But at the same time, Jerome is depicted as an archetype of a new relationship with the wild where human holiness confers harmony and peace between man and beast and the wild is tamed. Even the king of beasts—the lion—recognizes the authority of this saint, coming to him for healing, drawn by his holiness.

Weyden's image wonderfully captures the duality in the Christian tradition of the human relation to creation. From the Gospel narratives of the life of Christ, through the stories of the desert fathers and saints, the tradition attests to a cosmological reordering which sees the resurrected body of Christ as first fruit of a "new creation" in which the whole cosmos is recapitulated and Christians are set in a new relationship with the nonhuman world;—one that is nonviolent and harmonious. This new creation, and nature as a whole, is seen as a domain that is still subject to the exigencies of sin and that Christians are called both to subdue and to redeem, by their quest for sanctification, and by their work in the world.

The long artistic tradition of portraits of Saint Jerome intertwines the concepts of human dominion over nature with a saintly capacity to engender compassion and healing in the human and larger-than-human world. An analogous duality may be observed in the pioneering conceptions of nature of two North American conservationists, John Muir and Gifford Pinchot. Symbolizing starkly different philosophies of nature conservation, Muir and Pinchot began as friends, united in their zeal to stem the widespread deforestation that affected the United States in the 1800s (Nash 1982). But their friendship was short lived, and their different approaches to land use and wilderness eventually made them bitter public enemies. The terms of their debates are important as they continue to mark American attitudes to nature conservation today (Meyer 1997, Smith 1998).

THE COMPETING VISIONS OF JOHN MUIR AND GIFFORD PINCHOT

In his journals and letters John Muir describes the cathedral-like rocks, giant sequoias, and flowery meadows of the Californian Sierra Nevada as sacred. As for Jerome, the wilderness for Muir is a place of bodily asceticism and soul therapy. But Muir goes far beyond Jerome in his account of the presence of the divine in the pristine landscape of wilderness. In a letter to his transcendentalist mentor, Ralph Waldo Emerson, Muir invites Emerson, "in a month's worship with Nature in the high temples of the great Sierra Crown beyond our holy Yosemite" (quoted in Rusk 1994: 154–55). In making this claim, Muir articulates a new ecological sensibility in American nature writing: the Protestant God is remapped onto the wild lands of America, the wilderness becomes a savior, and liberal Protestant piety finds its incarnation through an ecstatic engagement with the natural sublime (Stoll 1993). It is as if the remnant of untouched or wild land is the only place where atonement may be found from the carnage the colonists had wrought on its previous inhabitants, and the heedless exploitation of so much of its forest, minerals, and soil. Whereas the portraits of Jerome indicate that the saintly man has become the healer of the world, for Muir it is the reverse: the holiness of wilderness becomes the source of the healing of man, and of Muir.

Muir commenced his long wilderness walks after an industrial accident that had nearly blinded him. This was a pivotal event in his life that led, after a period of sickness and depression, to a kind of conversion experience: as his sight returned he felt that he had "arisen from the grave," and the purpose of this rising was that he might put his eyes to their proper use, which was to seek the glory of God reflected in the wonders of God's creation. Muir felt the divine hand was pushing him out "into heaven's light" to start on a "long excursion" into the wild. As he put it in a letter to his employers, "God has to nearly kill us sometimes, to teach us lessons" (Stoll 1993). After recovering his sight, Muir gave up his intended work as an industrial inventor, bid farewell to his family who had emigrated from Scotland to the Wisconsin territory, and walked to the Gulf of Mexico. Thereafter, he traveled to California's Yosemite valley, from where his rhapsodic written dispatches to newspapers and magazines on the East Coast earned him fame and sufficient income to sustain him in the struggle he eventually took up to save the wilderness from the lumberjack, the miner, and the shepherd. Like a latter day John the Baptist, with his long flowing beard and wilderness lifestyle, Muir took up with evangelical fervor the role of preacher and prophet to industrialists, politicians, and the general public. His message was that the preservation of the wild lands of America was God's good work. According to Muir's nature gospel, the light of God shone from the ranges and valleys of the mountains and forests, and hence saving nature from exploitation would manifest salvation for Americans in this new land. Eventually for Muir, the wilderness usurps the cathedral and becomes *the* sacred place in which religious piety is truly stirred, the sentiment that is seen in this account of dusk falling in the Sierra Nevada:

> Now came the solemn, silent evening. Long, blue, spiky shadows crept out across the snow-fields, while a rosy glow, at first scarce discernible, gradually deepened and suffused every mountain-top, flushing the glaciers and the harsh crags above them. This was the alpenglow, to me one of the most impressive of all the terrestrial manifestations of God. At the touch of this divine light, the mountains seemed to kindle to a rapt, religious consciousness, and stood hushed and waiting like devout worshipers. (1911)

The core insight that passes from Muir's wilderness piety into the American imagination is the idea that wild nature has the right to exist and flourish untamed (Muir 1911, Nash 1982). And as he molded this romantic ideal, first voiced by Thoreau and Emerson, into a national preservation ethic, Muir felt that the only hope for saving the forests from the rapacious demands of farmers, foresters, and miners was an intervention by the federal government of the United States:

> Through all the wonderful eventful centuries since Christ's time and long before that God has cared for these trees, saved them from drought, diseases, avalanche and a thousand straining leveling tempests and floods, but he cannot save them from fools—only Uncle Sam can do that. (1897)

A contemporary of Muir's, Gifford Pinchot also held deep-seated convictions about the future of America's forests and wild lands, as evidenced through his key role in the establishment of what today is the United States Forest Service. Just as Muir helped popularize nature *preservation* through the federal system of parks and wilderness areas, Pinchot's efforts helped institutionalize nature *management* through the system of national forests. In a classic example of Pinchot's legacy, he skillfully maneuvered the transfer of the administration of forest reserves from the General Land Office of the Department of the Interior to the Division of Forestry in the Department of Agriculture, which he headed. In so doing, he convinced many in Washington, including his friend President Theodore Roosevelt, of his particular vision for conserving America's forests (Williams 1989). For the Department of Agriculture, and for Pinchot, America's wild forests were a merchantable crop. Where Muir saw intrinsic goodness and divine light in the unhewn primary forest and the untamed wild, Pinchot was a utilitarian for whom the forest was to serve the greater good of the American nation-state.

Pinchot's testimony before a congressional committee over the proposed damming of the Hetch Hetchy Valley of Yosemite National Park is particularly revealing. Pinchot as conservationist supports the damming of the Tuolumne river precisely because this would transform an inaccessible and little visited valley into a reservoir for the rapidly growing city of San Francisco: "The fundamental principle of the whole conservation policy is that of use, to take every part of the land and its resources and put it to that use in which it will serve the most people" (quoted in Nash 1982: 171). Whereas for Muir nature serves humanity best in its primal state as a spiritual guide to wisdom divine, for Pinchot nature only serves humanity when industry puts its resources into productive use. So for Pinchot, wise conservation necessarily involves wise use. For Pinchot, like the American Puritans before him (Taylor 1989: 221–35), it is as if old-growth forests, and indeed nature writ large, were divinely intended to be instruments of human work, and are so sanctified through their use. A table made from wooden planks, therefore, sanctifies the tree from which the planks were cut, fulfilling its purpose, intended by its creator. For Muir, however, ancient trees stand on sacred ground, and in setting aside that ground to be preserved from human labor, Muir seeks to fashion a new Eden.

To their credit, the competing visions of Muir and Pinchot were both instrumental in helping to bring about the sequestration of large areas of the United States from industrial and real estate use and for nature conservation of one kind or another. Combined, national parks, forests, wilderness areas, and wildlife refuges represent nearly 400 million acres, or roughly one fifth of the land area of the United States that is under federal nature management. If these areas had not been established through the convictions of Muir and Pinchot, there would potentially be fewer areas of the United States remaining that had not been logged, mined, ploughed under, or turned into real estate. Nonetheless their respective visions represent a profound ambivalence in the American ecological psyche;—the one giving rise to an aesthetic ethic of preservationism and what elsewhere we have called "wilderness fetishism" (e.g., Northcott 2002), the other promoting the instrumental value of nature as a human resource. Neither vision, however, nor the sequestration of such large land parcels has been able to prevent the ecological devastation of North America that began with the colonials and has been systematically advanced by the modern partnership of the nation-state and the economic corporation. The nation-state exercises an increasingly imperial dominion on the whole land of North America and its natural heritage. The ecological consequences have been dramatic: thousands of species have been pushed to the edge of extinction, water sullied, air toxified, aquifers drained, old-growth forests almost completely annihilated, native peoples extinguished, and oceans over-fished and over-burdened with topsoil and toxic waste washed from the industrial farms and factories of the American heartland (Pimm 2002).

Though the images of Jerome in the Washington National Gallery echo Muir's idea of wilderness sanctity, the sheer number of acquisitions of this image—the gallery owns some 107 images of Jerome[1]—suggests to us a sense of guilt, and perhaps a desire to assuage American history of its ecological sins. The large number of these holdings may also suggest a fellow feeling of the colonists for Jerome. He was the first of the early Latin fathers to move to the Holy Land, and he was consequently the first Christian pilgrim and the key transitional figure between the Latin Christianity of the first three centuries and the wilderness traditions of the Desert Fathers of both East and West. The Desert fathers had left the compromises of imperial Christianity for the ascetic solitude of the desert, but their networks of cells and hermitages began to transform the desert into a holy city in which the first monasteries were founded and where the monastic gardens and farms of later eras find their origins (Chitty 1966). Intending to tame their souls in the wild the Desert Fathers through their holy communities began to tame the wild, and to see the desert bloom. Analogously, the Pilgrim Fathers left the Babylon of Europe

1. See Washington National Gallery's current holdings and collections at http://www.nationalgallery.com.

for a Promised Land in which they would come to see themselves as a redeemer nation, redeeming the wild and untamed land of the New World by their industry and inventiveness, and redeeming the hemisphere from pagan religion and European colonialism. If Jerome is the first Pilgrim Father whose sanctity enables him to tame the wild, he is in this sense the patron saint of the American nature imagination. For the various icons of Jerome symbolize both Pinchot's nature tamed and Muir's holy wilderness. And this connection may point to an important problematic feature of Muir's vision of wilderness. For in romanticizing the American wilderness, Muir turns the mountains and forests he loved into a totem of American nationhood, and of the nation-state's colonization of the wild.

WENDELL BERRY AND ECOLOGICAL EVIL

The ambiguity of the colonists' taming of America is brilliantly evoked in the title of Wendell Berry's classic monograph *The Unsettling of America* (1983). According to Berry, the agrarian revolution of the last fifty years in American and global agriculture is unsettling as it dissolves and destroys the earlier agrarian community of land and people that the first colonists had established. The root of the destructive tendencies of American industrialism is not Americans' unwillingness to set aside wild nature to preserve it for posterity, but the duplicity of modern institutions. These institutions in one hand claim to steward the creation, through setting aside parks and preserves, yet with the other hand plot widespread nature destruction. Berry ascribes the motive power of this destruction to the triumvirate forces of the nation-state, science, and the economic corporation in the forms respectively of the United States Department of Agriculture, the modern university, and industry. The partnership of these forces generates a style of agriculture that is deeply disrespectful of fauna and flora, field and forest, while also deeply destructive of agrarian culture and of the traditional relationship of the cultures of food and farming communities.

Here Berry is firmly at odds with Pinchot's state-mediated utilitarian ethic. But, importantly, he also opposes the nation-state as the primary defender of the wild in the setting aside by federal and state governments of parts of nature as parks and wilderness areas. State protection of these delimited areas of the wild is merely the reverse side of its systematic utilitarian abuse of the rest of the land, and may even advance it by providing the state with the acquired sanctity of conserver of the nation's symbolic wild lands. Here Berry is opposed to elements of the wilderness ethic of Muir and what he sees as its formative role in the environmental psyche of modern America. If the wilderness ideal helps to produce a situation where the only sacred ecological spaces are institutionalized, then it colludes in the narrowing of an environmental ethic to one that views parks and wilderness areas as sacred, while the remaining natural areas are relegated as profane space, left for industrial desecration. In a pointed passage, Berry writes:

> Idolatry always reduces to the worship of something "made with hands," something confined within the terms of human work and human comprehension. Thus, Solomon and Saint Paul both insisted on the largeness and at-largeness of God, setting Him free, so to speak, from *ideas* about Him. He is not to be fenced in, under human control like a domestic creature; He is the wildest being in existence ... That is why the subduing of things of nature to human purposes is so dangerous and why it so often results in evil, in separation and desecration. (1993: 101)[2]

It is in this sense that the wilderness becomes a fetish and is incorporated in the larger totemic civil religion of the American nation (Marvin and Ingle 1996). Like other totems, this fetish mystifies the myriad ecological sacrifices that the nation-state elsewhere requires through its advancing of the corporate and consumer economy. The *idea* of wilderness cannot ultimately save nature from the instrumental dominion of the nation-state since, as a national or state park, the wilderness is also fenced in, subjected to government purposes and instrumental control, something that Edward Abbey records and protests in *Desert Solitaire* while working as a park ranger in Utah (1985). The black top roads and camp grounds that the National Parks Service rolled out through desert and forest effectively tamed the wild in the effort to draw car driving urbanites into the parks.

The crucial failing in the competing philosophies of Muir and Pinchot is that when married to the nation-state both produce forms of nature conservation that collude in the larger imperial conquest of

---

2. Here, Berry echoes the prophet Isaiah: "Their land is full of silver and gold, there is no limit to their treasures; their land is full of horses, there is no limit to their chariots. And their land is full of idols; they bow down to the work of their hands, to what their own fingers have wrought." (Is 2:7–8, Tanakh trans.)

nature. Thus modern silviculture of the kind advanced by Pinchot and the National Forest Service he founded is an exemplar of the collectivizing and reductionist tendencies of the science-informed nation-state. The forest of the forester is a monocrop designed so that it can be easily quantified and hence subjected to the accountant's rule. Although the plantation forest is less efficient than its more diverse counterpart, and less able to sustain life and to provide a range of goods for the builder, the fisherman, and the hunter, the forester looks on serried ranks of trees as a bankable economic resource (Scott 1999). Analogously the wilderness reserve is managed by rangers who, through the culling of certain species and the reintroduction of others, attempt to restore the wild and, through information centers and roads, to make it available for human enjoyment. Both ideologies legitimate technocratic forms of control of nature that are intrinsically exploitative and reductionist. They both represent and sustain the alienation of industrial civilization from nature and its systematic onslaught on biodiversity and on sustainable communities both human and wild.

As Berry suggests, the ideologies and practices of science-informed nature management interact with the moral climate of the consumer society in that they are meant to deliver the good of the land, independently of the culture of their communities or the ecology of their economy (Taylor 1989: 232). Neither wilderness preservation nor silviculture truly *conserves* because these practices neglect the relationship of biodiversity and human cultures. Societies cannot truly conserve nature absent of moral practices and communities in which individuals are directed towards love of goodness, beauty, and truth, which are part of the constitution of the divine creation and not just human constructs and sentiments. The capacity of humans to dwell in the land without excessive instrumentalization arises from their ability to see the species with whom they share the land as divinely made, and hence as fellow creatures and not as so-called natural resources. Seeing the world as God's creation involves seeing it as gift rather than a possession; it also involves recognizing that there are limits to nature's bounty (DeWitt 1998). The ability to receive gifts and to perceive limits are moral qualities that are eroded by the heedless greed and sloth encouraged by a machine-dominated consumer economy.

In his account of the intrinsic relation between human virtue and ecological richness, between good work and the health of the land, Berry sets an agrarian ideal against the pernicious partnership of the state, the scientist, and the corporation as they exploit the prairie and the forest to destruction. Against those who would suggest that his is a utopian vision that could never provide sufficient food for the 280 million who now live in America, Berry points to the farms of the Amish who have managed to farm the prairie in such a way as to preserve the soil while also being productive and successful farmers. The secret of their success is that they understand that there is a relationship between good farming and good politics, between cultivating the soil and nurturing human character. The Amish resist the institutional forms and technologies that the nation-state advances in its control of nature. For Berry, as for the Amish, this control represents an idolatrous subjection of the earth and its creatures to human design, and hence the unsettling of America ultimately manifests a spiritual and moral malaise. The core motive of idolatry is the desire to manipulate the human relation to the divine through the construction and control of natural objects. As Charles Taylor suggests, the desire to reduce nature to human control is analogous to a desire to control the human relation to God:

> The instrumental stance towards the world has been given a new and important spiritual meaning. It is not only the stance which allows us to experiment and thus obtain valid scientific results. It is not only the stance which gives us rational control over ourselves and our world. In this religious tradition, it is the way we serve God in creation ... *Instrumentalizing* things is the spiritually essential step. (1989: 232)

Against instrumentality, Berry, like the Amish, sets the recognition of the co-creaturehood of human and non-human; it is in the nature of creatures that they are not all-powerful or all-seeing, but rather dependent on the ecological contingencies the Creator has set into the creation.[3] Modern agronomists and modern foresters in their love of the monocrop and weed-killer set themselves on a constant treadmill of interventions designed to eradicate contingency, to supplant ecological food webs and traditional husbandry with flow charts, factory farms, and bankable utilities. Like the utilitarianism of the monocropper, the preservationist

---

3. Karl Barth has much to say about the contingency of creatures: "The creature is not self-existent. It has not assumed its nature and existence of itself or given it to itself. It did not come into being by itself. It does not consist by itself. It cannot sustain itself. It has to thank its creation and therefore its Creator for the fact that it came into being and is and will be" (2003: 94).

mindset also involves conquest and control, even seen in the advocacy by some conservation scientists of the need to exclude indigenous peoples from tropical forest preserves (e.g., Terborgh 1999, Karanth 2007). The assumption is that conservation is monoculturally related to the mindset of the conservation scientist just as the modern forester rejects the apparent inefficiency of the diverse natural forest for the quantifiable purity of the monocrop plantation (Scott 1999). Neither approach has ultimately proven effective in resisting the widespread depredation of nature (Van Houtan 2006). And for Berry the reason is clear: in its specialization of function and the dedication of its various functionaries—agronomists, conservationists, consumers, farmers, food manufacturers, foresters, politicians—to goals and procedures that are disparate from one another, modern America reproduces in its social structures the deeper alienation between modern human work and the good of the land.

The consequent ecocide is not directly intended by the individuals who find their careers in these agencies. Instead it appears an instance of what Hannah Arendt identified as the "banality of evil" in her dispatches from the trial of the Gestapo officer Adolf Eichmann. Though he had organized the transportation of so many Jews to the death camps, Arendt did not find Eichmann to be sociopathic, or even display a maligned personality. Rather, Eichmann was a bureaucrat who lacked the imagination to do anything other than follow the orders of Hitler and Himmler. Like genocide, ecocide is a consequence of chains of command and bureaucratic and economic procedures too long and complex for their consequences to be fully understood or mastered by any one of those who assent to the collective will. Instead we encounter in these imperial forms of command and control what liberation theologians call structural sin, or what Saint Paul called the "principalities and powers." The individual caught in these structures may not be a vicious or violent person, but in colluding with them, she assents to their forceful domination of the natural world.

John Steinbeck understands something profound in the complex social reality of sin in his novel *The Grapes of Wrath*. Through the story of the Joad family's attempt to cope with the Dust Bowl tragedy, Steinbeck presents an account of human suffering and the wasting of the land that is at once political and ecological, personal and social. Unlike so many moderns, Steinbeck seems to recognize the profundity of human evil. Contemporary conservationists and environmental philosophers, like most modern scientists and philosophers, refuse the central place given to sin and evil in the Jewish and Christian traditions as part of the theological worldview overturned by the Enlightenment (McFadyen 2000). The lack of a robust conception of sin and evil in modern nature philosophies is indicated in the widely shared assumption that reason and law can redeem the human–nature relationship from the overbearing dominion of modern industrial civilization. But with the recent attack of the Bush Junior administration on ecological regulations and its subversion of the effectiveness of the Environmental Protection Agency, this assumption looks increasingly misguided. Under the Bush administration nature preservation has become hotly contested terrain and "Uncle Sam" looks less like the savior of nature envisaged by John Muir than its rapacious destroyer. From the high point of the 1970s when major pieces of legislation such as the Clean Water Act and Clean Air Act were put in place, and the Environmental Protection Agency was created, the debate now in America has returned to the earlier more colonial emphasis on property rights. We are now seeing increasing prioritization of the economic rights of corporations and large individual landowners over the well-being of ecological and human communities of place.

BIBLICAL DOMINION VERSUS DOMINATION

Perhaps the most surprising feature of this new assertion of human dominion over nature is not only that it comes at a time of unprecedented ecological threat, in the form of global warming, but that it has attracted considerable support among millions of American Christians who, while conservative on matters of personal morality, are willing to embrace an economic creed that is revolutionary in its deracinating effects on rural and urban communities alike as both jobs and natural resources are culled in the pursuit of profit margins. And yet conservative Christians who place property rights before the rights of nature believe that they themselves are the ones pursuing a biblical mandate that sets humans in dominion over the earth.

This conception of dominion is, however, at odds with the core meanings of the Hebrew word *radah*, often translated as dominion. *Radah* carries a double meaning of both ascent and descent. In the context of the passage, and in the larger narrative of the Old Testament, the clear meaning is that when humans live righteously and humbly and justly on earth, they enjoy the fruits of the land and so they ascend in their likeness to and relation with the Creator. Conversely, when humans assert themselves forcefully and pridefully, neglecting the laws of the Creator that are set into the creation, they descend from their place of dominion and the likeness of the Creator is marred. As such, in their wickedness they subject the land to unjust burdens and so they loose their place in the land while the land loses its fertility. We already see this moral cosmology displayed in the story of the fall of Adam and Eve and their resulting exclusion from the Garden of Eden. Adam and Eve misappropriate the fruits of the garden, and this misappropriation leads to their expulsion to occupy a land where they must endure sweat and toil, fighting thorns and briars for sustenance (Hiebert 1996). Once true dominion is lost, and humanity falls, the land too is subject to futility. And from the second chapter of Genesis through the rest of the Old Testament, there is no point at which humans are said to regain just *radah*, true dominion, over the earth. The word dominion only recurs in the sense of descent; as an adjective used to describe the exploitative and oppressive rule of kings and emperors whose forms of rule stand opposed to the righteousness and justice of Yahweh, and seen in the Mosaic covenant. In the story of the fall and its playing out in the subsequent history of Israel, the original dominion offered by God to Adam is lost and never regained.

In the New Testament, the hues of *radah* find reference in the gospel accounts of Christ's temptation in the wilderness, where St. Mark records, "he was with the wild animals." The implication is that his Lordship of the earth is such that it is acknowledged by non-human creatures even though refused by humans whose minds are darkened by the inheritance of the Fall. The Lucan account of Christ's birth offers an interesting juxtaposition in this respect, displaying the birth of the Incarnate One in an animal stall among lowing creatures who need no revelation to recognize the Lord of the cosmos, an implication that is extensively drawn out in medieval depictions of the birth of Christ. The same artistic tradition depicts the adulation of foreign kings who, unlike the murderous Herod, submit their dominion to the cosmic rule of the Incarnate child. The implication, as in the Magnificat of Mary, is that the high are brought low on bended knee while the lowly—the animals and those who tend them—are exalted by the birth of the King amongst them. This theme is taken up in the earliest tradition of Christian art as Susan Power Bratton displays in chapter 6 in the present volume.

The American Christian account of dominion suffers from the same deficiencies we identify in the American accounts of nature conservation as seen in Muir and Pinchot. This is the recognition that no earthly form of sovereignty or dominion can escape the infection of sin and the Fall between the Resurrection and the eschaton. The confidence of conservative Christians in the rule of the corporation and the citizen consumer, and the lack of awareness of the ambiguities of any form of dominion other than that of Christ is a lacunae that is sharply at odds with the political theologies that informed the founding fathers of America. The Calvinist and covenantal theology that guided their deliberations played an important role in the creation of a three-fold separation of powers, and a further division of powers between federal and state governments, precisely because they understood the continuing infection of sin in human affairs and therefore believed that the only adequate restraint on the dominion of any branch of human government was the division of political power into multiple entities (e.g., Eleazar 1984).

THE MICROPOLITICS OF JOHN HOWARD YODER

The themes of dominion, politics, and sin that are missing in the conservation dialogue, and in the political theology of the Christian right, play a central role in the writing of the American Mennonite theologian John Howard Yoder. Yoder describes human history as if there are not one, but two, great falls. The first is in the Garden of Eden with Adam and Eve, involving their prideful assertion of the human creature over the will of the Creator. The second fall is the fall of the church, which occurs after the conversion of the Roman Emperor Constantine to Christianity. This second fall, in which Constantine sanctions the Christian God as one of the pantheon of gods recognized as legitimate by Rome. The eventual consequence was an emergent rupture between the anti-imperial, and less hierarchical, ethic of the first Christians and the ethics and politics of a more imperial Christianity in subsequent centuries. In both falls the biblical mandate of human dominion is radically compromised.

Against the politics of empire, and the partnership between church and state that this politics births, Yoder sets his account of the body politics of Christians. He suggests that the social forms of the Christian moral life after the death and resurrection of Christ involves a limited recovery by Christians of the God-given capacity to exercise divine authority on

Earth. In particular Yoder reads the words of Christ to the disciples "what you bind on earth shall be bound in heaven" as giving the church a "transcendent moral ratification" (Yoder 1984: 27) for decisions the church makes concerning the righting of wrongs, or practical moral reasoning. This location of moral authority in the practice of binding and loosing, or making judgments, is of foundational importance for Yoder's classically Anabaptist identification of the life of the church with the micropolitics of the local congregation. Yoder sets this account of practical moral reasoning against both "individualistic intuitionism" and rule-based accounts of moral reasoning. This means for Yoder that the micropolitics of local place-based moral communities are central to the Christian social ethic. This also reflects the central and guiding insight of the radical reformers from which the American Mennonites descended "who refuse to delegate 'being church' to the civil powers" (1984: 28). For Yoder then, there can be no contiguity between Christian dominion understood as the authority to bind and loose and the rule of the nation-state. On the contrary, the church is called constantly to witness to the moral ambiguity of all forms of community, corporation, institution, and state, as all run the risk of supplanting consensual conversation with coercive violence.

This account means that moral reasoning always involves a community process. And it is moreover a process that is "not reducible to a political science model projecting who promotes what interests, with how much power, through which procedures" (1984: 35). By contrast for Muir, moral authority and the battle to save nature are located in the individual's transcendent experience of the sublime and the sentiments it evokes, and for Pinchot, moral authority resides in the eminent domain of the nation-state to determine the greater good or the utility of the land. But as Yoder puts it in *The Christian Witness to the State*:

> The actual socialization of certain elements in the economy may be dictated by certain considerations of justice, efficiency, risk, or public welfare—Tennessee Valley Authority, national parks, public schools, roads, post office, public health, etc.—where competition or unsupervised private management would be harmful to the general welfare; but socialism as a panacea and centralized planning as the major economic development are open to challenge both theologically and practically. (1964: 58)

In this way Yoder's moral theories resonate powerfully with Wendell Berry's ecological essays. Like Yoder, Berry understands the need for vigilance to prevent any rule, procedure, or institution from turning into a form of prideful or idolatrous dominion. However, Yoder gives a clearer account than Berry for why this vision is necessary, and this is located in the fact that the only creature who legitimately exercises dominion after the Genesis fall is crucified on a cross. As he says, "only from within the community of resurrection. . . . is the cruciformity of the cosmos a key rather than a scandal" (1984: 36). For Yoder then, there is no guarantee that even Christians will not fall back into a false prideful dominion, other than their continual commitment to confess and practice what he calls the "cruciformity of the cosmos."

Although Yoder is theologically conservative, he is not a right-wing Christian, because he believes the limited role of the nation-state to involve the preservation of the fabric of the society and the cosmos from unrestrained power either of an economic or a political kind (1964: 5). Like Berry, Yoder also challenges the idea that it is possible to construct a moral society or to institutionalize a set of procedures without citizens themselves practicing morality in their micropolitics. As he puts it, "practical moral reasoning if Christian must always be expected to be at some point subversive" (1984: 40). The logic of universal moral reasoning is analogous to the logic of nation-state as empire. Both involve a coercive claim to subject human communities and relationships to procedures and rules that eschew the local particular and place-based character of being. The central significance of the cross for Yoder, as for Paul, is that Jesus Christ crucified makes captivity captive and dethrones the principalities and powers that usurp God's sovereignty in the world. This is why for Yoder the only way in which Christians rule legitimately is through confession, forgiveness, and reconciliation, and not through coercion, rules, and violence.

In the perspective of the agrarian ethic of Berry and the body politics of Yoder, the violence of the American nation-state against native peoples, non-human animals, and plants, as well as the use of eminent domain against it's own citizens, is crucially related to the millennialist claim that America is the biblical "New World," the new creation, and even the guarantor of the happiness of its own people (Northcott 2004). Muir's idea that Uncle Sam will defend nature from fools and industrialists generates a national park system that transforms nature into a symbolic spectacle, a source of entertainment and diversion and of national identity and pride in flag and empire. It then becomes acceptable to tarmac over land near

Old Faithful so that so people can come as spectators of a geyser. It likewise becomes acceptable that large RV parks are built within national parks to accommodate thousands of Americans who will not abandon a machine-dependent and electronically distracted consumer life style even to visit wilderness. Perhaps this is most obvious at Mount Rushmore National Memorial. Here, the first President Bush remarked that the Black Hills of the Dakotas, once dynamited and reshaped to the visages of American presidents, is a "communion with the very soul of America" (Bush 1991).

For Anthony Giddens, the roots of the structural violence of the modern nation-state lie in its increasing monopolization of sovereign power over the bodies of its citizens and the land they inhabit and its redistribution of that power among its principal agencies and partners (1987). Yoder argues that the state is a necessary locus of sovereignty for there must always be powers that stand in the place of God in human society; but in the world before the eschaton these powers are fallen and hence sinful. Christian witness to the state therefore always involves an insistence on the submission of the state to its divine mandate, which is to restrain evil, to conserve, and to preserve the fabric of human society. And such fabric we suggest, though Yoder does not, includes local communities and their natural context—all creatures. In this perspective, the central problem with the National Forests and the National Parks is that they are both *national*, possessive objects of the nation-state and beholden to its desires, its military, and its economic corporations.

This perspective can also help to explain why the Amish are such good conservers of the soil. In their efforts to resist the concentrated material power that mechanical devices such as tractors and trucks put in the hands of individual farmers, the Amish express in their farming techniques the implications of their cruciform micropolitics; hegemonic power of the kind the machine and the technologically advanced nation-state acquire over humans and nature is at odds with the virtues of humility, fidelity, and truthfulness that make possible the mutual subordination of the Amish one to another in their agrarian communities.

For Jerome, holiness comes through the cross of Christ and redemption comes through that wounded body, when all cosmic forces are subdued by the humility of the Son of God. For Christians space and time are remade during the hours between Good Friday and Easter Sunday. In the light of this remaking, dominion is restored to the creation but it is not the triumphant dominion of the Emperor but the victory of the

Lamb of God. That victory is not possible without the wounds of the cross. Conserving the memory of the cross and its implications for the sovereignty of all human institutions and powers enables Christians to practice the kinds of holiness that make it possible to create and sustain human communities that do not destroy but conserve the new creation that is first glimpsed in the resurrected body of Christ.

Response

Conservative Christians and Environmentalism, 1970–2005

SETH DOWLAND *and* BRANTLEY GASAWAY

THE "RHAPSODIC" DISPATCHES OF John Muir and "skillful maneuverings" of Gilbert Pinchot, described by Kyle Van Houtan and Michael Northcott in "Nature and the Nation-State," formed a two-pronged approach to ecological conservation that has captivated American environmentalists for over a century. Muir's romanticism and Pinchot's utilitarianism came together in a marriage that wed environmental protection to the American nation-state. Yet Van Houtan and Northcott contend that neither Muir nor Pinchot provides a Christian model for environmentalism. The authors, taking their cues from Wendell Berry and John Howard Yoder, argue that a Christological understanding of "dominion" involves self-sacrifice, and that such an understanding should guide Christians in their approach to creation care.

This theological argument is compelling to us. But as historians of American evangelicalism, our methodological commitments incline us to a different task than Van Houtan and Northcott's. Rather than making a normative theological statement, we intend here to provide a descriptive historical account of the way American evangelicals have approached environmentalism over the last three decades. We choose to focus on evangelicals both because our expertise lies in the history of contemporary American evangelicalism and because Van Houtan and Northcott suggest that conservative Christians ought to find Yoder's Christological understanding of "dominion" persuasive. Most evangelicals, contend the authors, do not. Van Houtan and Northcott argue that "millions of American Christians ... embrace an economic creed that is revolutionary in its deracinating effects on rural and urban communities alike."

We acknowledge—and document below—that many conservative Christians see preservation of the free market as the foremost consideration in environmental debates and thereby reject the understanding of "dominion" forwarded by the authors. Yet we also recognize that growing numbers of progressive evangelicals have wrestled with arguments similar to Van Houtan and Northcott's and have embraced new ways of thinking about environmental policy. Our job as historians, then, involves complicating the authors' claim to have identified "*the* American Christian account of dominion." We do so here by taking a closer look at the most politically powerful and numerically dominant subset of American Christians: evangelicals.[1]

This response highlights two divergent approaches to "creation care" among contemporary conservative Christians, approaches embodied by the Evangelical Environmental Network (EEN) and the Interfaith Council for Environmental Stewardship (ICES).[2] Both of these groups display pragmatic impulses and hold a historically Reformed understanding of Christians' relationship to culture, validating much of Van Houtan and Northcott's critique. Although the EEN has criticized American government and free-market capitalism, ICES, which represents a larger proportion of conservative Christians in America, has argued that democracy and capitalism emerged from a biblical approach to ordering society. Such characteristics place them at odds with the Anabaptist model of John Howard Yoder and have resulted in the approach toward environmentalism that Van Houtan and Northcott find so problematic.

Beginning in the late 1960s and with increasing frequency in the early 1970s, diverse evangelical leaders touted ecological concerns as essential to both human welfare and Christian discipleship. By 1970 the National Association of Evangelicals and *Christianity Today*, together representative of the conservative Christian mainstream, had issued statements in support of the ecological movement. "Scripture tells man

   1. Several scholars—many of them sociologists—have pointed to the diversity of American evangelicalism in recent studies. See: Greeley and Hout (2006), and Smith (2000).

   2. We use the terms "evangelicals" and "conservative Christians" interchangeably here to indicate Christians who share a high view of the Bible and believe in the necessity of personal regeneration for salvation. Media accounts often assume that theologically conservative Christians are necessarily politically conservative. Yet as our response makes clear, Christians who share a core theological conservatism are not always politically conservative.

to subdue the earth-not exploit it," editors of *Christianity Today* wrote, and "the Christian must remember that he is entrusted with the stewardship of God's earthly creation" (*Christianity Today* 1970). But many other evangelicals found reasons to distance themselves from the environmentalist movement. They worried about alliances with left-leaning environmentalists and claimed that the needs of humanity offered the primary (if not sole) rationale for ecological concern. Often arising in more fundamentalist enclaves, Christian critics of radical environmentalism argued that humans held unmitigated precedence over the rest of creation, that environmentalists worshiped nature, and that environmental problems signaled inevitable signs of impending apocalyptic events (*Christian Beacon* 1971, Houston 1972). By the end of the 1970s, then, two contrasting reactions to environmentalism had emerged among theological conservatives: servant stewardship and caring dominion.[3]

SERVANT STEWARDSHIP: THE EVANGELICAL ENVIRONMENTAL NETWORK

The concurrent publication of *Earthkeeping: Christian Stewardship of Natural Resources* and the creation of the Au Sable Institute of Environmental Studies in 1980 inaugurated a sustained and complex analysis of environmental ethics among a minority of conservative Christians. The scholars who authored *Earthkeeping* argued that God's creation had intrinsic value rather than merely a utilitarian purpose for humans. Stewardship, therefore, entailed servanthood as much as wise management (Wilkinson 1980). Many of the contributors to this book helped found the Au Sable Institute. Throughout the 1980s Au Sable hosted forums dedicated to theological exploration of environmental issues, and several of these conferences resulted in notable books such as *Tending the Garden: Essays on the Gospel and the Earth*. In its introduction Wesley Granberg-Michaelson reiterated that God intended human dominion for the service of all of creation and insisted that all of creation participated in God's redemption and restoration that has already broken into history.[4]

---

3. The best description and analysis of the rise of ecological concern among conservative Protestants is David Kenneth Larsen's unpublished dissertation "God's Gardeners: American Protestant Evangelicals Confront Environmentalism, 1967–2000" (2001: 173–74).

4. Granberg-Michaelson (1987) provided leadership to the emergent progressive evangelical network in the 1970s as an assistant to Senator Mark Hatfield, original signer

The efforts of Au Sable highlighted potential affinities between environmental activists and the mainstream conservative Christians and would culminate in the creation of the Evangelical Environmental Network (Larsen 2001: 175–230).

In 1993 the growing number of conservative Christian environmentalists joined together in the Evangelical Environmental Network (EEN). EEN published its core vision in the "Evangelical Declaration on the Care of Creation." Its authors confessed and repented of devaluing creation through greedy and perverted stewardship. The word "dominion" stood conspicuously absent, and instead the document claimed for humans a "unique responsibility" for creation. The statement avoided specifying a positive agenda beyond fostering "faithful stewardship" and working for undefined "responsible public policies which embody the principles of biblical stewardship of creation." Evangelical leaders ranging from *Christianity Today*'s editors to college presidents and professors have endorsed the declaration.[5]

Van Houtan and Northcott can find much to commend regarding EEN. The organization has gained the most influence among the minority wing of theological conservatives who, like John Howard Yoder, have eschewed right-wing politics and are wary of the power and economic ambitions of the American nation-state.[6] Perhaps most promising to Van Houtan and Northcott, EEN's leaders have expressed sentiments in accord with both their rejection of dominion as domination and their insistence upon the pervasive effects of humanity's fall into sin. Calvin DeWitt, one of the principal authors of the "Evangelical Declaration on the Care of Creation," criticized those who isolated Gen 1:28 and interpreted the concept of dominion as "oppressive domination." "Dominion as outright oppression is not advocated or condoned by the Scriptures," he wrote, and "the Christian model for dominion is the example of Jesus Christ" and his sacrificial love. Indeed, DeWitt noted that the dominion mandate

---

of the 1973 "Chicago Declaration of Evangelical Social Concern," and editor of *Sojourners* magazine.

5. For the full text of the "Evangelical Declaration on the Care of Creation" and list of prominent signers, see http://www.creationcare.org/resources/declaration.php.

6. Progressive evangelical organizations such as *Sojourners* and Evangelicals for Social Action have consistently opposed the politics of the New Christian Right over the past three decades. These groups and sympathetic leaders such as Tony Campolo have served as the primary evangelical advocates for environmentalism.

occurred *before* the Fall. Humans' corrupted nature thereby qualifies the command's implications (DeWitt 2000). Likewise, Ron Sider, the head of Evangelicals for Social Action, agreed that those who champion free-market economies and social progress as environmental solutions severely underestimate the impact of the Fall (Sider 1994, Aeschliman 1994).

EEN has balanced esteem for the micropolitics advocated by John Howard Yoder with political pragmatism. For instance, the organization supported local community projects to provide clean water and reduce pollution. It mailed "environmental awareness kits" to over 35,000 congregations and hosted training conferences for leaders and students, hoping that these efforts would encourage communal conversations regarding a biblical vision for environmentalism. But utilitarianism and a penchant for prophetic action have also led EEN to campaign on a national and political level. For example, leaders played a pivotal role in preventing Republicans from weakening the Endangered Species Act in 1996 and recently lobbied on behalf of public policies to curtail global warming. Van Houtan and Northcott seemingly reject such utilitarianism as manifestations of coercive rules. Perhaps, then, the authors would appreciate better the possibility for communal moral reasoning created by EEN's 2002 media campaign that asked "What Would Jesus Drive?" Despite espousing an environmental ethic closer to Northcott's and Van Houtan's proposal, however, EEN has had only moderate success among evangelicals. Thus the authors' critique rightly appraises the more typical environmental views among politically powerful conservative Christians, views expressed by the Interfaith Council for Environmental Stewardship.

CARING DOMINION: THE INTERFAITH COUNCIL FOR ENVIRONMENTAL STEWARDSHIP

While the EEN claimed that their vision represented a biblical model of stewardship, a substantial portion of conservative Christians countered that the needs of humanity offered the primary rationale for ecological concern. Through the 1980s and early 1990s, numerous politically conservative Christians questioned the rationale for environmental conservation. Most famously, James Watt, appointed head of the Department of the Interior by Ronald Reagan, raised the ire of environmentalists by advocating "wise use" of public lands and implying that the imminent return of Jesus sanctioned human consumption of natural resources.[7] Other opponents expressed misgivings about the ecological movement's alliances with leftist political groups repugnant to the New Christian Right. When the EEN issued the "Evangelical Declaration on the Care of Creation," E. Calvin Beisner denounced the document in the politically conservative evangelical magazine *World*. Beisner insisted that apart from human cultivation, nature would remain a wilderness rather than a garden yielding its fruits to humanity, a point he developed more fully in his 1997 book, *Where Garden Meets Wilderness*. Beisner gave voice to the sentiments of many conservative Christians who believed Christian environmentalists in the EEN discounted the unique honor God bestowed on humans in the creation. These conservatives developed anthropocentric, or human-centered, arguments for environmentalism to counter the doctrines of the EEN (Larsen 2001).

The formation of the Interfaith Council for Environmental Stewardship (ICES) in 2000 provided an institutional home for anthropocentric environmentalism. Comprised of conservative Protestants, Catholics, and Jews, ICES adopted "The Cornwall Declaration on Environmental Stewardship" (drafted in 1999 at a conference in West Cornwall, CT) as its fundamental statement concerning Christians' relationship to the environment. Rather than viewing humans as "consumers and polluters"—a dig aimed at EEN activists—the Cornwall Declaration maintained that humans are "producers and stewards." And unlike EEN, ICES did not shy away from the explicit language of dominion. "Sound environmental stewardship," said the Cornwall document, "must attend both to the demands of human well being and to a divine call for human beings to exercise caring dominion over the earth." Signers, including Protestant notables Charles Colson, James Dobson, and D. James Kennedy, insisted that environmentalists who ignored the biblical privileging of human beings over the rest of creation "deify nature" and "oppose human

---

7. Media reports omitted Watt's references to the indeterminate timing of the second coming of Jesus and his avowed commitment to preserve natural resources for coming generations. Nevertheless, Watt clearly believed that stewardship involved maximizing the use of natural resources for human good. "If we fail to make wise use of resources, we unduly penalize and impoverish our people, weaken our nation and deny ourselves the economic base essential to good stewardship," Watt told *The Saturday Evening Post*. "Only economically strong nations can be good stewards. It is in the economically deprived countries that environmentally devastating practices abound" (1982: 75).

dominion." These positions, said Cornwall signers, contradicted biblical teaching.[8]

ICES leaders placed concern for human health and well-being at the center of environmental discussions. Cornwall signers based their opposition to groups like EEN on biblical admonitions to care for the needy. Rich, Western environmentalists, said ICES leaders, overlooked the "unprecedented improvements in human health, nutrition, and life expectancy" offered to those "blessed by political and economic liberty."[9] Because the wages of sin is death, and because free-market economies have facilitated the improvement of human health and the extension of life expectancy, ICES leaders believed that Christians ought to "take very seriously the claim that free markets and liberal democracy are essential to human welfare and therefore have a moral priority on our thinking about how society ought to be ordered" (Beisner et al. 2000). Thus, any environmental program that threatened to staunch development or impede free markets aroused suspicion in these conservative circles. Anthropocentric environmentalists tended to see Third World poverty (and the resulting environmental damage) as evidence of the superiority of free-market capitalism rather than the result of American imperialism. ICES did not advocate the complete erasure of governmental checks on individual or corporate polluters. But the organization certainly worried that EEN environmentalists planned to throw the baby out with the bath water.

ICES leaders, like other politically conservative Christians, have seen themselves as custodians of the culture, charged by God to ensure that a broadly Christian culture existed in the United States. This position emerged both from a historically Reformed understanding of the Christian's relationship to government and from conservative Christians' understanding of God's work in history. Reformed theology holds that God sanctions governments and permits believers to work within the government, convictions shared by a majority of American Christians.[10]

---

8. *The Cornwall Declaration on Environmental Stewardship* 1999; available online: http://www.stewards.net/CornwallDeclaration.htm; Larsen (2001: 301–21).

9. ICES leaders did not claim to be downtrodden; rather, they accused radical environmentalists of patronizing poor people by denying them the benefits that Westerners enjoyed.

10. By "Reformed," we mean the theological tradition descended primarily from the sixteenth-century theologian John Calvin. Calvinists have exercised disproportionate theological influence among American Protestants.

Moreover, many conservative Christians believe divine Providence played a central role in the establishment of America. The Anabaptist model of a church standing outside the state apparatus—a model endorsed by Van Houtan and Northcott—has seemed nonsensical and even blasphemous to conservatives. "Any diligent student of American history," wrote conservative leader Jerry Falwell, "finds that our great nation was founded by godly men upon godly principles to be a Christian nation" (1980: 29). Though some Christians resisted Falwell's oversimplified reading of history (Noll et al. 1983), plenty more agreed that God guided the founding of this nation—and that cultural custodianship demanded working for the redemption of the nation.

Conservative Christians in the United States, then, have tended to couch their environmental activism in the context of American politics and citizenship. In 1992, for example, the Southern Baptist Convention's Christian Life Commission (now the Ethics & Religious Liberty Commission) published a collection of essays called *The Earth is the Lord's*. Morris Chapman, then president of the SBC Executive Committee, typified the instinctive connection many of the book's authors made between environmental stewardship and American citizenship. "By God's providence," he wrote, "we are blessed to be citizens of this great and glorious land." This language would hardly surprise those familiar with Southern Baptists, but its appearance in a book about the environment demands explanation. Chapman's belief that God had smiled on this nation colored his view of environmentalism. American Christians were to take stewardship seriously because they were Christians *and* Americans. As Chapman put it, "we have increased responsibility because God has blessed us as a country" (1992: 31). This stance predisposed Chapman and like-minded conservatives to reject environmentalist programs that diminished America's glory. Indeed, in a subsequent essay in *The Earth is the Lord's*, SBC leader Gary H. Leazer connected New Age spirituality to environmentalism, highlighting the two movements' shared taste for words like "unity," "planetary," and "interdependence." Even Earth Day came in for censure; Leazer said most observers of the April holiday held "a New Age World View" (1992: 107). Conservative American Christians' belief that God had favored their nation has led many to distance themselves from environmentalists who value the oneness of humanity and stress the interdependence of the planets' creatures.

CONCLUSION

Whereas Van Houtan and Northcott believe a "profound ambivalence" characterizes Americans' "ecological psyche," we contend that over the last thirty-five years, evangelical activists on both sides of the political divide have developed comprehensive responses to the problem of environmental destruction. ICES and like-minded believers have demonstrated that even the most politically conservative Christians now view care for the creation as a central facet of good stewardship. Yet their theology of culture renders them unable to view complicity with the nation-state as a shortcoming, validating Van Houtan and Northcott's critique of political conservatives. EEN activists, however, come closer to the ideal espoused by Van Houtan and Northcott, even if their political pragmatism does not always accord with Yoder's micropolitics. The authors themselves offer a few concessions to utilitarianism: they call the 1970s a "high point" in environmental policy even as they argue that policy solutions dependent on state support fall short of ideal. One senses that Van Houtan and Northcott would be pleased, if not altogether satisfied, if more American Christians gravitated towards the utilitarianism of EEN rather than the anthropocentrism of ICES. The conservative Christians who have risen to political power in recent years continue to define dominion as a position of power over the environment. But growing numbers of other evangelicals have proven willing to acknowledge limits to that power and, perhaps, even to imagine a world where the Lamb's self-sacrificing dominion reigns.

Eight

Biodiversity and the Kingdom of God

Laura Yordy

IN WHAT FOLLOWS, I shall move from an examination of biblical and doctrinal themes about the redemption of a diverse creation to ethical mandates for Christian churches based on these themes. These visions of redemption often differ from those of secular environmentalism; however, they comprise central elements of many Christian traditions, and thus are especially pertinent to ecotheologians—or other Christians who are seeking direction for their response to the scientific demonstration of biodiversity loss.

Eschatology is that branch of theology concerned with the "end times" or the "last things," the second coming of Christ, judgment and salvation, the consummation of creation, the taking up of all things into the divine being. Eschatology derives from the churches' interpretations of the promises of God to God's people, biblically narrated in both the Old and New Testaments. Although different Christian traditions perceive the eschatological vision quite differently, many agree that because Jesus Christ defeated death, the earth as it is will not continue forever, but its inhabitants will not vanish into nothingness. Something beyond—an "afterlife" of some sort—awaits at least some humans.[1] Moreover, many Christian traditions have always understood Christ as savior of the whole cosmos,

---

1. Some contemporary feminist theologians reject the possibility of "personal" continuation beyond death (Rosemary Radford Ruether, for instance). However, that route poses several problems, a few of which are clearly pointed out by Karras (2002). It is worth noting that not all feminist theologians reject unrealized eschatology or the personal aspects thereof. See, for instance Johnson (1992), LaCugna (1993), Jones (2007), and Young (2002). Moreover, many liberation theologies, such as African-American and Latino/a theologies, "are infused with eschatological hope" that includes the resurrection of the dead (Pedraja 2006, Evans 1992).

not only its human residents. As biblical scholar Bill T. Arnold comments, heaven "is the transformation of life as we know it today; a genuinely renewed creation, in which our resurrected bodies and this renewed earth enjoy peace and bliss eternally. The great Creator of heaven and earth will not abandon his material creation but transform it" (Arnold 2004: 104). This vision of the "New Creation" may appear implausible in light of contemporary physics, which predicts a "freeze or burn" ending to the universe, but it need not be so. Robert John Russell and Denis Edwards each demonstrate, in different ways, how theological understandings of the "end times" may cohere with scientific theories about the "end."[2] At any rate, biblical texts that sketch the eschaton do more than simply note the inclusion of nonhuman creation in a vision of the Kingdom of God. They bear directly on questions of human response to biodiversity loss and conservation, and they offer a rich resource for theological and ethical reflection.

Scripture writers provide clear parameters of the character of the "life to come," though not the specifics of how it will take place. What the biblical authors describe, though, is the redemption and consummation of the whole creation, not only humans or their souls.[3] Moreover, the original creation and its consummation are, as reflections of the Trinitarian Creator, characterized by profound diversity and interdependence—a theological parallel to the biodiversity named by science. Honoring the biodiversity of the created world may comprise, therefore, a necessary component of Christian witness to the eschaton, to what is understood as God's plan and promise for all creation.

In order to understand the mandate to honor biodiversity, it is important to understand the theological description of both creation (the

---

2. For instance, Russell writes, "The regularity of natural processes is ultimately the result of God's faithfulness, even if God bequeaths a significant degree of causal autonomy to nature.... if this is so, and if God is free to act in radically new ways (which of course God is!) not only in human history but in the ongoing history of the universe, then the future of the cosmos will not be what science predicts. Instead the cosmic far future will be based on a radically new kind of divine action which began with the resurrection of Jesus, and this new act of God cannot be reduced to, or explained by, the current laws of nature, that is by God's action in the past history of the universe" (Russell 2008: 307). See also Edwards (2006).

3. See, for instance, Rom 8:37–39 and Eph 1:10. Also see O'Donovan (1992: 13–14) and Pope Paul XXIII, Lumen Gentium, sections 17 and 48. A contemporary examination of this aspect of eschatology in relation to recent science is offered by Russell (2008).

divine process) and creation (the result). God's creation is diverse in its very origin, and for many Christians this diversity reflects the Trinitarian character of its Creator and the activity of its coming into being.[4] This Trinitarian aspect fundamentally connects creation and eschaton, so creation is eschatological in nature: it points toward its fulfillment in Christ at a time determined by God. To put this another way, this cosmos comes about through *Trinitarian* activity: the loving interplay of the three divine persons (Father, Son, Holy Spirit) creates the biophysical universe. Rather than describing creation as the work of God "in general," many New Testament writers affirm the distinctive role of Christ in creation, confessing "one Lord, Jesus Christ, through whom are all things" (1 Cor 8:6).[5] The Nicene Creed, developed in the fourth century, corresponds with these texts, saying "We believe in one Lord, Jesus Christ. . . . Through him all things were made." And the activity of the Spirit appears at the very beginning, when "a wind from God swept over the face of the waters" (Cunningham 1998: 58). From the very early days of the Church, Christians—from Athanasius through Basil, Calvin, Joseph Sittler, Colin Gunton, to Jürgen Moltmann and Elizabeth Johnson—have attested to the agency or mediation of Christ in the act of creation, and the activity of the Spirit in sustaining and enlivening creation, as well as the role of the First Person of the Trinity in the originating move of creative activity.[6]

In particular, affirming that Christ is the agent of creation strengthens the link between creation and salvation, for it is Christ who achieves both. Moltmann writes that "if Christ is the ground of salvation for the whole creation, for sinful men and women, and for 'enslaved' non-human creatures, he is then also the ground or the existence of the whole creation, human beings and nature alike" (Moltmann 1981: 102). Similarly, many New Testament authors speak about creation in past, present, and even future tenses, linking God's "original" creation of the world through Christ with God's continuing sustenance of the world-again through Christ—with its future reclaiming by Christ. This connection becomes explicit in wisdom Christology, where "the mediation of glory and cre-

---

4. My claim here is different from "Creationism," which removes Genesis 1 and 2 from their narrative context and attempts to read the texts as scientific explanation.

5. John 1:1-18; 1 Cor 8:6; Col 1:15-20; Phil 2:6-11; and Heb 1:2-4.

6. Cf. Ps 104:30: "when you [God] send forth your spirit, [all things] are created, and you renew the face of the ground." See also Athanasius (1971: 129-31), Basil the Great (1980: 39), Calvin (1963), Johnson (1993: 9), and Bonting (2006).

ation are one and the same" (103). Jesus Christ is the One through whom God creates and orders the world, *and* through whom God will one day glorify the world (Cunningham 1998: 82). Creation, then, is Christological and eschatological; it has its beginning and end (both future and goal) in Christ. Moreover, the New Creation is not unrelated to the old: it is *this* world that was created by Father, Son, and Holy Spirit, and *this* world that is redeemed by Jesus's death and resurrection, and *this* world that will be taken up into final consummation with the Trinity (Rossing 2004, Russell 1996, Polkinghorne 2003).[7] The new creation begins with the resurrection of Christ's body after his death, but will not be completed until the day of judgment (Romans 5–8). Creation and salvation are not discrete divine projects, but an extended activity of God through Christ in time and space.

Another reason for remembering that creation is Trinitarian activity is epistemological: on this view, the universe can only be understood in Trinitarian terms (Cunningham 1998: 90ff). It is only through an understanding of God's activity through Christ in the Spirit that creation can be understood at all. That is to say, Trinity is the Christian God, the source of all being, the foundation of all there is, and the Trinity is the mutually indwelling, self-giving communion of divine persons. The universe is thoroughly, essentially Trinitarian (Edwards 2006). This assertion need not contradict modern scientific views of the universe. God's infinite power surely includes such means as "big bangs" and evolution, just as it includes forgiveness, mitosis, and dung beetles. Nothing under the sun (and over it) lies outside the sovereignty of God.

But why does it matter that creation is Trinitarian? This is not, after all, the most common focus of Christian writings on creation or ecology.[8] It matters, especially for discussions of ecological ethics, because the Trinitarian character of creation manifests itself in diversity and mutuality. The Trinity—the dance of three divine persons in intimacy and mutual love—overflows in creation and becomes expressed in the dance of the

---

7. This is part of the argument against the reading of Revelation that sees the current earth as being completely destroyed. Rowan Williams also points out that in that in the post-resurrection appearance stories, Jesus meets the disciples where he met them before: in the upper room, in Galilee, on the hill, on the seashore. All the sites of terror and betrayal become sites of reconciliation and repair. The new age begins on the ruins of the old age, with the old stones (1995: 49).

8. In addition to Cunningham (1998), exceptions include Moltmann (1993) and Powell (2003).

universe. As Denis Edwards writes, the abundance of life on earth "springs ultimately from the abundance of the divine communion. It expresses the ecstatic nature of the divine life. The divine Persons are ecstatic not only in their being-with-each-other, but in choosing to be with a world of creatures" (2006: 77). The Trinity is characterized by supreme dynamic unity, supreme communicability, co-equality, and co-eternity (e.g., Gunton 1993, Zizoulas 1997).[9] Therefore, relations of mutual love, persons indwelling without loss of distinction, are the foundation of everything—not only human life, not only earthly life, but divine life as well, insofar as humans comprehend God's self-revelation. Relationship is the *primary* metaphysical category. Elizabeth Johnson explains it this way: the God who is three times personal signifies that relatedness, rather than the solitary ego, is the heart of all reality. In this universal relatedness, mutuality and distinction are not opposites, but they require each other. Genuine mutuality of relationship involves real dynamic distinctions (LaCugna 1993). Contrary to what contemporary Western culture seems to claim, difference does not imply either competition or inequality; instead, difference and love are equally characteristic of God and of the universe. The fact that human cultures tend to view nature as agonistic and hostile results, in part, from their imperfect perception (whether scientific, political, religious, or aesthetic) and, in part, because creation has "fallen" from its true self. Yet behind/beyond all the indifference or antagonism lies difference in loving communion—Father, Son, and Holy Spirit.

Christian traditions suggest not only that creation is Trinitarian, but that God created everything *ex nihilo*, out of nothing. Creation *ex nihilo* is not explicitly asserted in the Genesis accounts.[10] However, Jewish scholar Peter Ochs argues that the Hebrew of the beginning of Genesis is best translated "In the beginning of [the activity of] God's creating heaven and earth—[when] the earth was unformed and void" (2000: 8).[11] The question of any prior status of heaven and earth is left open; God may have already created the unformed "stuff" before shaping it into the universe. Creation *ex nihilo*, at any rate, has been a strong belief in Christian traditions, at least since the third century. Jettisoning this could imperil Christian understanding of God's sovereignty and gracious providence,

9. This "social" understanding of the Trinity is more recent and contrasts with hierarchical understandings of pre-modern Christians.

10. 2 Macc 7:28; Rom 4:17; Heb 11:3.

11. See also Eichrodt (1984).

although it would probably not, in our scientific age, revive the particular pagan notion of the world as eternal.[12]

Continuing to affirm creation *ex nihilo* is important to the relationship in theological ethics between creation and eschatology. The doctrine emphasizes the uniqueness of God's creating work: creating the universe is *not* like a sculptor shaping clay, or even a geneticist "producing" hybrid mice.[13] Therefore, the world creatures live in *and* the world to come each bears a strong element of mystery and surprise. Just as the natural processes and "laws" of this world originate in God's loving will, so does the nature of the eschaton (Russell 2008: 307). Perhaps humans cannot suppose *how* predation could be absent from the Kingdom, but they can trust that God, the author of nature, is not limited by what already exists.

The second point about creation *ex nihilo* is that because chaos is not something that pre-exists God, there is no force of evil that somehow escapes divine dominion. Rather, chunks of disorder temporarily mar the goodness of God's works. This is not to diminish the severity of evil, but to limit its scope: evil does not precede, overcome, or outlast the good.[14] All material existence has its ground in God: there is no other, competing, order of being (Schwöbel 1997: 163).

Thus far, I have tried to show that God's creative activity is Trinitarian, unfettered by temporal/spatial categories, and that Christian traditions see a unified arc of God's action from creation through final consummation. What, though, about the created world itself? How do these Christian perspectives on creation correlate with the scientific imperative to conserve biodiversity? The next several sections argue from Christian doctrine that in its goodness, diversity, particularity, even in its corruption, creation exhibits its participation in God's intentions to redeem the divine word—that is, its eschatological character.

---

12. In fact, divine sovereignty and "creation *ex nihilo*" go hand in hand; theologians who are uncomfortable with the former often reject the latter. My own view, evident throughout this article, is that "traditional" doctrine offers untapped resources to ecotheology, so need not be discarded just yet.

13. Brueggemann writes, "while it may be used synonymously with 'make' or 'form,' the verb 'create' [bara'] is in fact without analogy. It refers to the special action by God and to the special relation which binds these two parties [creator and created] together" Brueggemann (1982: 17).

14. Of course, this is part of Augustine's definition of evil as the privation of good. See also Haas (2001).

Diversity and Dominion

To begin with, both scripture and Christian traditions affirm that the world is good, although fallen and disordered. The author of Genesis 1 asserts seven times that "God saw that it was good" (Brueggemann 1982: 31). On the other hand, as early as Gen 6:11, "the earth was corrupt in God's sight, and the earth was filled with violence." Yet that corruption was insufficient to nullify all the earth's goodness (Brueggemann 1982: 76). And so it has continued to this day. Earthly reality pulses in a constant tension between the goodness of its creation and the disorder of its fall. It is appropriate, therefore, that one of Christianity's most consistent positions has been the qualified endorsement of the created world; it is not evil, yet not wholly good.[15] It operates according to a natural order that should be honored and respected, yet not understood as ideal.

It is important for those of us who are not scientists to remember that despite many generalizations about "the created world," it is in fact comprised of a myriad of creations, each with its own character and particular destiny in God. The Priestly account of creation narrates God's creating a great variety of things-stars, seas, assorted plants, animals of many different types, over a span of time, and in relation to one another. (Gen 1:1–2:4a) This matches the understanding of the Israelite authors of the Old Testament, for whom the idea of "nature" as a single category of creatures, elements, and forces governing their behavior was quite foreign (Gregorios 1991). Land was the key concept, and everything else—climate, animals, plants, soil and rocks—was perceived in relation to the land and its fertility. Further, what controlled the land was not a set of abstract mathematical laws, but the will of God (Brueggemann 1977). So rather than seeing the universe as a single thing, Old Testament writers tended to see a myriad of creatures and forces united by their divine origin and governance. What categories are seen in the Old Testament match the perspectives of herding and farming cultures: garden is different from wilderness, and domestic animals from wild animals and predators.[16] Animals are rarely regarded simply as generic "animals," much less

---

15. Ever since the early church confronted gnosticism in the second century CE, it has struggled to hold in balance these contradictory qualities of creation. Its success in this endeavor has been highly variable over the years and across strands of Christian tradition. See Williams (1972), Coates (1998), and Santmire (2000).

16. The distinction between garden and wilderness carried profound implications for Christian treatment of their biophysical environment in the colonial era, when unfamiliar lands were viewed as ungodly wilderness awaiting transformation into blessed gardens. Not only was this approach disastrous for the land's prior occupants, it distorted the

an undefined part of a generic "nature."[17] Similarly, animals and plants in Jesus's parables tend to behave according to their kind: "sparrows drop dead, dogs scavenge and lick the wounds of beggars, and eagles gather over a carcass…There is a certain realism here, and a respect for the way things are, since that is the way God has made them" (Muddiman 1998: 30). And the way God made things is an amazing number of ways that humans have not even begun to understand.[18]

This is a point at which recent secular environmentalism and Christian theology may concur: the caution against abstracting biophysical specificities into a single thing called "nature." As Will Friesen points out:

> We [humans] do not really experience abstractions like "biosphere" and "environment," especially when we are describing the experience of crisis. Rather, we experience concrete and particular changes within the horizons of a particular place—horizons which are never so broad as to be captured by the word "environment." So when we sound the alarm of crisis, what we mean to say is that something has happened to the places in which we live, that something has come between us and the fields and forests and the rivers, and between here and the mountains that have marked for generations the places we call home. (1992: 48)

It is important to note that the categories discovered or imposed by humans may not match the diversity of God's creation. That is, Christians cannot presume to know, to have mastered epistemologically, God's "map" of this created universe. Racial categorization is one of the more striking examples of attributing a human construct of difference to divine intent, with horrible consequences. On the other hand, mistakenly identifying sameness can also have tragic results. Gorillas, for instance, are much more similar to human children than to geckos, yet they have been lumped together as "animals," and seen as equally fit to live in cages

---

Bible's own narrative. In both Old Testament and New Testament writings, both garden *and* wilderness were suffused with God's presence and under God's care. Biblical writers may have understood what subsequent generations forgot, that the garden-wilderness distinction holds with regard for human endeavors, but not necessarily for God's providential intentions.

17. Where the text reads "animals," the reference is usually to livestock, as the context makes clear.

18. In Job 38–39, the writer repeatedly emphasizes the vast difference between Job's (human) understanding of the universe and God's own. Also see Wirzba (2003: 41ff).

under human scrutiny and for human study and amusement.[19] All human characterizations of God's creations, no matter how scientifically or theologically "certain," must remain open to revision. What Christians can say, based on Trinitarian faith, is that God's creations seem intended to differ and converge in ways they do not comprehend; that differences do not necessitate conflict or inequality; and that all of God's creations are united in their common origin and destiny in Christ.[20]

Because creation's variety reflects its divine origins, that variety is good. From the early years of Christianity, Christian traditions have suggested that the diversity of creatures reflects the immeasurable richness of their Creator. Creation is good because all created entities mirror, in some way, the divine Trinity and its infinite goodness. However, the infinite distance between God's goodness and created goodness means that only a plethora of good creations can reflect, even imperfectly, the divine excellence. C. S. Lewis describes Richard Hooker's sixteenth-century vision of the world: "We meet at all levels the divine wisdom shining out through 'the beautiful variety of all things' in their manifold and yet harmonious dissimilitude" (Lewis 1954: 460). Each creature, each of the innumerable bits of created matter, each community and ecosystem, retains and exhibits a minute portion of its Creator's bounty. In a famous passage at the end of *The City of God*, Augustine writes in awestruck praise:

> Shall I speak of the manifold and various loveliness of sky, and earth, and sea; of the plentiful supply and wonderful qualities of the light; of sun, moon, and stars; of the shade of trees; of the colors and perfume of flowers; of the multitude of birds, all differing in plumage and in song; of the variety of animals, of which the smallest in size are often the most wonderful—the works of ants and bees astonishing us more than the huge bodies of whales? (1958: 529)

---

19. In addition to the many studies of gorillas, a wonderful source of insight on other primates and birds is Linden (1999).

20. Unfortunately, theologians continue to frame ecological issues as "humans" in relation to "nonhuman" or even "nature" as if, even while acknowledging the difficulties of the Cartesian dualism, they are simply unable to imagine beyond it (e.g., P. Scott unpub. manuscript, Zizoulas 1990). Interestingly, the tendency to think solely in human versus nonhuman terms seem associated with less attention to the Biblical texts. Both Scott and Zizoulas are deeply concerned to explain the rationality of God's action (rather than, perhaps, describe an appropriate response to it).

It is important not to forget that creation is as much or more a creation-and-sustaining of relationships as it is of bodies. Here again, Christian theology and recent secular ecological work find agreement. Richard Hooker wrote, "God hath created nothing simply for it selfe: but ech thing in all things and of everie thing ech part in other hath such interest that in the whole world nothing is found whereunto anie thing created can saie, 'I need thee not'" (1977: 333). The interdependence of creatures is not a new discovery; what is perhaps being *re*-discovered (in Western culture, at least) is that humanity is not exempt from this interdependence. The great difference, of course, is that many Christians believe these interrelationships to be not a self-generating blossoming of the earth, but part of the gift of life from God. The "web of creation" is strung and restrung in the gracious care of the Holy Spirit. In Athanasius's words, "... it is [Christ] who has established the order of all things, reconciling opposites and from them forming a single harmony" (Athanasius 1971: 113). So as creation's beauty and diversity is Christological, and Christ is the author and agent of ultimate peace, then creation reflects—in a dim and fractured fashion—its Christic purpose.

It seems obvious, however, that what people observe in the "natural" world is only occasionally good (in these terms), only occasionally "genuine mutuality of relationship." Often, relationships among creatures are competitive, antagonistic, or parasitic. Traditional theology does not deny this reality (although it is worth noting that nineteenth-century scientists, including Charles Darwin, viewed the world in even more hostile terms than do current naturalists). Many Christians, though, contend that the harshness of earthly existence is not the last word; while undoubtedly real, nature's waste, suffering and death are, in a sense, a deviation from the more profound truth of the universe, which is love. The world has fallen away from its "authentic self" as articulated biblically and theologically and thus operates in a painful and bloody manner.

If theologians define "Fall" in the narrow sense, the question is whether the sin of the first humans corrupts not only the rest of humankind, but the entire cosmos and its inhabitants irrevocably, until God's final saving action. The (Yahwist) author of Gen 3:15–19 describes the effects of Adam and Eve's disobedience on nonhuman creation: enmity between the serpent and the woman and between their offspring, and a curse upon the ground such that its "natural" fruitfulness is diminished.[21]

Most early Christian interpretations of the passage read it to mean that *all* of creation was perpetually damaged as a result of Adam's sin.[22] In subsequent centuries, Christian attitudes toward the post-fall status of creation varied, although the view that creation had escaped the fall was typically a minority opinion, especially after the Reformation. Either view raises serious difficulties. On the one hand, to suppose that human beings managed to corrupt the whole creation that was otherwise in good order, conforming to God's intentions, seems incredibly anthropocentric. It also knots up any attempt to view God's creative activity as a gradual, developmental process from "primitive" to "advanced." The choice seems to be: either millions of years of life got derailed by those disobedient humans, or else the Edenic narrative must be completely ahistoricized. On the other hand, to suppose that only humans suffer the consequences of human sin is manifestly false, especially from an ecological perspective. Such a view also introduces its own sort of alienation between humans and nonhumans, as if the moral status of humans is disconnected from their bodily existence-and that of other creatures.

However, it is not necessary to resolve this question here. What matters is not so much whether earth was corrupted by human sin, but whether earth is corrupted at all. That is, Christians can broaden their definition of "fallen" and ask whether creation is other than it should be-disordered, less than ideal, or contrary to God's purpose and plan. "Fallen" in this sense is different than finite, at least logically different. Many Christian theologians hold that the finitude of the world is part of God's creative intent. The understanding that the universe and its creatures has a beginning and end was an important component of Hebrew and Christian faith from the earliest times. That God created this world and is in charge of the world's end sharply contrasted with both ancient ideas of the cosmos being in some sense divine and the Greek idea of earth's eternity.[23] Anything

---

21. Anderson notes that "God's word of judgment to 'ādām is: "cursed is the soil ['ādāmâ] on your account," because of what you have done . . . In short, violence is a disease, as it were, that affects all those living in the same *oikos*" (1994: 145–46).

22. See Romans 5 and 8. Also, in the intertestamental *Life of Adam and Eve*, Seth gets attacked by a "beast." When Eve chastises the beast, it retorts that its hostility is the result of Eve and Adam's own behavior. This is discussed in Charlesworth (1985: 273).

23. See Aristotle (2004: 8.6, 258b26–259a9).

created is not God and therefore not perfect or eternal. However, it is possible to imagine a finite world in which lives are limited, creatures are born, live peacefully, and die, but without the vast conflicts and suffering that life on this world seems to entail. Moreover, it seems clear that the corruption of natural reality contradicts God's intentions for the world. Recall, first, the Old Testament admonishments to treat domestic animals kindly. The Book of Deuteronomy, for instance, includes animals in the Sabbath rest, and prescribes ways to care for animals' physical and psychological welfare.[24] As Terence Fretheim notes, "the explicit provision for the care of the animals, both domestic and wild ... is one of the more neglected themes in the law. Such concerns are rooted in Israel's general understanding that God provided for the animals in the ordering of the world ... even God's salvific activity includes them" (Fretheim 1990: 251). Then consider the repeated assertions by the Old Testament prophets that the Israelites' unfaithful behavior bore severe consequences for the land.[25] If drought or famine is a penalty for sin (even a God-given penalty), it cannot be desirable in itself. Creation's suffering and disorder are indications of things gone wrong in the created world. Finally, as I will argue below, God's promises consistently include not only justice among people, but abundant life for all creatures and harmonious relations between species. These promises reverse the present order *because* the present order contradicts God's ultimate intentions.[26] In Galloway's words, "the symbol of cosmic fall is the complement of the symbol of cosmic redemption" (Galloway 1951: 21).

To put it another way, creation did not avoid the fall; nonhuman creation suffers corruption and distortion just as humans do, even though both remain within the compass of God's love and care and are, therefore, good.[27] This understanding of creation makes important theological points. It underscores that "the very nature of creation is always ambiguous; it points both ways; it affirms and denies God at one and the same time. It affirms God because God loves and cares for it but it also neces-

---

24. Deut 5:14, 22: 6, 25:4. The injunction in 22:6 against taking a mother bird from her nest, when collecting eggs or young birds, ensures the continuity of the food source (and species!) for the human community (Miller 1990: 170). See also Exod 23:12, Prov 12:10.

25. See, for instance, Deut 6:2–3, Amos 6:4–14, Hosea 4:1–3, Isa 24:1–7, Lev 18:26–28, Ezek 33:25–28, Jer 4:23–26, 5:23–25, 12:4. See also Northcott (1996: 187ff.).

26. For an opposing view, Fern (2002).

27. Rom 8:19–25.

sarily denies God because it is not divine" (Linzey 1994: 81). This pervasive ambiguity of nature also means that natural and human evil are never completely distinguishable. So what humans do matters-has meaning-in ways that transcend the personal, social, political, or "spiritual" realms. It matters in and to the world beyond human culture. Conversely, humans are *necessarily* subject to the conditions of earthly life. Whether her sins are horrible or minor, any human being will suffer the effects of natural corruption and death. This is both comforting and sobering news. It is sobering because nothing in the created world, no environmental ethic, no human power, no evolutionary shift, can "cure" creation. "A new and special act of God, accomplished in the death and resurrection of Christ, is necessary to purge creation of the corrupting effects of sin" (Haas 2001: 339). In this rather backhanded way, creation is shown again to be eschatological; none of God's creatures can in themselves fulfill God's purposes for them. Yet it is comforting to realize, as Stephen Webb says, "that nature is fallen, and that nature's distortions transcend the many harms humans contribute to it, so that Christians should deplore the human abuse of nature but they should not think that humans cause all of nature's problems" (Webb 1996: 240).

This is a tricky point. Overemphasizing the corruption of creation (as may be claimed of Calvin and, in his wake, Jonathan Edwards) can lead toward an undervaluing of the biophysical world, and thus an abdication of human responsibility for the effects of human behavior on the rest of creation.[28] This attitude appears in some "wise use" literature: if species extinctions happen anyway, why are human-caused extinctions any cause for concern or remorse?[29] Obviously, this argument cannot withstand logical scrutiny (the existence of evil does not generally justify the commission of evil acts), nor, from a Christian perspective, does it adequately describe God's relationship with all of creation. One of the fundamental tenets of Christian faith, after all, is that God loves *despite* the imperfections of the beloved. Rather than being impeded by the corruption of the

---

28. Tied into his stress on the corrupt character of creation is Calvin's implicit view that creation serves more to demonstrate God's justice than God's charity. For a different view, see Schreiner (2001).

29. For a similar argument, see Fitzsimmons (2001). The "wise use" movement is a quasi-Christian anti-environmentalist movement that prioritizes financial profit and individual political freedom over state regulation or restraint. It characterizes environmentalism as pagan, extremist, and seeking excessive state control of citizens. The phrase "wise use" was coined by Ron Arnold in the late 1980s (Burke 1993).

beloved, God's charity is directed precisely toward the sinfulness and corruption so that the beloved may be sanctified and redeemed by grace. On the other hand, underemphasizing the fallen character of creation is also dangerous. It can yield a romantic view of "nature" that contrasts the goodness of the nonhuman with the sinfulness of the human-at once re-inscribing the human-nonhuman dualism and misrepresenting the complex character of the nonhuman world. This romanticism parades itself as a nature-friendly, sympathetic perspective, yet it diminishes the very real struggle, suffering and waste that constantly occur in nonhuman creatures. In a sense, it denies God's care of the universe because it denies the universe's need for that care. Both errors, then, produce the same result. Over-emphasizing or under-emphasizing creation's fall refuses the expansiveness and depth of God's unlimited love for the world, and therefore nullifies the eschatological dimension of creation. From both theological and ecological standpoints, the most helpful view may be that creation is neither ideal nor completely corrupt. Hugh Montefiore writes that "Christianity doesn't teach that this is the best of all possible worlds. It teaches rather that God's potentially good creation needs to be redeemed and sanctified, and that these are costly processes" (1975: 36).

In sum, the fundamental Christian characterization of God's creation is that it reflects and partakes of the goodness of its Trinitarian Creator, but the reflection is currently dimmed and distorted, and can never be restored by natural means. As a result, the extent to which the current natural order can function as normative is limited. This posts a strong warning for environmental ethics: Christians do well to honor the "natural" processes and relationships among species that science reveals, and make great effort to preserve them, yet understand that those processes are not in themselves the ultimate word. Honoring nature is the best humans can do (and we are manifestly inept at the task); glorifying and consummating nature is what God can and will do. So, for instance, Christian environmentalists strive to conserve predator species that keep ecosystems in balance by killing individual animals, *without* believing that predation is the ultimate will of God.

God's creation is suffused with purpose and promise: all of creation, including humans, is made for the glory of God. In the words of Steven Bouma-Prediger, "God is the center of the cosmos, and our [human] task and privilege is to worship the Maker of heaven and earth in concert with all other creatures" (2001: 174).[30] I take it as given here that nonhuman creation does not exist solely to assist in human salvation, or to chastise "man," as has been argued occasionally in the Christian tradition. Biblical writers as well as ancient and contemporary theologians argue decisively that nonhuman creation serves God, praises God, and will partake in the Kingdom of God.[31] According to many Christian traditions, all creatures, living or nonliving, sentient or not, live in doxological (praising) response to God's gift of creation and promise of redemption. In Ps 96:11–13, for instance, earth and heaven sing joyfully in response to God's faithfulness:

> Let the heavens be glad, and let the earth rejoice; let the sea roar, and all that fills it; let the earth exult, and everything in it. Then shall all the trees of the forest sing for joy before the Lord; for he is coming, for he is coming to judge the earth. He will judge the world with righteousness, and the peoples with his truth. (Mays 1989: 309)

The book of Revelation also paints wonderful images of "every creature in heaven and on earth and under the earth and in the sea" singing praises and worshipping the Lamb at (or even "after") the end time (Rev 5:13–14). The purpose of creation is the glorification of God, and that purpose is fulfilled partially in earthly life, and only completely in the final consummation. So the universe is doxological and eschatological in its very being.

The details of this claim are important. Christian eschatology differs from Aristotelian teleology in that its telos is granted as gift from God. Scientists speak of the "inner" drive of an organism to survive and reproduce, but this is different from creation's eschatological goal, which transcends the organism, species, even the category of earthly life. As Conyers explains, the world does not find its purpose in itself. It is "eccentric"

---

30. Wynne-Tyson (1989: 9) quotes St. Basil who prayed, "O God, enlarge within us the sense of fellowship with all living things, our brothers the animals, to whom you gave the earth as their home in common with us. We remember with shame that in the past we have exercised the high dominion of man with ruthless cruelty, so that the voice of the earth, which should have gone up to you in song, has been a groan of travail. May we realize that they live not for us alone but for themselves and for you and that they love the sweetness of life."

31. The point that God's care for nonhuman creatures transcends humanity was one of the first arguments by ecological theologians in this century. The argument rests soundly on biblical and early church sources which were largely ignored in the centuries since Descartes.

because it centers outside of itself; it centers in God (Conyers 2002: 15). The universe, then, is not a closed system; it is always open to the gracious presence of the Spirit in accord with the intentions of the Trinitarian God. What I am describing here is very close to the traditional idea of divine providence; yet I want to emphasize that *the entire* universe is under God's providential care, not just human lives and interests.

I have argued thus far that according to the doctrine of creation, God's creation is Trinitarian in character, continuous, and out of nothing. Creation itself is good because it reflects the goodness of its creator, yet also fallen and subject to evil and suffering. It is incredibly various and particular, with all things in the universe held in relation to each other and to God through Christ. Finally, it is eschatological: sustained by the Spirit until the fulfillment of all things comes with the eschaton. This last claim cannot be overstated: it is not as though there exists an entity (creation) which plays a role in God's redemptive purposes. It is that God's providential care and intentions call the creation into being and sustain it until it is drawn fully into its consummated relationship with the Trinity.

Christian environmentalists, then, may want to read "their" story of nature and humans through the biblical narrative of the promised second coming and the eschaton. Two initial caveats here: knowledge of the Kingdom of God requires faithful practices, and human understanding will never match the divine intention. That is, knowledge of God and God's kingdom comes about through discipleship; it is when Christians follow Jesus that they learn where Jesus is going. So the Kingdom of God can never be depicted in abstraction from what is being done in witness to the Kingdom. Further, because of human sinfulness, the finitude of earthly existence, and the infinity of the divine, humans will never acquire perfect knowledge of the Kingdom, no matter what they do. On the other hand, Christians are not left simply with vague promises of "eternal life" or "new creation." The Scripture writers, in fact, relate a good deal about the eschaton, and not only in the "eschatological" texts. The whole creation/redemption story is the basis of an adequate grasp of the eschatological vision. It is important to keep in mind that God's possibilities are infinite and unbounded by history, while human visions of the Kingdom of God are invariably constrained by the context of finite, earthly life. So it is good to proceed here, as in all theological matters, confident of God's truthfulness yet well aware of humanity's own distorted perceptions.

Most visions of the eschaton contain a set of familiar elements: peace, justice, abundance, righteousness, communion with God, reconciliation, and love. A psalmist writes:

> surely his salvation is at hand for those who fear him,
> that his glory may dwell in our land.
> Steadfast love and faithfulness will meet;
> righteousness and peace will kiss each other.
> Faithfulness will spring up from the ground,
> and righteousness will look down from the sky.
> The Lord will give what is good,
> and our land will yield its increase.
> Righteousness will go before him,
> and will make a path for his steps. (Ps 85:9–13)

All of these characteristics pertain not only to humans, but to *all* of creation. Recall the famous passage from Isaiah 11, describing the world after the coming of a messiah:

> The wolf will live with the lamb,
> the leopard will lie down with the goat,
> the calf and the lion and the yearling together;
> and a little child will lead them.
>
> The cow will feed with the bear,
> their young will lie down together,
> and the lion will eat straw like the ox.
>
> The infant will play near the hole of the cobra,
> and the young child put his hand into the viper's nest.
> They will neither harm nor destroy
> on all my holy mountain,
> for the earth will be full of the knowledge of the LORD
> as the waters cover the sea. (Isa 11:6–9)

This passage presents a clear image, however improbable, of interspecies peace and companionship in the world to come.[32] As Walter Brueggemann explains, "The poet imagines a coming time, under good governance, when all relationships of hostility and threat, in the animal world as in the human environment, shall be overcome. There will be conciliation and peaceableness among these species that have been at war with each other since the beginning of time" (Brueggemann 1998: 102).[33]

---

32. The image is echoed in Isa 65:25.
33. Brevard Childs also writes, "... the portrayal of universal peace in this chapter is

Belief in the reconciliation and redemption of all creation has been part of Christian traditions from the beginning. Although it has not always been the predominant view, it has never disappeared, even in times when a purely spiritualized notion of the eschaton seemed to prevail.[34] The following section describes the different key aspects of the Kingdom as expressed by the prophets and testified to by Jesus.

John Howard Yoder writes, "concern for peace ... is part of the purpose of God for all eternity" (Yoder 1985: 34). According to the Genesis story, the world was created, after all, not through a battle between gods, but out of the irenic, extravagant love of Father, Son, and Holy Spirit. Because the Trinitarian God is prior to-before, after, beyond-the created world, peace *is* the ultimate reality. Violence and warfare (nature red in tooth and claw) may seem like the way of the world, but many Christian traditions hold that they are results of the fall-contrary to God's intentions and destined for defeat. Christians themselves have not been very peaceful over the centuries, and apocalyptic fervor sometimes envisions the end of the world in spectacularly violent scenarios. Nonetheless, the Kingdom itself-after the dust of Armageddon settles-is always a realm of peace. Isaiah 60:17-18 is one of several prophetic texts whose author depicts that future for Zion: instead of slavery and warfare, "I will appoint Peace as your overseer, and Righteousness as your taskmaster. Violence shall no more be heard in your land, devastation or destruction within your borders." From the perspective of many Christians, Jesus's incarnation fulfilled this divine promise.[35] Jesus preached peace and demonstrated peace in his refusal to take up arms against his accusers and in his fellowship with outcasts. Above all, in his death and resurrection, Christ conquered war

---

set within an eschatological context ... and is an expansion of the picture of the future harmony among the peoples who flow to the holy mountain .... In Chapter 11 the vision of the future is greatly expanded to include not only the nations but creation itself, in which the entire world, not only the righteous king and his people, is filled with the knowledge of Yahweh (Isa. 11:9)" (Childs 2007: 104).

34. There is no comprehensive treatment of the history of Christian beliefs in the redemption of all creation. Partial treatments can be found in Galloway (1951) and Santmire (1985).

35. I am not arguing here, in a kind of anachronistic exegesis, that the meaning of the passage is Jesus Christ, or that the author intended it as such. However, many Christian traditions have understood this passage to reflect the sort of promises of peace that God makes and will fulfill.

with peace and death with life.[36] Even if just war is a "necessary evil" in an imperfect world, it is not part of the eschaton (NCCB 1983: 8).

The peace of Christ is not nuclear deterrence, nor is it complacency. It is not a smooth surface laid over violent tensions underneath. The peace of Christ, rather, is the unity of Christ: all things united in their source, savior, and destiny. It is the result of reconciling differences and healing ruptures, of divine justice and mercy. This peace is not only interpersonal, but interspecies: not the wary tolerance of animals forced to share a waterhole, but shared communion with God. Richard Bauckham argues persuasively that the vision of Isa 11:6–9 is borne out by Mark 1:13 in which Jesus is "with the wild beasts" during his temptation in the wilderness:

> The expression "to be with someone" (*einai meta tinos*) frequently has the strongly positive sense of close association or friendship or agreement or assistance ... Just as he resists Satan not as merely an individual righteous person but as the messianic Son of God on behalf of and for the sake of others, so he establishes, representatively, the messianic peace with wild animals. (1998: 58)

It is worth stating the obvious fact that if various species are to abide in peace, these species must be *present* at the eschaton. The lion and the lamb, the viper and the child, are all members of the Kingdom of God. The Old Testament prophets make this clear, as do the visions in the Book of Revelations. The author of Revelations depicts New Jerusalem as a green and fertile city, with trees of different sorts growing along a river of purest water (Rev 22:1–2). Even when read metaphorically, the image is unquestionably multifaceted and pluriform; the New Jerusalem is an eschatological ecosystem with many different sorts of inhabitants, all interacting harmoniously, to the benefit of all (Rossing 2000: 216).

Because God's peace is essential rather than superficial, it results from divine justice and liberation. According to the Old Testament prophets, divine justice "does not consist primordially in pronouncing an impartial verdict, but in the protection given to the poor, to widows and orphans" (Sobrino 1993: 83). Rather than "equal distribution" to an already unequal world, God's justice re-creates the world in accordance with mercy and righteousness. Divine justice, however, is not content with turning losers into winners, but in reconciling all conflicting parties. Scott Bader-Saye

---

36. The "Christus Victor" view is not, of course, the only interpretation of the atonement, but it is one of the three most prominent in Christian history.

notes that for Jesus "to "justify" is to make right, to reconcile, to bring back a proper ordering of human life and relationships" (Bader-Saye 1997: 540). Moreover, this biblical vision of reconciliation includes non-human creation. Old Testament writers, especially Isaiah, *presume* that the redemption of material creation is part of God's intention and plan, as is the restoration of relationships within and among creation's species. Thus the famous "peaceable kingdom" verses in Isaiah (11:6–9).

The New Testament writers also foretell the redemption of all creation through Christ, for he is Lord of all. Relationships between lands and their animal inhabitants, between human communities and their non-human neighbors, all are reconciled into the unity of Christ. In LaCugna's words, "the reign of God promises the life of true communion among human beings and all creatures" (1991: 399).

The eschaton is also a realm of material abundance. All the references to heaven as a "banquet" or feast, the miracles of loaves and fishes, even the disciples' habit of journeying with few provisions-all these point to the Kingdom as the "land of milk and honey."[37] To the millions of people who are starving or whose children suffer continual hunger, the prospect of abundant food is indeed a matter of hope, rather than expectation. Nearly two-thirds of the world's people live where clean water, food, or arable land is insufficient, either through "natural" or social causes, or a combination of both. Their prayer for daily bread is heartfelt. Moreover, hunger bears directly on issues of biodiversity, as the desperate need for fuel and food overwhelms long-term concerns about the health of local ecosystems.

In addition, material abundance as a property of the eschaton is much more subversive than it might appear. Modern Western capitalism is premised on the assumption of enduring scarcity-that, at bottom, there are not enough resources to satisfy the desires of all, because "unlimited desire is a natural quality" of humans (Achterhuis 1995: 106). So competition is the norm; the market adjudicates between supply and demand; and affluent people are encouraged to amass wealth for "security" against the possibility of hardship. People taking more than they need (if they have the money to do so) becomes, on this view, a mark of prudence rather than greed. There are winners and losers, and the goal is to be on the winning side. We may contrast this to the eschatological New Jerusalem

37. Isa 25:6; Luke 9, 14; Matt 10:8–10; 14. In the Gospel of John, Jesus himself is the feast (John 7:37).

where the water of life flows through the city and is given without cost to all who desire it,[38] or contrast scarcity with the vision in Amos 9:13–15, where "the mountains shall drip sweet wine, and all the hills shall flow with it."[39]

Note that eschatological abundance is not limited to human lives. Animals, too, receive ample food and water, and comfortable surroundings.[40] Irenaeus makes a beautiful comment on the fact that predators (including humans) will be vegetarians in the Kingdom: ". . . that the lion shall [then] feed on straw. And this indicates the large size and rich quality of the fruits. For if that animal, the lion, feeds upon straw [in the eschaton], of what a quality must the wheat itself be whose straw shall serve as suitable food for lions?" (2004: ch. 33).[41] To think of a world that is infinitely fruitful strains many modern sensibilities. Recall, however, the Christian insistence on God's freedom in creation. This world and all its arrangements are both contingent on God's providence and fallen from God's intention; it is part of many Christians' faith that God's reign will establish fecundity and plenty for all creation.

Just as peace is not merely the "temporary cessation of hostilities," so righteousness is not merely the restraint of sinfulness. The Bible often pairs righteousness with justice: righteousness delivers justice that releases the oppressed and restores community (Stassen and Gushee 2003: 42). But biblical righteousness is a wide-ranging ideal, including right relationships with God and neighbor, and faithfulness and consistency in all areas of life. Righteousness, therefore, cannot be limited to human-human or human-divine interaction. In fact, the very idea of salvation as restoration of right relationships has ecological overtones (LaCugna 1991). If all things on heaven and earth will be united with God through Jesus Christ, then right relationship—mutuality, fellowship, union without homogeneity—with all God's creation, beyond all current imaginings, will comprise the very "atmosphere" of the eschaton.[42]

---

38. Rev 21:6; 22:17. See also Rossing (2000: 216).

39. See also Joel 3:18.

40. Joel 2:22; Ezek 47:9–12. For a discussion of approaches to the question of the redemption of animals see Willey and Willey (1998).

41. Note, too, that since the prohibition against eating flesh was not lifted until after the Flood, the animals on Noah's ark would have all been vegetarian.

42. The emphasis on right relationship as a quality of the Kingdom and on relationality as central to Christian understanding of the Trinity (e.g., Johnson [1992], Schwöbel

Eternal communion with God is not another attribute of the Kingdom; it *is* the Kingdom. This is often described in the Old Testament as God's glory or light shining over all, or God's presence with his people in an intimate fashion, far beyond anything possible in this world (e.g., Isa 9:2; 30:26; 32:15; 42:16; 53:11; 60:20). From the perspective of Paul and other Christians, Christ's lordship over all things in the reign of God puts all things under subjection to God, and draws *all creation* into the loving communion between Father, Son, and Spirit. (1 Cor 15:27–28) This intimate contact with God is promised, yet mysterious; it has been described as seeing God clearly, as theosis (divinization), as becoming friends with God, and as abiding in God.

Because communion is not union, and because the fundamental reality of the universe is Trinity, eschatological union with God does not entail removal of all distinctions (LaCugna 1993: 299). Resurrected persons are in some way continuous with their earthly selves, and so each is unique. Likewise, there is no strong theological reason to suppose that nonhumans will lose their individuality. Biodiversity, therefore, is part of the eschaton, just as are cultural and social diversity. If the diversity of creation is part of its goodness, as I argued above, and God has promised to take up all that is good into the New Creation, then diversity itself is a quality of the Kingdom. The Kingdom is a realm of innumerable transformed selves, landscapes, and relationships, suffused with the light of God's presence.

At this point, some might object: Fine, God made the world with diverse species and habitats, and the Kingdom of God will include a variety of life forms, but why should that have any bearing on human life here and now? If (as you argue) God can do anything, why not let species die out until the eschaton, when God can resurrect them or create new ones? This argument ("wise-use gets eschatology") would mis-state the whole idea of Christian ethics. After all, the same logic could advocate letting the poor die off until their resurrection into new life. On the contrary, Christians are invited to feed the hungry, clothe the naked, and welcome

---

[1997], LaCugna [1993]) triggers a concern. Does it risk trivializing matter once again? For instance, does it matter if tigers get redeemed as long as we can have tiger-ish relationships with another? The response, I suspect, is that even in the eschaton, perhaps especially in the eschaton, tiger-ish relationships involve real tigers. The point of the emphasis on relationality is not to make bodies disappear, but to recognize the profoundly ecological point that bodies always already live within relationships to others.

the stranger as a witness to the Kingdom. The actions of human beings, minuscule as they seem individually, are ways to honor the goodness of this creation *and* to demonstrate the possibilities of the New Creation. According to the Gospel writers, Jesus commanded his disciples to "preach the Kingdom" wherever they went (e.g., Matt 10:7, Luke 9:2) and preaching the Kingdom entails honoring God's creations both here and in the eschaton. The New Creation fulfills the old, consummating what is already good and purifying evil. Christian discipleship witnesses God's sustaining love of this earthly life as prelude to God's glorifying love in the Kingdom.

Many Christians believe that God opposes injustice, oppression, suffering, and death. They come to this belief by reading the prophets and by following the example of Jesus Christ. So they, too, undertake resistance to these evils. Church traditions teach that God favors generosity and forgiveness, so Christians, too, strive to be generous and forgiving people. I have argued that God created the universe with biodiversity "built in," and intends the eschaton as a glorious environment of diverse inhabitants. Therefore, Christians may choose, as part of their lives and ministry, to preserve biodiversity wherever possible. This is not an environmentalist mandate wrapped in Christian garb, but a Christian imperative grounded in God's creation and salvation of the world.

How, then, can churches conserve the variety of God's creation in ways that testify to the peace, abundance, and righteousness of the eschaton? Believing communities cannot "save the earth," (any more than anyone else can) but they can exhibit, in small ways, what a "saved" earth might look like.

Creation's diversity exists at every level, from local population to global species, and because Christ reigns over people's own backyards as well as the entire universe. Christian concern for biodiversity, therefore, ought to be expressed at both the local and global levels. On the one hand, it is easy to lament the destruction of Amazonian rainforest while busily eradicating endangered species in our own locales. On the other hand, it is also easy to ignore the literally far-reaching consequences of our actions. It is helpful to envision the world as God's ecosystem, where multiple communities (of multiple species) interact and intersect. Witnessing to the diversity of God's kingdom requires attention to the needs of the local and the distant, wherever the practices of the church affect the life of the community. What follows are just a few suggestions along these lines.

Peaceful witness to the diversity of the kingdom requires, at least, a minimizing of violence toward the parish's local land, creatures, and ecosystems. The intensive use of pesticides and herbicides causes undeniable long-term damage to ecosystems and their diverse populations. And the eradication of forests leads to global warming, hotter micro-climates, unbalanced local ecosystems, and threats to plant and animal species. Therefore, rather than aiming for the "green" lawns of English country estates (which were deliberate indicators of wealth and earthly dominance), churches should aim for "green" practices of fostering native plant habitats, organic fertilizers (if required), wildlife feeding stations where appropriate, minimal use of non-native plant species, and the most gentle "development" of church property-mulch paths rather than sidewalks, gravel screen rather than paved parking, trees and underbrush uncut. In this way the church can physically present a (partial and imperfect) sign of the eschaton, where species live as neighbors rather than enemies.

Peaceful witness also requires the minimization of animal death at the hands of the church.[43] Aside from the theological arguments about vegetarianism, there are good reasons for churches to reduce their consumption of meat. Large corporate pork farms cause immense destruction to local ecosystems, largely through the spread of hog waste in streams and rivers. Moreover, the world's appetite for beef is a significant factor in the deforestation of Amazonian rainforest and the degradation of land in the American west. Without sufficient forest protection in countries such as Brazil, the tropical trees are cut down to make way for beef cattle. Churches can testify against these harmful practices of meat production by offering vegetarian meals rather than barbecues or "pig pickings." If meat is served, it can be obtained from local organic sources instead of distant factory farms, so the church is not supporting food production systems that reduce biodiversity, as well as create widespread animal misery and suffering.[44]

---

43. For an excellent historical analysis of meat-eating and vegetarianism, see Adams (2000). For good Christian arguments on vegetarianism, also see Linzey (1994).

44. Vegetarianism is not the focus of my work here. However, Carol Adams makes an excellent point about modern methods of meat production. She writes, "we come to see that a piece of 'meat' turns the miracles of the loaves and fishes on its head. Where Jesus multiplied food to feed the hungry, our current food-producing system reduces food sources and damages the environment at the same time, producing plant food to feed terminal animals" (2000: 156). In effect, factory farming creates scarcity where abundance formerly occurred.

In terms of affecting biodiversity at the local level, parishes should attend to the endangered plants and animals of their own regions. Most people are unaware of endangered creatures in their own communities, except for extremely well-known or charismatic examples (such as the Ivory-billed Woodpecker or Florida Panther). Part of a church's eco-discipleship might be to include at-risk habitats and species in its corporate prayers, in its outreach efforts, and as part of its education programs. Children already learn the story of Noah's protection of the animals on the ark; they can also learn what nonhuman neighbors need their protection today.

Clearly, these steps toward peaceful conservation of biodiversity are only the beginning. Yet already, the churches' "green discipleship" displays its eschatological character: in adopting these conservation practices, Christians demonstrate an alternative way of life in Christ-the way of life of the eschaton. Creation in its essence is eschatological, because it is Trinitarian in origin and destiny. The "difference in communion" that is the Christian God, on this view, carries through the universe as it is created, sustained, and redeemed by God. In proclaiming the hopeful message about the Kingdom, parishes can witness to the biodiversity that is part of the promised life to come. It is important, therefore, to protect the biodiversity that is given to earthly life now, before the hoped-for final consummation in Christ.

Response

Biodiversity and the Ministry of Reconciliation

FRED VAN DYKE

TWENTY YEARS AGO *BIOSCIENCE* ran a debate between Norman Levine, Professor Emeritus at the College of Veterinary Medicine, University of Illinois, and noted conservationist Norman Myers. Their exchange, entitled "Evolution and Extinction," was a clash of secular eschatologies. Levine's view was this: "Some nature lovers weep at this passing [of recently exterminated creatures] and collect money to save species. They make lists of animals and plants that are in danger of extinction and sponsor legislation to save them. I don't. What the species preservers are trying to do is to stop the clock. It cannot and should not be done. Extinction is an inevitable fact of evolution, and it is needed for progress. New species continually arise, and they are better adapted to their environment than those that have died out ... Evolution exists, and it goes on continually. People are here because of it, but people may be replaced someday. It is neither possible nor desirable to stop it, and that is what we are doing when we try to preserve species on their way out" (Levine 1989: 38).

Levine's conclusion is logical if you accept his premises. Interestingly, that is just what Myers did, arguing that humans should not "impoverish" or "unbalance" the evolutionary process by causing too many extinctions. Besides that, Myers notes, almost as afterthought, these rare species may be valuable to us someday. "An endangered species of evening primrose ..." wrote Myers, "offers materials with potential to counter eczema, coronary heart disease, multiple sclerosis, schizophrenia, and possibly even alcoholic hangovers" (Myers 1989: 40). Is that why I and thousands of others have engaged our lives, our careers, and our fortunes in the conservation enterprise, so that we can enjoy the abuse of alcohol on Saturday night and not suffer the consequences on Sunday morning, because we saved the right species of primrose?

In my judgment, Levine won this debate hands down, not because his argument is valid, but because Myers choose to play according to his rules. Myers accepted Levine's eschatological vision, a future without redemption, hope, or meaning, a future in which there is no purpose but survival.

Myer's failure in this exchange serves as a snapshot of the same failure that plagues the conservation community today. It is an ethical failure. Biodiversity conservation is a celebration of nature's individuality. But if the start of every evolutionary lineage is speciation, then the end of every lineage is extinction. We cannot praise the first and condemn the second and appear, to an onlooking public, as people who know what we are talking about.

Laura Yordy's, "Biodiversity and the Kingdom of God," offers a biblically accurate and ethically insightful Christian response to one of the most fundamental questions of environmental ethics. Namely, what is the ultimate end of nature? Yordy, unlike Myers, provides a meaningful answer. Nature, and all its non-human citizens, have a future in the kingdom of God. Speaking of Christ to the Christians as Colossae, Paul explained the basis for this hope:

> He is the image of the invisible God, the firstborn of all creation. For by him all things were created, in the heavens and on earth, visible and invisible, whether thrones or dominions or rulers or authorities - all things have been created through him and for him. He is before all things, and in him all things hold together. He is also head of the body, the Church; and he is the beginning, the firstborn from the dead, so that he himself will come to have first place in everything. For it was the Father's good pleasure for all the fullness to dwell in him, and through him to reconcile all things to himself, having made peace through the blood of his cross; through him, I say, whether things on earth or things in heaven. (Col 1:15–20)

The cosmic nature and consequences of Christ's lordship are common themes of Paul's epistles.[1] What this passage of scripture makes more explicit is that the reconciliation and redemption achieved through the

---

1. Rom 5:12–21; Rom 8:19–23; 1 Cor 8:6; Eph 1:18–23; Phil 2:6–11.

death and resurrection of Christ affect every created thing, in other words, all creatures, not merely human kind. The recurring Greek phrase *ta panta*, translated in English as "all things," remains the same throughout the doxology. Thus, Paul asserts, first, that Jesus Christ created *ta panta* (Col 1:16). Second, Jesus Christ sustains *ta panta* (or, in more literal Greek, 'in him all things consisted') (Col 1:17). Third, the *ta panta* that Jesus created and sustains are the same *ta panta* that he reconciles "through the blood of his cross" (Col 1:20).

Christians, particularly those of an evangelical stripe, have shown an historic tendency to separate the doctrines of creation and redemption. In his review of twenty books on evangelical theology published between 1970 and 2000, theologian John Davis noted that nearly all treated the doctrine of creation as primarily a discussion of *creation and evolution*, and treated the doctrine of redemption primarily as the doctrine of *personal substitution* through which Christ atones for the sins of individual persons (Davis 2000). In contrast to this dichotomous and hyper-individualistic theological perspective, Paul links the doctrines of creation and redemption by making Christ the agent of both. While evangelical theology has long tended to describe the effects of the atonement in personal terms that achieve reconciliation between God and human beings, Paul describes the atonement's effects in cosmic terms that achieve reconciliation between God and the entire created order. Paul thus makes the atonement more than a personal sacrifice for human beings. He elevates it to the means through which Christ redeems the cosmos.

Throughout the Old Testament, non-human and human creatures are explicitly linked in fall and consequent judgment, creating a common need of redemption for both. "Cursed is the ground because of you," God declares to Adam. "In toil you shall eat of it all the days of your life."[2] Non-human creation not only becomes a means through which God expresses his judgments against human sin (Joel 1:4), but is itself a victim of that sin and suffering from the consequences of it. That is why Paul declares, in his letter to the church at Rome, that "the anxious longing of creation waits eagerly for the for the revealing of the sons of God. For the creation was subjected to futility, not willingly, but because of him who subjected it, in hope that the creation itself will be set free from its slavery to corruption into the freedom of the glory of the children of God" (Rom 8:19–21). It

---

2. Gen 3:17.

is because of the New Testament doctrine of creation's inclusion in the redemptive purpose of God that we know that the vision of Isaiah 11 is, indeed, just as Yordy asserted, not a metaphor, but a description of relationships in the kingdom of God.

THE RESPONSE OF THE CHRISTIAN COMMUNITY TO BIODIVERSITY CONSERVATION

Aldo Leopold, speaking of the content of conservation education some fifty years ago, wrote, " . . . the content is substantially this: obey the law, vote right, join some organizations, and practice what conservation is profitable on your own land: the government will do the rest. Is not this formula too easy to accomplish anything worthwhile? It defines no right or wrong, assigns no obligation, calls for no sacrifice, implies no change in the current philosophy of values. In respect of land-use it urges only enlightened self-interest" (Leopold 1966: 243). From this state of affairs, Leopold moved to this oft-quoted conclusion. "No important change in ethics was ever accomplished without an internal change in our intellectual emphasis, loyalties, affections, and convictions. The proof that conservation has not yet touched these foundations of conduct lies in the fact that philosophy and religion have not yet heard of it. In our attempt to make conservation easy, we have made it trivial" (246).

In these words, Leopold reveals something of his own eschatology. He betrays a hope, albeit sarcastically expressed, that perhaps one day religion and philosophy will hear of conservation and will make its acquaintance, and, in doing so, conservation will be elevated from being little more than "enlightened self-interest" to become an intrinsic, life-changing perspective grounded in the most fundamental things we know about wisdom, truth, and God. Yordy is in a position to make this transformation at the end of her essay. Regrettably, she seems to shrink back from it, and instead offers advice about the appropriateness of serving coffee and meat at church fellowships meals. One is left with the impression that the Christian community has nothing to offer conservationists except an enthusiastic "Amen!" when it comes to actually protecting biodiversity. What then is the content of Christian conservation?

This oversight recalls Myers's response to Levine. Yordy does not challenge the conservation community's eschatology, as if that vision and the current efforts it inspires were untainted by human sinfulness and rebellion against God. It is not. Much of the modern conservation effort is ineffective because it is tragically amiss in moral understanding. If that effort is going to succeed, it will do so only if Christian theologians and the Church help set the broken ethical bone right in both theory and practice, not by applauding how well conservation is running the race in spite of its obvious moral limp. Kyle Van Houtan has said as much in the pages of *Conservation Biology*: "To succeed as a social cause, conservation needs a hope that academic science itself cannot provide. Conservation needs a cultural legitimacy that inspires enthusiasm, allegiance, and personal sacrifice—in other words, actual changes in human behavior" (2006).

So, why can't the conservation community inspire the general public to the kind of enthusiasm, allegiance, and personal sacrifice needed to save biodiversity? To paraphrase that famous Clinton campaign slogan, "It's the eschatology, stupid!" If natural selection ends in extinction, including our own, why not sooner than later? In the eschatology of evolution, nothing endures and there is no particular significance to the world's present array of biodiversity. Given this view, it is no wonder that the public is as unmoved by conservation's successes as by its failures. In the end all efforts will fail. "The race is not to the swift, or the battle to the strong, nor does food come to the wise . . . but time and chance overtake them all" (Eccl 9:11).

I am a conservation biologist and I do not think that most of my colleagues really view nature or biodiversity as Norman Levine does. But they do not believe Norman Myers either. We don't want to save species just to keep the evolutionary process running. And we don't want to save beautiful plants because they might provide a cure for hangovers or Hodgkins' disease or eczema someday. We want to save species because we love them now. The more we study their lives, the more we stand in rapt and wondrous awe at the marvel of what they are, for each one is the outcome of a series of the most improbable events, "threading the needle," as E. O. Wilson put it, of survival and adaptation against a hostile, changing world. Thus, every species is a celebration of its own existence, a triumph, if only temporarily, over competition death. And the lives of all this myriad of non-human creatures (that we refer to collectively with inexcusable verbal sterility as "biodiversity") fill the world with the joy and gladness of their collective lives, if only we take the time to study and share that joy with them.

But just as we are touched by the joys of their existence, the sadness and sorrow of our fellow creatures touch us also, when we understand what such sadness and sorrows are. And the thought of their loss from this world is the greatest sorrow of all. The present situation looks bleak. The future looks even more so. But our affection for these non-human species of birds and fish and plants and fungi, our identification with them as part of the family of life, is so great we can do nothing but carry on the fight. Despite the hopeless odds and deteriorating conditions for many of the world's species, we view the world much as the British essayist G. K. Chesterton described it, as ". . . not a lodging house at Brighton, which we are to leave because it is miserable. It is the fortress of our family, with the flag flying on the turret, and the more miserable it is, the less we should leave it. The point is not that this world is too sad to love or too glad not to love: the point is that when you do love a thing, its gladness is a reason for loving it, and its sadness a reason for loving it more" (Chesterton 1995: 72).

One of most striking developments in biodiversity conservation in the last ten years has been the rise of the faith-based conservation organization. Such "FBOs" are arising in all major religions and denominations, none more so than Christianity. Perhaps the best example is A Rocha, an organization of Christians in conservation currently engaged in cooperative efforts to save dozens of species of plants and animals on five continents through its national chapter organizations now active in eighteen countries. A Rocha and other Christian environmental FBOs share a concomitant tendency to employ a "bottom-up" approach to conservation in which ultimate responsibility for conservation practice is placed in the hands of local residents who will directly benefit, or suffer, from the consequences of their decisions. Such faith-based conservation organizations often succeed where traditional conservation organizations fail because they empower communities to protect and benefit from their own local biodiversity, and, in the process, design regulations suited to local needs and conditions (Abuyan 2006). Christian FBOs take this approach because they see a future of reconciliation for human and non-human creation in the coming Kingdom of God, not a series of "preserves" from which human presence must be forever excluded.

This pattern of engagement is consistent with a worldview that perceives the problem to be solved as one of relational reconciliation, not the technical application of improved conservation tactics. The role and contribution of local churches, then, is not merely to provide an environmentally sensitive menu at the potluck or to reduce the use of pesticides on the church lawn, or perhaps even to use better light bulbs, but to enable Christians engaged in conservation to understand and discover the full implicational force of their own transforming eschatology. Ironically, it is this vision of a future reconciliation that infuses conservation effort with a sense of present hope. In the words of Simon Stuart, Senior Advisor on Biodiversity Assessment for the IUCN Species Survival Commission, and other Christian conservationists in a recent contribution to *Conservation Biology*, ". . . Christians are committed by their biblical beliefs not only to the conviction that God himself cares for his universe in a daily and ongoing way but also that he helps and guides people in their conservation efforts. We are therefore not on our own against the relentless forces of unsustainable development and rapacious materialism. Every time we celebrate a conservation success story such as the recovery of the white rhinoceros in southern Africa, we are strengthened in this present hope that God is working with us to redeem his creation" (Stuart et al. 2005). It is precisely this message of hope based on a Christian eschatology of the reconciliation of the entire created order to God, that represents a unique contribution, and vital perspective, to the current conservation effort.

Bibliography

(1970). "Fulfilling God's Cultural Mandate." *Christianity Today* 16.24:25.
(1971). "Ecology, the Anti-Christian." *Christian Beacon* 36.19:1–2.
Abbey, E. (1985). *Desert Solitaire*. New York: Ballantine.
Abraham, D. (1997). *The Spell of the Sensuous: Perception and Language in a More-Than-Human-World*. New York: Vintage.
Abuyan, A. T. (2006). "Faith Based Organizations, International Development Agencies, and Environmental Management." PhD diss., University of Southern California.
Achterhuis, H. (1995). "Scarcity and Sustainability." *Global Ecology: A New Arena of Political Conflict*. W. Sachs. London: Zed.
Adams, C. J. (2000). *The Sexual Politics of Meat: A Feminist-Vegetarian Critical Theory*. New York: Continuum.
Aischliman, G. (1994). "Somebody Got Shot in the Head." *Prism* (December, January): 7.
Alvarado, R. C. (1986). "Environmentalism and Christianity's Ethic of Dominion." *Journal of Christian Reconstruction* 11:201–15.
Arendt, H. (1958). *The Human Condition*. Chicago: University of Chicago Press.
Aristotle (2004). *Physics*. Whitefish, MT: Kessinger.
Arneil, B. (1996). *John Locke and America: The Defence of English Colonialism*. Oxford: Clarendon.
Arnold, B. T. (2004). "Vegetarians in Paradise." *Christianity Today* 48.10:104.
Arnold, R. and A. Gottleib (1994). *Trashing the Economy: How Runaway Environmentalism Is Wrecking America*. Washington, DC: Free Enterprise.
Athanasius (1971). *Contra Gentes and De incarnatione*. Oxford: Clarendon.
Attfield, R. (2000). "Evolution, theodicy, and Value." *Heythrop Journal* 41.3:281–96.
Augustine (1958). *City of God*. New York: Doubleday.
Bader-Saye, S. C. (1997). "Aristotle or Abraham: Church, Israel, and the Politics of Election." PhD diss. Durham, NC: Duke University Press.
Barbour, I. (1997). *Religion and Science: Historical and Contemporary Issues*. San Francisco: HarperCollins.
Barth, K. (1981). *Church Dogmatics, IV/4*. Grand Rapids: Eerdmans.
———. (2003). *Church Dogmatics, III/1*. London: T. & T. Clark.
Baruffa, A. (2000). *The Catacombs of St. Callixtus: History, Archeology, Faith*. Vatican City: Liberia Editrice Vaticana.
Basil the Great (1980). *On the Holy Spirit*. Crestwood, NY: St. Vladimir's Seminary Press.
Bate, J. (2000). *The Song of the Earth*. Cambridge: Harvard University Press.

Bibliography

Bauckham, R. (1998). "Jesus and the Animals II: What Did He Practise?" In *Animals on the Agenda: Questions about Animals for theology and Ethics*, edited by A. Linzey and D. Yamamoto, 49–60. Urbana: University of Illinois Press.

Bauman, Z. (1998). *Globalization: The Human Consequences*. New York: Columbia University Press.

———. (2000). *Liquid Modernity*. Cambridge: Polity.

Beacham, R. C. (1999). *Spectacle Entertainments of Early Imperial Rome*. New Haven: Yale University Press.

Beisner, E. C., M. Cromartie, et al. (2000). "A Biblical Perspective On Environmental Stewardship." In *Environmental Stewardship in the Judeo-Christian Tradition: Jewish, Catholic, and Protestant Wisdom On the Environment*, edited by M. B. Barkey. Grand Rapids: Acton Institute For Religious Liberty.

Belise, M., and S. Mcdowell (1989). *America's Providential History (Including Biblical Principles of Education, Government, Politics, Economics, and Family Life)*. Charlottesville, VA: Providence Foundation.

Bennet, T., L. Grossberg, et al. (2005). *New Key-Words: A Revised Vocabulary of Culture and Society*. Oxford: Blackwell.

Bernall, M. (1999). *She Said "Yes."* Rifton, NY: Plough.

Berry, R. J., Ed. (2000). *The Care of Creation: Focusing Concern and Action*. Leicester, UK: InterVarsity.

Berry, W. (1969). *The Long-Legged House*. New York: Harcourt Brace.

———. (1983). *The Unsettling of America*. San Francisco: Sierra Club.

———. (1993). *Sex, Economy, Freedom, and Community: Eight Essays*. New York: Pantheon.

———. (2002). "The Idea of a Local Economy." In *The Art of Commonplace: The Agrarian Essays of Wendell Berry*, edited by N. Wirzba, 249–61. Washington, DC: Counterpoint.

———. (2003). *Citizenship Papers*. Washington, DC: Shoemaker & Hoard.

Best, S., and D. Kellner (1997). *The Postmodern Turn*. New York: Guilford.

Birch, C. (1990). "Christian Obligation For the Liberation of Nature." In *Liberating Life: Contemporary Approaches To Ecological Theology*, edited by C. Birch, W. Eakin, and J. B. McDaniel. Maryknoll, NY: Orbis.

Bisconti, F. (2002). "The Decorations of Roman Catacombs." In *The Christian Catacombs of Rome: History, Decoration, Inscriptions*, edited by V. F. Nicolai and F. Bisconti, 71–145. Regensburg, Germany: Schnell & Steiner.

Blake, W. (1991). *Everlasting Gospel & Other Poems*. Santa Barbara: Bandanna.

Boddy, J. (1989). *Wombs and Alien Spirits: Women, Men, and the Zar Cult in Northen Sudan*. Madison: University of Wisconsin Press.

Bonting, S. L. (2006). "Spirit in Creation." *Zygon* 46:713–26.

Botkin, D. (1990). *Discordant Harmonies: a New Ecology For the 21st Century*. New York: Oxford University Press.

Bouma-Prediger, S. (2001). *For the Beauty of the Earth: A Christian Vision for Creation Care*. Grand Rapids: Baker.

Bourdieu, P. (2000). *Pascalian Meditations*. Translated by Richard Nice. Cambridge: Polity.

Bratton, S. P. (2007). *Environmental Values in Christian Art*. Albany: State University of New York Press.

Bibliography

Brueggemann, W. (1977). *The Land: Place As Gift, Promise, and Challenge in Biblical Faith.* Philadelphia: Fortress.

———. (1982). *Genesis.* Interpretation: A Bible Commentary For Teaching and Preaching. Louisville: Westminster John Knox.

———. (1998). *Isaiah.* Westminster Bible Companion. Louisville: Westminster John Knox.

Buechner, F. (2006). *Secrets in the Dark: A Life in Sermons.* New York: HarperSanFrancisco.

Burke, W. K. (1993). "The Wise Use Movement: Right Wing Anti-Environmentalism." *The Public Eye* 7.2 (June).

Bush, G. H. W. (1991). "Remarks at the Dedication Ceremony of the Mount Rushmore National Memorial in South Dakota." July 3, 1991.

Bush, L. R. (1992). "Humanistic and New Age Ideas and Ecological Issues." In *The Earth Is the Lord's*, edited by R. D. Land and L. A. Moore, 55–67. Nashville: Broadman & Holman.

Bush, V. (1945). *Science, the Endless Frontier.* Washington, DC: U.S. Government Printing Office.

Calame-Griaule, G. (1965). *Ethnologie Et Language: La Parole Chez Les Dogon.* Paris: Gallimard.

Calvin, J. (1963). *Calvin's Commentaries On the Book of Genesis.* Translated and edited by John King et al. Grand Rapids: Eerdmans.

Carletti, S. (2000). *Guide to the Catacombs of Priscilla.* Vatican City: Pontifical Commission For Sacred Archeology.

Chapman, M. (1992). "Salt and Light in Our World." In *The Earth Is the Lord's*, edited by R. D. Land. Nashville: Broadman & Holman.

Charlesworth, J. H. (1985). *The Old Testament Pseudepigrapha,* Vol 2. New York: Doubleday.

Chesterton, G. K. (1995). *Orthodoxy.* San Francisco: Ignatius.

Childs, B. S. (2007). *Isaiah.* Louisville: Westminster John Knox.

Chitty, D. (1966). *The Desert, a City.* Crestwood, NY: St. Vladimir's Seminary Press.

Christensen, N., J. K. Agee, et al. (1989). "Interpreting the Yellowstone Fires of 1988." *Bioscience* 39:678–85.

Cissé, Y. (1973). "Signes, Graphiques, Representations, Concepts, et Tests Relatifs a la Personne Chez les Malinke et les Bambara Du Mali." In *La Notion De Personne En Afrique Noire*, edited by Germaine Dieterlen. Paris: Éditions du Centre national de la recherche scientifique.

Coates, P. (1998). *Nature: Western Attitudes Since Ancient Times.* Berkeley: University of California Press.

Collingwood, R. G. (1944). *The Idea of Nature.* Westport, CT: Greenwood.

Collins, C. (1990). "Break the Chains of Debt: International Jubliee 2000 Campaign Demands Deeper Debt Relief." *Africa Recovery.* New York: United Nations.

Constanza, R., R. d'Arge, et al. (1997). "The Value of the World's Ecosystem Services and Natural Capital." *Nature* 387:253–60.

Conyers, A. J. (2002). "Living Under Vacant Skies." *Heaven and Hell.* Waco, TX: Baylor University.

Csikszentmihalyi, M. (1990). *Flow: The Psychology of Optimal Experience.* New York: Harper & Row.

Bibliography

Cunningham, D. (1998). *These Three Are One: the Practice of Trinitarian Theology*. Oxford: Blackwell.

Daily, G. C. (1997). *Nature's Services: Societal Dependence On Natural Systems*. Washington, DC: Island.

Darwin, C. (1958). *Autobiography of Charles Darwin*. New York: Norton.

———. (1987). *The Origin of Species*. London: Penguin.

Davis, J. J. (2000). "Ecological Blind Spots in the Structure and Content of Recent Evangelical Systematic Theologies." *Journal of the Evangelical Theological Society* 43:273–86.

Deweese, T. (2003). "Green Invasion of Church Intensifies." *Deweese Report* 4(10).

Dewitt, C. (1998). *Caring For Creation: Responsible Stewardship of God's Handiwork*. Grand Rapids: Baker.

Dewitt, C. (2000). "*Creation's Environmental Challenge to Evangelical Christianity*." In *The Care of Creation: Focusing Concern and Action*, edited by R. J. Berry. Leicester, UK: InterVarsity.

Dewitt, C. B. (1991). *The Environment and the Christian: What Does the New Testament Say About the Environment?* Grand Rapids: Baker.

Diamond, J. (2005). *Collapse: How Societies Choose to Fail or Succeed*. New York: Viking.

Diamond, S. (1995). "Dominion Theology." *Zmagazine* (February).

Dillard, A. (1974). *Pilgrim at Tinker Creek*. New York: Harper & Row.

Dunlap, R. E. (1994). International Attitudes To Environment and Development. In *Green Globe Yearbook of International Co-Operation On Environment and Development 1994*, edited by O. Bergesen and G. Parmann. Oxford: Oxford University Press.

Dunlap, R. E., G. H. Gallup, et al. (1992). *The Health of the Planet Survey: A Preliminary Report On Attitudes To the Environment and Economic Growth By Surveys of Citizens in 22 Nations*. Princeton: Gallup International Institute.

Edwards, D. (2006). *Ecology at the Heart of Faith: The Change of Heart That Leads to a New Way of Living on Earth*. Maryknoll, NY: Orbis.

Eichrodt, W. (1984). "In the Beginning: A Contribution to the Interpretation of the First Word of the Bible." In *Creation in the Old Testament*, edited by B. W. Anderson. London: SPCK.

Eleazar, D. J. (1984). *American Federalism: A View From the States*. New York: Harper & Row.

Ellul, J. (1964). *The Technological Society*. Translated by J. Wilkinson. New York: Vintage.

———. (1986). *The Subversion of Christianity*. Translated by G. W. Bromiley. Grand Rapids: Eerdmans.

Emerson, R. W. (1995). *Essays and Poems*. London: J. M. Dent.

———. (2003). *Selected Writings*. New York: Signet.

Evans, J. H. (1992). *We Have Been Believers: An African-American Systematic Theology*. Minneapolis: Fortress.

Falwell, J. (1980). *Listen, America!* Garden City, NY: Doubleday.

Fasola, U. M. (2002). *The Catacombs of Domitilla and the Basilica of the Martyrs Nereus and Achilleus*. Vatican City: Pontifical Commission On Sacred Architecture.

Fern, R. (2002). *Nature, God, and Humanity: Envisioning an Ethics of Nature*. Cambridge: Cambridge University Press.

Fitzsimmons, A. (2000). "Ecological Confusion Among the Clergy." *Journal of Markets & Morality* 3:2.

Fleming, D. (1961). "Charles Darwin, the Anaesthetic Man." *Victorian Studies* 4:219–36.

Bibliography

Fluckinger, J., E. Monnin, et al. (2002). "High-Resolution Holocene N_2O Ice Core Record and Its Relationship With CH^4 and CO^2." *Global Biogeochemical Cycles* 16.
Franzen, A. (2003). "Attitudes in International Comparison: An Analysis of the ISSP Surveys 1993 and 2000." *Social Science Quartlery* 84:2:297–308.
Fretheim, T. E. (1991). *Exodus*. Interpretation. Louisville: Westminster John Knox.
Freud, S. (1961). *Civilization and Its Discontents*. New York: Norton.
Friesen, W. (1992). "What Are We Fighting For?" *Direction* 21:2:48.
Fujimura, M. (2004). Columbine Dream. New York: 60.2cmx72.6cm. Mineral Pigments, Gold, Oyster Shell White On Kumohada.
Galloway, A. D. (1951). *Cosmic Christ*. New York: Harper.
Giddens, A. (1987). *The Nation State and Violence*. Cambridge: Polity.
———. (1990). *The Consequences of Modernity*. Palo Alto: Stanford University Press.
Goostein, L. (2005). "Evangelical Leaders Swing Influence behind Effort to Combat Global Warming." *New York Times*, March 10.
Granberg-Michaelson, W. (1987). *Tending the Garden: Essays on the Gospel and the Earth*. Grand Rapids: Eerdmans.
Greeley, A. M., and M. Hout (2006). *The Truth about Conservative Christians: What They Think and What They Believe*. Chicago: University of Chicago Press.
Gregorios, P. M. (1991). "Nature." In *Dictionary of the Ecumenical Movement*. Edited by N. Lossky, 715–18. Geneva: World Council of Churches.
Griffiths, P. (2004). *Lying: An Augustinian Theology of Duplicity*. Grand Rapids: Brazos.
Gunton, C. (1993). *The One, the Three and the Many: God, Creation, and the Culture of Modernity*. Cambridge: Cambridge University Press.
Haas, G. (2001). "The Significance of Eschatology For Christian Ethics." In *Looking into the Future: Evangelical Studies in Eschatology*, edited by D. W. Baker. ETS Studies. Grand Rapids: Baker Academic.
Hall, D. J. (1986). *Imaging God: Dominion As Stewardship*. Grand Rapids: Eerdmans.
Halweil, B. (2004). *Eat Here: Homegrown Pleasures in a Global Supermarket*. New York: Norton.
Hansen, R. (2008). *Exiles: A Novel*. New York: Farrar, Strauss & Giroux.
Harris, P. (2000). *Under the Bright Wings*. Vancouver, Canada: Regent College Publishing.
———. *Kingisher's Fire*. Oxford: Monarch.
Harvey, D. (1990). *The Condition of Postmodernity*. Cambridge, Blackwell.
Hauerwas, S. (1999). *Prayers Plainly Spoken*. Downers Grove, IL: InterVarsity.
———. (2001b). "A Story-Formed Community: Reflections on *Watership Down*." In *The Hauerwas Reader*, edited by J. Berkman and M. Cartwright, 171–99. Durham: Duke University Press.
———. (2001a). "Why Truthfulness Requires Forgiveness: a Commencement Address For the Graduates of a College of the Church of the Second Chance." In *The Hauerwas Reader*, edited by J. Berkman and M. Cartwright, 307–17. Durham: Duke University Press.
Hiebert, T. (1996). *The Yahwist's Landscape*. New York: Oxford University Press.
Hillary, E. (1975). *Nothing Venture, Nothing Win*. New York: Coward, Mccann, & Geoghegan.
Hillel, D. (1991). *Out of the Earth: Civilization and the Life of Soil*. London: Arum.
Hindle, M. (1992). *Introduction to Frankenstein, By Mary Shelley*. Harmondsworth, UK: Penguin.

Bibliography

Hooker, R. (1977). "Sermon On Pride." In *The Folger Library Edition of the Works of Richard Hooker, Vol. V*, edited by W. S. Hill. Cambridge: Harvard University Press.

Hopkins, G. M. (1917). "God's Grandeur." In *The Oxford Book of English Mystical Verse*, edited by D. H. S. Nicholson and A. H. E. Lee. Oxford: Oxford University Press.

Horkheimer, M., and T. Adorno (1972). *Dialectic of Enlightenment*. New York: Herder & Herder.

Houston, J. (1972). "The Environmental Movement: Five Causes of Confusion." *Christianity Today* 16:24:8–10.

Howard, A. (2006). *The Soil and Health: A Study of Organic Agriculture*. Lexington: University Press of Kentucky.

Irenaeus (2004). *Against Heresies, Book V*. Whitefish, MT: Kessinger.

IUCN (2007). *The IUCN Red List of Threatened Species*. Gland, Switzerland: International Union For the Conservation of Nature and Natural Resources.

Jackson, M. (2007). "A Walk on the Wild Side: The Idea of Nature Revisited." In *Excursions*, 135–53. Durham: Duke University Press.

Jaspers, K. (1955). *Reason and Existenz: Five Lectures*. Translated by W. Earle. New York: Noonday.

Jenson, R. M. (2000). *Understanding Early Christian Art*. London: Routledge.

Johnson, E. A. (1992). *She Who Is: The Mystery of God in Feminist Theological Discourse*. New York: Crossroad.

Johnson, E. A. (1993). *Women, Earth, and Creator Spirit*. Madeleva Lecture in Spirituality. Mahwah, NJ: Paulist.

Jones, B. F. (2007). *Marks of His Wounds: Gender Politics and Bodily Resurrection*. New York: Oxford University Press.

Karanth, K. K. (2007). "Making Resettlement Work: the Case of India's Bhadra Wildlife Sanctuary." *Biological Conservation* 139:3–4:315–24.

Karras, V. A. (2002). "Eschatology." In *The Cambridge Guide To Feminist Theology*, edited by S. F. Parsons. Cambridge UK: Cambridge University Press.

Kennedy, R. F. (2004). *Crimes against Nature*. New York: Random House.

Kessler, H. L. (2007). "The Word Made Flesh in Early Decorated Bibles." In *Picturing the Bible: The Earliest Christian Art*, edited by J. Spier, 140–68. New Haven: Yale University Press.

Kingsolver, B. (2007). *Animal, Vegetable, Miracle: A Year of Food Life*. New York: Harper Collins.

Klein, D. R. (1968). "The Introduction, Increase, and Crash of Reindeer On St. Matthew Island." *Journal of Wildlife Management* 32:350–67.

Knord, D. P. (1998). "Benevolent Capital: Financing Evangelical Book Publishing in Early Nineteenth-Century America." In *God and Mammon: Protestants, Money, and the Market 1790–1860*, edited by M. Noll, 147–70. New York: Oxford University Press.

Kyle, D. (2001). *Spectacles of Death in Ancient Rome*. London: Routledge.

Kyung, C. H. (1994). "Ecology, Feminism, and African and Asian Sprituality: Towards a Spirituality of Eco-Feminism." In *Ecotheology: Voices From South and North*, edited by D. G. Hallman. Maryknoll, NY: Orbis.

Lacugna, C. M. (1993). *God for Us: The Trinity and the Christian Life*. New York: HarperOne.

Land, R. D. (1992). "Overview: Beliefs and Behaviors." In *The Earth Is the Lord's: Christians and the Environment*, edited by R. D. Land and L. A. Moore. Nashville: Broadman & Holman.

Bibliography

Land, W. G. (1936). *Harvard University Handbook.* Cambridge: Harvard University Press.
Larsen, D. K. (2001). "God's Gardeners: Christian Stewardship of Natural Resources 1967–2000." PhD diss., University of Chicago.
Leazer, G. (1992). "The New Age Movement and the Environment." In *The Earth Is the Lord's*, edited by R. D. Land. Nashville: Broadman Holman: 107.
Leonhardt, D., J. Mouawad, et al. (2005). "To Conserve Gas, President Calls For Less Driving." *The New York Times.*
Leopold, A. (1966). *A Sand County Almanac.* New York: Ballantine.
Leopold, A. (1987). "Foreword." In *Companion To a Sand County Almanac: Interpretive and Critical Essays*, edited by J. B. Callicott. Madison: University of Wisconsin Press.
Levine, N. D. (1989). "Evolution and Extinction." *Bioscience* 39:38.
Lewis, C. S. (1954). *English Literature in the Sixteenth Century, Excluding Drama.* Oxford: Oxford University Press.
Lind, M. (2004). "Did Jesus Wear Birkenstocks?" *New York Press*, December 17.
Linden, E. (1999). *The Parrot's Lament: And Other True Tales of Animal Intrigue, Intelligence, and Ingenuity.* New York: Dutton.
Linzey, A. (1995). *Animal Theology.* Urbana: University of Illinois Press.
Logan, W. B. (1995). *Dirt: The Ecstatic Skin of the Earth.* New York: Riverhead.
Long, K. T. (2001). "Turning . . . Piety in to Hard Cash: The Marketing of Nineteenth-Century Revivalism." In *God and Mammon: Protestants, Money, and the Market 1790–1860*, edited by M. Noll, 236–64. New York: Oxford University Press.
Louth, A. (1990). *Discerning the Mystery: An Essay on the Nature of Theology.* New York: Oxford University Press.
Malinowski, B. (1922). *The Argonauts of the Western Pacific.* London: Routledge and Kegan Paul.
Mancenelli, F. (1981). *The Catacombs of Rome and the Origins of Christianity.* Florence, Italy: Scala.
Marcuse, H. (1966). *Eros and Civilization: A Philosophical Inquiry into Freud.* Humanitas. Boston: Beacon.
Marvin, C., and D. W. Ingle (1996). "Blood Sacrifice and the Nation: Revisiting Civil Religion." *Journal of the American Academy of Religion* 64:4:767–80.
Matthews, T. F. (1999). *The Clash of the Gods.* Princeton: Princeton University Press.
Mays, J. L. (1994). *Psalms.* Interpretation. Louisville: Westminster John Knox.
McDaniel, J. (1989). *Of God and Pelicans: A theology of Reverence For Life.* Louisville: Westminster John Knox.
McFadyen, A. I. (2000). *Bound to Sin: Abuse, Holocaust, and the Christian Doctrine of Sin.* Cambridge: Cambridge University Press.
McFague, S. (1987). *Models of God: Theology for an Ecological, Nuclear Age.* Minneapolis: Fortress.
———. (1997). *Super, Natural Christians: How We Should Love Nature.* Minneapolis: Augsburg Fortress.
———. (2001). "New House Rules: Christianity, Economics, and Planetary Living." *Daedalus* 130:124–40.
Meggit, M. (1964). "Male-Female Relationships in the Highlands of Australian New Guinea." *American Anthropologist* 66. 4:204–24.
Merchant, C. (1989). *Ecological Revolutions: Nature, Gender, and Science in New England.* Chapel Hill: University of North Carolina Press.

Bibliography

Meyer, J. M. (1997). "Gifford Pinchot, John Muir and the Boundaries of Politics in American Thought." *Polity* 30.
Miller, P. D. (1990). *Deuteronomy*. Interpretation. Louisville: Westminster John Knox.
Moltmann, J. (1981). *The Trinity and the Kingdom*. San Francisco: Harper & Row.
———. (1993). *God in Creation*. Minneapolis: Fortress.
Montefiore, H., editor. (1975). *Man and Nature*. London: Collins.
Montgommery, D. (2007). *Dirt: the Erosion of Civilizations*. Berkeley: University of California Press.
Moyers, B. (2005a). "Battlefield Earth." *Alternet* Jan 20.
———. (2005b). "Welcome To Doomsday." *New York Review of Books* 52.
Muddiman, J. (1998). "A New Testament Doctrine of Creation?" In *Animals on the Agenda*, edited by A. Linzey and D. Yamamoto. Urbana: University of Illinois Press.
Muir, J. (1897). "The American Forests." *Atlantic Monthly* 80:145–57.
———. (1911). *My First Summer in the Sierra Nevada*. Boston: Houghton Mifflin.
Myers, N. (1989). "Extinction Rates Past and Present." *Bioscience* 39:40.
Myers, N., R. A. Mittermeier, et al. (2000). "Biodiversity Hotspots For Conservation Priorities." *Nature* 403:853–58.
Nash, J. (1992). *Loving Nature: Ecological Integrity and Christian Responsibility*. Nashville: Abingdon.
Nash, R. (1982). *Wilderness and the American Mind*. New Haven: Yale University Press.
National Conference of Catholic Bishops (1983). "The Challenge of Peace: God's Promise and Our Response." Washington, DC: United States Catholic Conference.
Newey, G. (1997). "Political Lying: A Defense." *Public Affairs Quartlerly* 11:93–116.
Niebuhr, R. (1944). *The Children of Light and the Children of Darkness: A Vindication of Democracy and a Critique of Its Traditional Defence*. New York: Scribner.
Noll, M. (2001). "Protestant Reasoning About Money and the Economy, 1790–1860: A Preliminary Probe." In *God and Mammon: Protestants, Money, and the Market 1790–1860*, edited by M. Noll. New York: Oxford University Press.
Noll, M., N. O. Hatch, et al. (1983). *The Search For Christian America*. Westchester, IL: Crossway.
North, G. (1987). *Inherit the Earth: Biblical Blueprints for Economics*. Fort Worth, TX: Dominion.
———. (1990). *Tools of Dominion: The Case Laws of Exodus*. Tyler, TX: Institute for Christian Economics.
Northcott, M. S. (1996). *The Environment and Christian Ethics*. Cambridge: Cambridge University Press.
———. (2002). "Wilderness, Religion and Human Dwelling." *Dialogue* 19.
———. (2004). *An Angel Directs the Storm: Apocalyptic Religion and American Empire*. London: Tauris.
———. (2006). "Soil, Stewardship and Spirit in the Era of Chemical Agriculture." In *Environmental Stewardship: A Critical Reader*, edited by R. J. Berry, 213–19. London: T. & T. Clark.
———. (2008). "Earth Left Behind? Ecological Readings of the Apocalypse of John in Contemporary America." In *The Book of Revelation: As Told by Its Reception History*, edited by J. Okland and W. J. Lyons. Sheffield: Phoenix.
NRDC (2003). *Rewriting the Rules, Year-End Report 2002: the Bush Administration's Assault On the Environment*. New York: Natural Resources Defense Council.
Ochs, P. (2000). "Genesis 1–2, Creation as Evolution." *The Living Pulpit* 8.

Bibliography

O'Donnovan, O. (1993). *Resurrection and Moral Order: An Outline for Evangelical Ethics.* Grand Rapids: Eerdmans.
Olson, D. M., E. Dinerstein, et al. (2001). "Terrestrial Ecoregions of the World: A New Map of Life On Earth." *Bioscience* 51:933-38.
Orr, D. (1991). *Ecological Literacy: Education and the Transition to a Postmodern World.* Albany: State University of New York Press.
Orr, D. (2005). "Armageddon Versus Extinction." *Conservation Biology* 19:290-92.
Ostrom, E., T. Dietz, et al., Eds. (2002). *The Drama of the Commons.* Washington, DC: National Academy Press.
Page, S. (2004). "Churchgoing Closely Tied To Voting Patterns." *USA Today*, February 2.
Parker, G. W. (2003). "Grading the Government." *University of Chicago Law Review* 70: 1345-486.
Parker, R. (2004). "Does the GOP Have a Bloc On God: 'Religious Vote' Could Surprise Us." *Boston Globe.*
Parmesan, C., and G. Yohe (2003). "A Globally Coherent Fingerprint of Climate Change Impacts Across Natural Systems." *Nature* 421:37-42.
Pauly, D. (1995). "Anecdotes and the Shifting Baseline Syndrome of Fisheries." *Trends in Ecology and Evolution* 10.10:430.
Pedraja, L. G. (2006). "Eschatology." In *Handbook To Latina/o Theologies,* edited by E. D. Aponte and A. Delatorre. Atlanta: Chalice.
Pimm, S. L. (2001). *The World according To Pimm.* New York: McGraw Hill.
Pimm, S. L. et al. (2001). "Can We Defy Nature's End?" *Science* 293:2207-8.
Placher, W. (1996). *The Domestication of Transcendence: How Modern Thinking about God Went Wrong.* Louisville: Westminster John Knox.
Polkinghorne, J. (2003). *The God of Hope and the End of the World.* New Haven: Yale University Press.
Pollan, M. (2006). *The Omnivore's Dilemma.* New York: Penguin.
———. (2008). *In Defense of Food: An Eater's Manifesto.* New York: Penguin.
Powell, S. (2003). *Participating in God: Creation and Trinity.* Minneapolis: Fortress.
Preston, C., and W. Ouderkirk, Eds. (2007). *Nature, Value, Duty: Life on Earth with Holmes Rolston, III.* Dordrecht, Netherlands: Springer.
Rachels, J. (1990). *Created from Animals: The Moral Implications of Darwinism.* Oxford: Oxford University Press.
Rawson, P. (1968). *Erotic Art of the East.* London: Weidenfeld & Nicholson.
Regan, T. (1990). "Christianity and Animal Rights." In *Liberating Life: Contemporary Approaches to Ecological Theology,* edited by C. Birch, W. Eakin, and J. B. McDaniel. Maryknoll, NY: Orbis.
Roheim, G. (1971). *The Origin and Function of Culture.* New York: Doubleday.
Rolston, H. (1987). *Science and Religion: A Critical Survey.* Philadelphia: Temple University Press.
———. (1992). "Disvalues in Nature." *Monist* 75:2.
———. (1992). "Wildlife and Wildlands." In *After Nature's Revolt,* edited by D. Hessel. Minneapolis: Fortress.
———. (1994). "Challenges in Evironmental Ethics." In *Environmental Philosophy: Animal Rights to Radical Ecology,* edited by M. Zimmerman. Englewood Cliffs, NJ: Prentice Hall.
———. (1994). "Does Nature Need to Be Redeemed?" *Zygon* 29:2: 205-29.
———. (1999). *Genes, Genesis, and God.* Cambridge: Cambridge University Press.

Bibliography

———. (2003). "Naturalizing and Systematizing Evil." In *Is Nature Evil? Religion, Science, and Value*, edited by W. B. Drees. London: Routledge.

Rossing, B. (2000). "River of Life in God's New Jerusalem: An Eschatological Vision for Earth's Future." In *Christianity and Ecology: Seeking the Well-Being of Earth and Humans*, edited by D. Hessel and R. R. Ruether. Cambridge: Harvard University Press.

Rossing, B. (2004). *The Rapture Exposed: The Message of Hope in the Book of Revelation*. Boulder, CO: Westview.

Roth, W. E. (1897). *Ethnological Studies Among the North-West-Central Queensland Aborgines*. Brisbane, Australia: Edmund Gregory.

———. (1903). "Superstition, Magic, and Medicine." *North Queensland Ethnography Bulletin* 5:3–42.

Ruether, R. R. (1994). *Gaia and God: An Ecofeminist Theology of Earth Healing*. San Francisco: HarperSanFrancisco.

Rushdoony, R. J. (1984). *The Institutes of Biblical Law*. Vol. I. Phillipsburg, NJ: Presbyterian and Reformed.

Rusk, R., Ed. (1994). *The Letters of Ralph Waldo Emerson*. Vol 6. New York: Columbia University Press.

Russell, D. M. (1996). *The 'New Heavens and New Earth': Hope For the Creation in Jewish Apocalyptic and the New Testament*. Philadelphia: Visionary.

Russell, R. J. (2008). *Cosmology: From Alpha to Omega. The Creative Mutual Interaction of Theology and Science*. Theology and the Sciences. Minneapolis: Fortress.

Sachs, J. (2005). *Investment in Development: A Practical Plan To Achieve Millenium Development Goals*. London: Earthscan Publications Ltd.

Santmire, H. P. (2000). *The Travail of Nature: The Ambiguous Ecological Promise of Christian Theology*. Minneapolis: Fortress.

Sartre, J.-P. (1983). *Between Existentialism and Marxism*. London: Verso.

Schaeffer, F. (1970). *Pollution and the Death of Man: the Christian View of Ecology*. Wheaton, IL: Tyndale House.

Schaeffer, F., and U. Middleman (1992). *Pollution and the Death of Man (New Expanded Edition)*. Wheaton, IL: Crossway.

Scheper-Hughes, N., and M. L. Ferreira (2003). "Domba's Spirit Kidney: Transplant Medicine and Suya in dian Cosmology." *Folk* 45:125–57.

Scherer, G. (2003). "Why Eco-Cide Is 'Good News' For the GOP." *E Magazine*, May 5.

———. (2004). "The Godly Must Be Crazy: Christian-Right Views Are Swaying Politicians and Threatening the Environment." *Grist*, October 27.

Schlosser, E. (2001). *Fast Food Nation: The Dark Side of the All-American Meal*. New York: Houghton Mifflin.

Schreiner, S. E. (2001). *Theater of His Glory: Nature and the Natural Order in the Thought of John Calvin*. Grand Rapids: Baker.

Schumacher, E. F. (1979). *Good Work*. New York: Harper & Row.

Schwöbel, C. (1997). "A Christian Ethic of Createdness." In *The Doctrine of Creation*, edited by C. Gunton. Edinburgh: T. & T. Clark.

Scott, J. C. (1999). *Seeing Like a State*. New Haven: Yale University Press.

Scully, M. (2002). *Dominion: the Power of Man, the Suffering of Animals, and the Call To Mercy*. New York: St. Martin's Press.

Seligman, A. B. (1997). *The Problem of Trust*. Princeton: Princeton University Press.

Bibliography

Sellers, C. (1991). *The Market Revolution: Jacksonian America 1815–1846*. Oxford: Oxford University Press.
Shaw, R. (2002). *Memories of the Slave Trade: Ritual and Historical Imagination in Sierra Leone*. Chicago: University of Chicago Press.
Shellenberger, M., and T. Norhaus (2004). "The Death of Environmentalism: Global Warming Politics in a Post-Environmental World." In *Environmental Grantmakers Association*. Kauai, Hawaii.
Sider, R. (1994). "Another View." *World* 8:22–24.
Sideris, L. (2003). *Environmental Ethics, Ecological Theology, and Natural Selection*. New York: Columbia University Press.
Simmel, G. (1991). "The Alpine Journey." *Theory, Culture, and Society* 8.3:95–98.
Sittler, J. (1961). *The Ecology of Faith*. Philadelphia: Muhlenberg.
Slobodkin, L. (2003). *A Citizen's Guide To Ecology*. New York: Oxford University Press.
Smith, C. (2000). *Christian America? What Evangelicals Really Want*. Berkeley: University of California Press.
Smith, J. (1997). "Christian Evangelicals Preach a Green Gospel." *High Country News* 29.8:2–14.
Smith, M. B. (1998). "The Value of a Tree: The Public Debates of John Muir and Gifford Pinchot." *The Historian* 60.
Sobel, D. (2004). *Place-Based Education: Connecting Classrooms and Communities*. Great Barrington, MA: The Orion Society.
Sobrino, J. (1983). *Jesus the Liberator: A Historical-Theological Reading of Jesus of Nazareth*. Maryknoll, NY: Orbis.
Southgate, C. (2002). "God and Evolutionary Evil: Theodicy in the Light of Darwinism." *Zygon* 37.4:803–24.
Spier, J., Ed. (2007). *Picturing the Bible: the Earliest Christian Art*. New Haven: Yale University Press.
Stark, R. (1997). *The Rise of Christianity*. San Francisco: HarperCcollins.
Starke, L., Ed. (2007). *State of the World: Our Urban Future*. New York: Norton.
Stassen, G. H., and D. P. Gushee (2003). *Kingdom Ethics: Following Jesus in Contemporary Context* Downers Grove, IL: InterVarsity.
Stegner, W. (1988). *The American West as Living Space*. Ann Arbor: University of Michigan Press.
Steinbeck, J. (1951). *The Grapes of Wrath*. New York: Harper.
Stoll, M. (1993). "God and John Muir: A Psychological Interpretation of John Muir's Journey." In *John Muir: Life and Work*, edited by S. M. Miller. Albequerque: University of New Mexico Press.
Strathern, M. (1992). *After Nature: English Kinship in the Late Twentieth Century*. Cambridge: Cambridge University Press.
Stuart, K. (1984). "My Friend, the Soil: A Conversation With Hans Jenny." *Journal of Soil and Water Conservation* (May-June) 158–65.
Stuart, S., G. W. Archibald, et al. (2005). "Conservation Theology for Conservation Biologists: A Reply to David Orr." *Conservation Biology* 19:1690–91.
Swift, J. (1710). "On Political Lying." *London Examiner*, November 9.
Taussig, M. (1980). *The Devil and Commodity Festishism in South America*. Chapel Hill: University of North Carolina Press.
Taylor, C. (1989). *Sources of the Self*. Cambridge: Harvard University Press.
Terborgh, J. (1999). *Requiem for Nature*. Washington, DC: Island.

Bibliography

Terrell, T. (2002). "Stewardship and the Environment." *Chalcedon Report* 439.
———. (2003). "Christian Evangelism against Statism." *Christian Statesman*, May-June.
Thoreau, H. D. (1991). *Walking*. Boston: Beacon.
Toulmin, S. (1990). *Cosmopolis, the Hidden Agenda of Modernity*. New York: Free Press.
Turcan, R. (2000). *The Gods of Ancient Rome*. Edinburgh: University of Edinburgh Press.
Twain, M. (2003). *A Tramp Abroad*. New York: Modern Library.
Van Houtan, K. S. (2006). "Conservation As Virtue: a Scientific and Social Process For Ethics." *Conservation Biology* 20:1367-72.
Van Houtan, K. S. and S. L. Pimm (2006). "The Various Christian Ethics of Species Conservation." In *Religion and the New Ecology: Environmental Responsibility in a World in Flux*, edited by D. Lodge and C. Hamlin, 116-47. South Bend, IN: University of Notre Dame Press.
Van Der Weyden, R. (1450). St. Jerome and the Lion: Oil On Oak Panel.
Wackernagel, M., N. B. Schulz, et al. (2002). "Tracking the Ecological Overshoot of the Human Economy." *Proceedings of the National Academy of Sciences USA* 99(9266-9271).
Watt, J. (1982). "Ours Is the Earth." *Saturday Evening Post* 254(1): 75.
Webb, S. H. (1996). "Ecology vs. The Peaceable Kingdom: Toward a Better Theology of Nature." *Soundings* 79.
Whelan, R. (1996). "Greens and God." In *The Cross and the Rainforest: A Critique of Radical Green Spirituality*, edited by R. Whelan, J. Kirwan, and P. Haffner. Grand Rapids, Acton Institute For Religious Liberty.
Whitehead, A. N. (1971). *The Concept of Nature*. Cambridge: Cambridge University Press.
Wilkinson, L., Ed. (1980). *Earthkeeping: Christian Stewardship of Natural Resources*. Grand Rapids: Eerdmans.
Willey, P. and E. Willey (1998). "Will Animals Be Redeemed?" In *Animals On the Agenda: Questions About Animals For Theology and Ethics*, edited by A. Linzey and D. Yamamoto. Urbana: University of Illinois Press.
Williams, G. C. (1993). "Mother Nature Is a Wicked Old Witch." In *Evolutionary Ethics*, edited by M. H. Nitecki and D. V. Nitecki. Albany: State University of New York Press.
Williams, G. H. (1972). "Christian Attitudes Toward Nature." *Christian Scholar's Review* 2(1):112-36.
Williams, M. (1989). *Americans and their Forests*. Cambridge: Cambridge University Press.
Williams, R. (1995). *A Ray of Darkness*. Boston: Cowley.
Wirzba, N., Ed. (2003). *The Essential Agrarian Reader: The Future of Culture, Community, and the Land*. Lexington: University Press of Kentucky.
———. (2007). "An Economy of Grattitude." In *Wendell Berry: Life and Work*, edited by J. Peters. Lexington: University Press of Kentucky.
Wordsworth, W. (1850). *The Prelude: Or Growth of a Poet's Mind*. New York: Appleton.
Worster, D. (1986). *Rivers of Empire*. New York: Pantheon.
Wright, N. T. (2008). *Surprised By Hope: Rethinking Heaven, the Resurrection, and the Mission of the Church*. New York: HarperOne.
Wright, R. T. (1995). "Tearing Down the Green: Environmental Backalsh in the Evangelical Sub-Culture." *Perspectives On Science and Christian Faith* 49:80-91.

Bibliography

Wynne-Tyson, J., Ed. (1989). *The Extended Circle: A Commonplace Book of Animal Rights*. New York: Paragon.

Yoder, J. H. (1964). *Christian Witness To the State*. Scottdale, PA: Herald.

———. (1984). *The Priestly Kingdom*. South Bend: University of Notre Dame Press.

———. (1985). *He Came Preaching Peace*. Scottdale, PA: Herald.

Young, P. D. (2002). "The Resurrection of Whose Body? A Feminist Look At the Question of Transcendence." *Feminist Theology* 30:44–51.

Ziman, J. (1984). *An Introduction To Science Studies: The Philosophical and Social Aspects of Science and Technology*. Cambridge: Cambridge University Press.

Zinn, H. (1980). *A People's History of the United States*. New York: Harper & Row.

Zizoulas, J. D. (1990). "Preserving God's Creation: Three Lectures On Theology and Ecology." *King's Theological Review* 13.

———. (1997). *Being As Communion: Studies in Personhood and the Church*. Crestwood, NY: St. Vladimir's Seminary Press.

Contributors

SUSAN P. BRATTON is Professor and Chair of the Department of Environmental Studies at Baylor University. Dr. Bratton is the author of three books on Christianity and environmental ethics, the most recent is *Environmental Values in Christian Art*. Her career began with the U.S. National Park Service, when she served as director of a field laboratory in Great Smoky Mountains National Park, and as coordinator of a research cooperative at the Institute of Ecology, University of Georgia. Bratton is interested in subjects ranging from fire management, exotic plant species, ocean ethics, and Christian ecotheology and the Hebrew Scriptures.

NORM CHRISTENSEN is Professor of Ecology and the founding Dean of the Nicholas School of the Environment and Earth Sciences at Duke University. Christensen's research focuses on the effects of disturbance on structure and function of populations, communities and ecosystems. Ongoing studies include an analysis of patterns of forest development following agricultural abandonment and comparative studies of ecosystem responses to varying fire regimes across temperate North America. In addition to these interests in basic ecological science, Christensen has written widely on the importance of natural disturbance in the management of forests, shrublands, and wetlands. He is interested in the application of basic ecological theory and models to management, and has collaborated with others in the development of the concept of ecosystem management.

SETH DOWLAND is a Lecturing Fellow and Associate Director of the University Writing Program at Duke University. Professor Dowland holds a PhD in American religious history, and his research focuses on the emergence of the Christian right in the American South. In his 2007

Contributors

dissertation, *Defending Manhood: Gender, Social Order, and the Rise of the Christian Right in the South*, Dowland argues that issues related to gender and sexuality, such as opposition to abortion, feminism, and gay rights, attained prominence in the Christian right's agenda during the 1970s. Dowland has published an article in the collection *Southern Masculinity: Perspectives on Manhood in the South since Reconstruction* and is working on a book about the Christian right.

MAKOTO FUJIMURA is an artist in New York City. Fujimura graduated from Bucknell University and received an MFA in from Tokyo National University of Fine Arts and Music where he became a National Scholar. His thesis painting was purchased by the university and he was invited to study in the Post-MFA program, a first for a foreign student in this prestigious traditional program. In his books *River Grace* and *Refractions* he details his journey of mastering the Nihonga technique that uses carefully stone-ground minerals including azurite, malachite and gold, and his deep wrestling with art and faith issues. His works are represented by Dillon Gallery in New York as well as Tokyo. Public collections include The Saint Louis Museum, Museum of Contemporary Art in Tokyo and the Time Warner-AOL-CNN building in Hong Kong. Fujimura currently serves as the president of the National Council on the Arts.

BRANTLEY GASAWAY an assistant Professor in the Religion Department at Bucknell University. His research and teaching focuses on religion in American public life, politics, and law. Supported by a fellowship from the Louisville Institute for the Study of American Religion, his dissertation *An Alternative Soul of Politics: The Rise of Contemporary Progressive Evangelicalism* analyzed how a progressive minority of evangelical leaders has embraced a public theology of community that prioritizes social justice and environmental stewardship. He has published articles concerning the political implications of evangelical epistemology, religious architecture, and the history of fundamentalism in the United States.

STANLEY HAUERWAS is the Gilbert T. Rowe Professor of Theological Ethics at the Duke Divinity School. Professor Hauerwas has sought to recover the significance of the virtues for understanding the nature of the Christian life. This search has led him to emphasize the importance of the church, as well as narrative for understanding Christian existence. His work cuts across disciplinary lines as he is in conversation with systematic theology, philosophical theology and ethics, political theory, as well as the philosophy of social science and medical ethics. He was named "America's Best Theologian" by Time magazine in 2001. Dr. Hauerwas, who holds a joint appointment in Duke Law School, delivered the prestigious Gifford Lectureship at the University of St. Andrews, Scotland in 2001. His book, *A Community of Character: Toward a Constructive Christian Social Ethic*, was selected as one of the 100 most important books on religion of the 20th century.

MICHAEL JACKSON is the Distinguished Visiting Professor of World Religions at Harvard Divinity School. A graduate of the Universities of Auckland and Cambridge, Jackson has carried out ethnographic fieldwork in Sierra Leone and Aboriginal Australia. The author of numerous books of anthropology, including the prize-winning *Paths Toward a Clearing* and *At Home in the World*, he has also published three novels and six books of poetry (*Latitudes of Exile* was awarded the Commonwealth Poetry Prize in 1976, and *Wall* won the New Zealand Book Award for Poetry in 1981). Michael Jackson's work has been strongly influenced by critical theory, American pragmatism, and existential-phenomenological thought. His ethnographies have consistently sought to make thought answerable to the world—to show how reflection and research can engage with the everyday issues, exigencies and struggles that characterize human life in every society, irrespective of their historical and cultural differences.

ROBERT B. JACKSON is the Nicholas Professor of Global Environmental Change in the Nicholas School of the Environment and Earth Sciences and a Professor in the Biology Department at Duke University. His research examines feedbacks between people and the biosphere, including studies of the global carbon and water cycles, biosphere-atmosphere interactions, and global change. He is currently Director of Duke's Center on Global Change and Duke's Stable Isotope Mass Spectrometry Laboratory. In his quest for solutions to global warming, he also directs the new U.S. Department of Energy-funded National Institute for Climatic Change Research for the southeast and co-directs the Climate Change Policy Partnership, working with energy and utility corporations to find practical strategies to combat climate change.

Contributors

MICHAEL S. NORTHCOTT is Professor of Ethics in the School of Divinity at the University of Edinburgh, Scotland. He has been visiting professor at Dartmouth College, Claremont School of Theology, Duke University, Flinders University, and the University of Malaya. His work focuses on the interface between theological ethics and the human and natural sciences. His book *The Environment and Christian Ethics* is a well established text in environmental theology and ethics is now in its fourth printing. He has written more than seventy scholarly articles and chapters on bioethics, the ethics of food, aquaculture, and genetic modification, on fair trade, globalisation, place, the sociology of religion, theological ethics, and urbanism. His most recent book is *A Moral Climate: The Ethics of Global Warming*. He is currently working, with Van Houtan, on a project on the ethics of species extinction, and with biologist R. J. Berry on an edited collection entitled *Theology After Darwin*.

WILLIAM H. SCHLESINGER is the President of the Cary Institute for Ecosystem Studies and a member of the U.S. National Academies of Sciences. Before coming to the Institute, he served as the James B. Duke Professor of Biogeochemistry and Dean of the Nicholas School of the Environment and Earth Sciences at Duke University. Throughout his career, he has investigated the circulation of the chemical elements in natural ecosystems—a field now widely known as biogeochemistry. His work has focused on the carbon stored in soils which contain a major pool in the global carbon cycle, and has provided global estimates of the storage of organic and inorganic carbon in soils, losses of soil carbon to runoff, changes in soil carbon with conversion of land to agriculture, and accumulations of carbon during soil development. His work more recently examines changes in soils that will accompany plant growth at elevated levels of atmospheric CO_2, and evaluates carbon sequestration as a means to control the accumulation of atmospheric CO_2 to mitigate the potential for global warming.

LISA SIDERIS is an assistant Professor in the Department of Religious Studies at the University of Indiana. Sideris is broadly interested in the value and ethical significance of natural processes. Much of her research focuses on the intersection of religion, science and environmental ethics and how religious environmental thought incorporates, or fails to incorporate, knowledge from the natural sciences, particularly evolution-

Contributors

ary theory and ecology. Her 2003 book, *Environmental Ethics, Ecological Theology, and Natural Selection* examines the way in which much of Christian environmental ethics, or "ecotheology," misconstrues, or simply ignores, Darwinian theory, and the problems this creates for developing a realistic ethic for nature and animals. More recently, Sideris has focused on the life and work of Rachel Carson. She is co-editor, with Kathleen Dean Moore, of *Rachel Carson: Legacy and Challenge* and author of several essays on Carson's life and legacy.

FRED VAN DYKE is Professor and Chair of the Department of Biology at Wheaton College. Van Dyke's research, publications, and professional experience focus on the management and conservation of animal populations, the study of successional processes to manage and preserve biodiversity in plant and animal communities, the effects of environmental disturbance on plant and animal populations, the values and ethics of conservation, and the development of a comprehensive ethic of Judeo-Christian environmental stewardship. In his personal life, Dr. Van Dyke enjoys hiking, camping, and backpacking, especially in the Absaroka-Beartooth Wilderness of Montana. He serves as a Sunday school teacher and small group leader at his local church in Wheaton, Illinois.

KYLE S. VAN HOUTAN is a fellow with the President's Strategic Initiative on Science and Religion and holds appointments in the Center for Ethics and Biology Department at Emory University. Dr. Van Houtan seeks to understand the processes leading to the loss of species and ecosystems largely through geospatial models of ecological patterns in time. His work has unexpectedly led him to the practical ethics of language and social traditions, especially those of science and religion. His research crosses the disciplines of conservation biology, ecology, environmental ethics, and theological ethics and has been published in *Conservation Biology*, *Nature*, *Ecology Letters*, *Current Biology*, *New Scientist*, and the *New York Times*. He previously served as a biologist with the Smithsonian Institution and the U. S. Geological Service and he received a Harvey Fellowship for his doctoral dissertation in 2005. With Michael Northcott, Van Houtan is currently writing *The Ethics of Extinction: Christian Ethics and the Ends of Species*.

Contributors

JEFFREY D. VICKERY is an adjunct professor in the Department of Philosophy at Western Carolina University and co-pastor of Cullowhee Baptist Church. In Vickery's professional, academic, and congregational roles, he attempts to offer thoughtful Christian reflection to questions of ethics, theology, and community. When not teaching or preaching, Dr. Vickery is often exploring the trails and waterfalls of the Pisgah National Forest in western North Carolina, or training for another marathon.

NORMAN WIRZBA is Research Professor of Theology, Ecology, and Rural Life at Duke Divinity School. He is the author of *The Paradise of God: Renewing Religion in an Ecological Age* and *Living the Sabbath: Discovering the Rhythms of rest and Delight* and editor of *The Essential Agrarian Reader: The Future of Culture, Community, and the Land*. His teaching and research develop an agrarian cultural vision, particularly as it is manifested in theological and philosophical reflection. To this end he is the General Editor of the book series published by the University Press of Kentucky, *The Culture of the Land: A Series in the New Agrarianism*. He is currently at work on two books *The Grace of Good Food: Eating and the Life of Faith*, and *For the Health of the World: An Agrarian Manifesto*.

LAURA YORDY is an assistant Professor in Religion and in Philosophy at Bridgewater College in Virginia. Professor Yordy works on the intersections of Christian ethics, ecology, and theology—especially the areas of christology, eschatology, and ecojustice. She is also interested in the contextualization of virtues in terms of gender, race, class, and culture. Her book, *Green Witness: Ecology, Ethics, and the Kingdom of God* was published in 2008. She is currently writing about the domesticating of patience and its recovery as an ungendered, ecological Christian virtue.

www.ingramcontent.com/pod-product-compliance
Lightning Source LLC
Chambersburg PA
CBHW031356230426
43670CB00006B/555